Risk, Uncertainty and Profit

Frank H. Knight

Vernon Press

First published in 1921 by Hart, Schaffner & Marx, Boston; Houghton Mifflin Company, The Riverside Press, Cambridge.

www.vernonpress.com

In the Americas:
Vernon Press
1000 N West Street,
Suite 1200, Wilmington,
Delaware 19801
United States

In the rest of the world
Vernon Press
C/Sancti Espiritu 17,
Malaga, 29006
Spain

Library of Congress Control Number: 2014932231

ISBN: 978-1-62273-004-9

Author's Preface

There is little that is fundamentally new in this book. It represents an attempt to state the essential principles of the conventional economic doctrine more accurately, and to show their implications more clearly, than has previously been done. That is, its object is refinement, not reconstruction; it is a study in "pure theory." The motive back of its presentation is twofold. In the first place, the writer cherishes, in the face of the pragmatic, philistine tendencies of the present age, especially characteristic of the thought of our own country, the hope that careful, rigorous thinking in the field of social problems does after all have some significance for human weal and woe. In the second place, he has a feeling that the "practicalism" of the times is a passing phase, even to some extent a pose; that there is a strong undercurrent of discontent with loose and superficial thinking and a real desire, out of sheer intellectual self-respect, to reach a clearer understanding of the meaning of terms and dogmas which pass current as representing ideas. For the first of these assumptions a few words of elaboration or defense may be in place, in anticipation of the essay itself.

The "practical" justification for the study of general economics is a belief in the possibility of improving the quality of human life through changes in the form of organization of want-satisfying activity. More specifically, most projects of social betterment involve the substitution of some more consciously social or political form of control for private property and individual freedom of contract. The assumption underlying such studies as the present is that changes of this character will offer greater prospect of producing real improvement if they are carried out in the light of a clear understanding of the nature and tendencies of the system which it is proposed to modify or displace. The essay, therefore, endeavors to isolate and define the essential characteristics of free enterprise as a system or method of securing and directing cooperative effort in a social group. As a necessary condition of success in this endeavor it is assumed that the description and explanation of phenomena must be radically separated from all questions of defense or criticism of the system under examination. By means of first showing what the system is, it is hoped that advance may be made toward discovering what such a system can, and what it cannot, accomplish. A closely related aim is that of formulating the data of the problem of economic organization, the unchangeable materials with which, and conditions under which, any machinery of organization has to work. A sharp and clear conception of these fundamentals is viewed as a necessary foundation for answering the question as to what is reasonably to be expected of a method of organization, and hence of whether the system as such is to be blamed for the failure to achieve ideal results, of where if at all it is at fault, and the sort of change or substitution which offers sufficient chance for improvement to justify experimentation.

The net result of the inquiry is by no means a defense of the existing order. On the contrary, it is probably to emphasize the inherent defects of free enterprise. But it must be admitted that careful analysis also emphasizes the fundamental difficulties of the problem and the fatuousness of over-sanguine expectations from mere changes in social machinery. Only this foundation-laying is within the scope of this study, or included within the province of economic theory. The final verdict on questions of social policy depends upon a similar study of other possible systems of organization and a comparison of these with free enterprise in relation to the tasks to be accomplished. This one "conclusion" may be hazarded, that no one mode of organization is adequate or tolerable for all purposes in all fields. In the ultimate society, no doubt, every conceivable type of organization machinery will find its place, and the problem takes the form of defining the tasks and spheres of social endeavor for which each type is best adapted.

The particular technical contribution to the theory of free enterprise which this essay purports to make is a fuller and more careful examination of the role of the *entrepreneur* or enterpriser, the recognized "central figure" of the system, and of the forces which fix the remuneration of his special function. The problem of profit was suggested to the writer as a suitable topic for a doctoral dissertation in the spring of 1914 by Dr. Alvin Johnson, then Professor of Economics in Cornell University. The study was chiefly worked out under the direction of Professor Allyn A. Young after Dr. Johnson left Cornell. My debt to these two teachers I can only gratefully acknowledge. Since the acceptance of the essay as a thesis at Cornell in June, 1916, and its submission in the Hart, Schaffner & Marx competition in 1917, it has been entirely rewritten under the editorial supervision of Professor J. M. Clark, of the University of Chicago. I have also profited much by discussions with Professor C. O. Hardy, my colleague at the same institution, and by access to his unpublished "Readings on Risk and Risk-Bearing." Professor Jacob Viner, of the University of Chicago, has kindly read the proof of the entire work. My obligations to various economists through their published work are very inadequately shown by text and footnote references, but are too comprehensive and indefinite to express in detail.

F. H. KNIGHT

Iowa City, Iowa

January, 1921.

Contents

Part I. Introductory

Chapter 1. The Place of Profit and Uncertainty in Economic Theory

ECONOMICS, or more properly theoretical economics, is the only one of the social sciences which has aspired to the distinction of an exact science. To the extent that it is an exact science it must accept the limitations as well as share the dignity thereto pertaining, and it thus becomes like physics or mathematics in being necessarily somewhat abstract and unreal. In fact it is different from physics in degree, since, though it cannot well be made so exact, yet for special reasons it secures a moderate degree of exactness only at the cost of much greater unreality. The very conception of an exact science involves abstraction; its ideal is analytic treatment, and analysis and abstraction are virtually synonyms. We have given us the task of reducing to order a complex mass of interrelated changes, which is to say, of analyzing them into uniformities of sequence or behavior, called laws, and the isolation of the different elementary sequences for separate study.

Sometimes the various elementary constituents of our complex phenomenon are met with in nature in isolation complete or partial, and sometimes artificial experiments can be devised to present them either alone or with attendant conditions subject to control. The latter is, of course, the characteristic procedure of physical science. Its application to the study of industrial society is, however, generally impracticable. Here we must commonly search for manifestations of the various factors in our complex, under varying associations, or rely upon intuitive knowledge of general principles and follow through the workings of individual chains of sequence by logical processes.

The application of the analytic method in any class of problems is always very incomplete. It is never possible to deal in this way with a very large proportion, numerically speaking, of the vast complexity of factors entering into a normal real situation such as we must cope with in practical life. The value of the method depends on the fact that in large groups of problem situations certain elements are common and are not merely present in each single case, but in addition are both few in number and important enough largely to dominate the situations. The laws of these few elements, therefore, enable us to reach an approximation to the law of the situation as a whole. They give us statements of what "tends" to hold true or "would" hold true under "ideal" conditions, meaning merely in a situation where the numerous and variable but less important "other things" which our laws do not take into account were entirely absent.

Thus, in physics, the model and archetype of an exact science of nature, a relatively small and workable number of laws or principles tell us what would happen if simplified conditions be assumed and all disturbing factors eliminated. The simplified conditions include specifications as to dimensions, mass, shape, smoothness, rigidity, elasticity and properties generally of the objects worked with, specifications usually quite impossible to realize in fact, *yet absolutely necessary to make*, while the "disturbing factors" are simply anything not included in the specifications, and their actual elimination is probably equally impossible to realize, and, again, equally *necessary* to *assume.* Only thus could we ever obtain "laws," descriptions of the separate elements of phenomena and their separate behavior. And while such laws, of course, never accurately hold good in any particular case, because they are incomplete, not including all the elements in the case, yet they enable us to deal with practical problems intelligently because they are approximately true and we know how to discount their incompleteness. Only by such approximations, reached by dealing analytically with the more important and more universal aspects of phenomena, could we ever have attained any intelligent conception of the behavior of masses of matter in motion and secured our present marvelous mastery over the forces of nature.

In a similar way, but for various reasons not so completely and satisfactorily, we have developed a historic body of theoretical economics which deals with "tendencies"; i.e., with what "would" happen under simplified conditions never realized, but always more or less closely approached in practice. But theoretical economics has been much less successful than theoretical physics in making the procedure useful, largely because it has failed to make its nature and limitations explicit and clear. It studies what would happen under "perfect competition," noting betimes respects in which competition is not perfect; but much remains to be done to establish a systematic and coherent view of what is necessary to perfect competition, just how far and in what ways its conditions deviate from those of real life and what "corrections" have accordingly to be made in applying its conclusions to actual situations.[1]

The vague and unsettled state of ideas on this subject is manifest in the difference of opinion rife among economists as to the meaning and use of theoretical methods. At one extreme we have mathematical economists and pure theorists[2] to whom little if anything outside of a closed system of deductions from a very small number of premises assumed as universal laws is to be regarded as scientific economics at all. At the other extreme there is certainly a strong and perhaps growing tendency to repudiate abstraction and deduction altogether, and insist upon a purely objective, descriptive science. And in between are all shades of opinion.

In the present writer's view the correct "middle way" between these extreme views, doing justice to both, is not hard to find. An abstract deductive system is only one small division of the great domain of economic science, but there is opportunity and the greatest necessity for cultivating that field. Indeed, in our analogy, theoretical mechanics is a very small section of the science of physical nature; but it is a very fundamental section, in a sense the "first" of all, the foundation and prerequisite of those that follow. And this also may very well hold good of a body of "pure theory" in economics; it may be that a small step, but the *first* step, toward a practical comprehension of the social system is to isolate and follow out to their logical conclusion a relatively small number of fundamental tendencies discoverable in it. There is abundant need for the use

[1] Cf . Mackenzie, Introduction to Social Philosophy, p. 58. Also Bagehot, Economic Studies, no. 1: "The Presuppositions of English Political Economy."

[2] There are three types or schools of mathematical economic theory.

of both deduction and induction in economics as in other sciences, if indeed the two methods are theoretically separable. As Mill has well argued[3] we must reason deductively as far as possible, always collating our conclusions with observed facts at every stage. Where the data are too complex to handle in this way induction must be applied and empirical laws formulated, to be connected deductively with the general principles of "ethology" (we should now say simply "human behavior"). Emphasis being laid on the provisos, in both cases, that in using deduction the conclusions must be constantly checked with facts by observation and premises revised accordingly, while the empirical laws resulting from induction must in turn be shown to follow from the general principles of the science before they can be credited with much significance or dependability, we see that there is little divergence left between the two methods.[4]

[3]Logic, book vi, chaps, ix and x.

[4]The relations between deduction and induction are intimate, and a rigid separation or contrast between the two methods is misleading. A more careful study of the fundamentals of scientific method will be undertaken hereafter (chapter vii). We shall see that there is ultimately no ,such fact as deduction as commonly understood, that inference is from particulars to particular, and that generalization is always tentative and a mere labor-saving device. The fact is, however, that we can study facts intelligently and fruitfully only in the light of hypotheses, while hypotheses have value more or less., in proportion to the amount of antecedent concrete "Knowledge of fact on which they are teased. The actual procedure of science thus consists of making and testing hypotheses .] The first hypotheses in any field are usually the impressions of "common sense"; i.e., of that superficial knowledge forced upon intelligence by direct contact with the world. Study, in the light of any hypothesis, corrects or refutes the guiding generalization and suggests new points of view, to be criticized and tested in the same way, and so the organization of the material proceeds. The importance of generalization arises from the fact that as our minds are built, it is nearly fruitless to attempt to observe phenomena unless we approach them with questions to be answer id. This is what a hypothesis really is, a question. Superficial observation suggests questions which study answers. If and so long as it answers a question affirmatively and the answer is not contradicted by the test of practical application or casual observation, we have a law of nature, a truth about our environment which enables us to react intelligently to it in our conduct.

There is, then, little if .any use for induction in the Baconian sense of an exhaustive collection and collation of facts, though in some cases this may be necessary and fruitful. On the other hand, there is equally little use for deduction taken as doing more than suggesting hypotheses, subject to verification. It is to be noted, however, that our common-sense generalizations have a very high degree of certainty in some fields, giving us, in regard to the* external world, for instance, the "axioms" of mathematics. Even more important in the present connection is the r61e of common sense or intuition in the study of

The method of economics is simply that of any field of inquiry where analysis is in any degree applicable and anything more than mere description possible. It is the scientific method, the method of successive approximations.[5] The study will begin with a theoretical branch dealing with only the most general aspects of the subject matter, and proceed downward through a succession of principles applicable to more and more restricted classes of phenomena. How far the process is carried will be a matter of taste and of the practical requirements of any problem. In science generally it does not pay to elaborate laws of a very great degree of accuracy of detail. When the number of factors taken into account in deduction becomes large, the process rapidly becomes unmanageable and errors creep in, while the results lose in generality of application more significance than they gain by the closeness of approximation to fact in a given case. It is better to stop dealing with elements separately before they get too numerous and deal with the final stages of the approximation by applying corrections empirically determined.

The theoretical method in its pure form consists, then, in the complete and separate study of general principles, with the rigid exclusion of all fluctuations, modifications, and accidents of all sorts

---

human phenomena. Observation and intuition are, indeed, hardly distinguishable operations in much of the field of human behaviour. Our knowledge of ourselves is based on introspective observation, but is so direct that it may be called intuitive. Its extension to our fellow human beings is also based upon the interpretation of the communicative signs of speech, gesture, facial expression, etc., far more than upon direct observation of behaviour, and this process of interpretation is highly instinctive and subconscious in character. Many of the fundamental laws of economics are therefore properly "intuitive" to begin with, though of course always subject to correction by induction in the ordinary sense of observation and statistical treatment of data.

These brief statements must not be thought of as dealing with philosophical problems. The writer is, like Mill, an empiricist, holding that all general truths or axioms are ultimately inductions from experience. By induction as a method is meant deliberate, scientific induction, the planned study of instances for the purpose of ascertaining their "law." And deduction means reaching new truth by the application of general law to particular cases. In the present view both of these processes are regarded as suggestive merely, exhaustive induction and conclusive deduction being alike impossible.

[5]The reader will recall Comte's arrangement of the sciences in the order of generality of the principles they establish. Mathematics, 1 he properties of space and of quantity in the abstract, is applicable to all phenomena and tells us correspondingly little about any of them. The laws of matter, of living matter, etc., are less general and more concretely real. The same principles are applicable within any grand division of knowledge.

due to the influence of factors less general than those under investigation at any particular stage of the inquiry. Our question relates to the advisability of using this method in a tolerably rigid form in economics. The answer to this question depends on whether in the phenomena to be studied general principles can in fact be found of sufficient constancy and importance to justify their careful isolation and separate study. The writer is strongly of the opinion that the question must be answered affirmatively. Economics is the study of a particular form of organization of human want-satisfying activity which has become prevalent in Western nations and spread over the greater part of the field of conduct. It is called free enterprise or the competitive system. It is obviously not at all completely or perfectly competitive, but just as indisputably its *general principles* are those of free competition. Under these circumstances the study, as a first approximation, of a perfectly competitive system, in which the multitudinous degrees and kinds of divergences are eliminated by abstraction, is clearly indicated. The method is particularly indicated in a practical sense because our most important questions of social policy hinge directly upon the question of the character of the "natural" results of competition, and take the form of queries as to whether the tendencies of competition are to be furthered and supplemented or obstructed and replaced.

That such a theoretical first approximation is indicated in a theoretical sense, that it is the natural logical way of going at the problem, conforming to the workings of our thought processes, is sufficiently evidenced by the fact that this is what economists have always in fact done, ever since there has been such a science or such a social system to be studied. They have, to be sure, been criticized for doing it, and severely. But in the present writer's judgment theorists of the past and present are to be justly criticized not for following the theoretical method and studying a simplified and idealized form of competitive organization, but for not following it in a sufficiently self-conscious, critical, and explicit way. In their discussions of methodology the historic economists have, indeed, been as clear and explicit as could be desired,[6] but in the use of the method

[6]Cf. Mill's Essays on Unsettled Questions, no. 5, which really leaves little to be said on the subject. Also Cairnes, on the Character and Logical Method of Political Economy, and the discussions of methodology of the English economists generally. The conception of the "economic man" was one way of emphasizing the abstract and simplified character of the premises of the science. Keynes's Scope and Logical Method of Political Economy is an admirably clear and conclusive

as much cannot, unfortunately, be said.

It should go without saying that in the use of the scientific method of reasoning from simplified premises, it is imperative that it be clear to the reasoner and be made unmistakable to those who use his work what his procedure is and what presuppositions are involved. Two supreme difficulties have underlain controversies regarding method in the past. The first is the strong aversion of the masses of humanity, including even a large proportion of "scholars," to all thinking in general terms. The second difficulty, on the other side, is the fact referred to above, that the persons employing methods of approximation in economics have not themselves adequately and always recognized, and still less have they made clear to their readers, the approximate character of their conclusions, as descriptions of tendency only, but have frequently hastened to base principles of social and business policy upon very incomplete data. The evil results of the failure to emphasize the theoretical character of economic speculation are apparent in every field of practical economics. The theorist not having definite assumptions clearly in mind in working out the "principles," it is but natural that he, and still more the practical workers building upon his foundations, should forget that unreal assumptions were made, and should take the principles over bodily, apply them to concrete cases, and draw sweeping and wholly unwarranted conclusions from them. The clearly untenable and often vicious character of such deductions naturally works to discredit theory itself. This, of course, is wrong; we do not allow perpetual motion schemes to discredit theoretical mechanics, which is built upon the assumption of perpetual motion at every stage. But in economics a distrust of general principles, fatal as it is to clear thinking, will be inevitable as long as the postulates of theory are so nebulous and shifting. They can hardly be made sufficiently explicit; it is imperative that the contrast between these simplified assumptions and the complex facts of life be made as conspicuous and as familiar as has been done in mechanics.

The present essay is an attempt in the direction indicated above. We shall endeavor to search out and placard the unrealities of the postulates of theoretical economics, not for the purpose of discrediting the doctrine, but with a view to making clear its theoretical limitations. There are several reasons why the approximate character of theoretical economic laws and their inapplicability without

---

discussion of this whole subject.

empirical correction to real situations should be especially emphasized as compared, for instance, with those of mechanics. The first reason is historical and has already been indicated. The limitations of the results have not always been clear, and theorists themselves as well as writers in practical economics and statecraft have carelessly used them without regard for the corrections necessary to make them fit concrete facts. Policies must fail, and fail disastrously, which are based on perpetual motion reasoning *without the recognition that it is such.*

In the second place, the allowances and corrections necessary in the case of theoretical economics are vastly greater than in the case of mechanics, and the importance of not losing sight of them is correspondingly accentuated. The general principles do not bring us so close to reality; there is a larger proportion of factors in an economic situation which are of the variable and fluctuating sort.

Again, in spite of the greater contrast between theory and practice in the study of the mechanics of competition, as compared with the mechanics of matter and motion, the contrast is less familiar and more easily overlooked. Our race has been observing and handling in a rude way the latter type of phenomena ever since it has lived on the earth, while competitive relations among men were established only a few generations ago. In consequence the habit of clear thinking according to scientific method, the use of hypotheses and separation of fundamental principles from the accidents of particular instances, has become in some measure built up in the minds of at least a respectable body of the more cultivated division of the race. Perhaps it is even in some degree instinctive in certain strains.[7]

[7]It is necessary to admit that in fact only a pitifully small fraction of the race have any particular theoretical sense in the mechanical field either. Certainly a vast majority of literate adults with elementary experience with machinery have no real comprehension of the most fundamental principles of the transformation and equivalence of forces. As far as their own insight is concerned, they could easily be taken in with crude perpetual motion schemes, and an astonishing proportion are willing to back their own judgment in such matters against what they know to be the unanimous verdict of the scientific world. The recurrent discussion of such projects in our National Congress are familiar. A certain mechanical "handiness" is probably all that is to be found in any but the rare scientific minds, and these handy men are precisely the ones who seem most likely to waste their lives and means over palpably absurd enterprises. A large proportion even of competent engineers have neither comprehension nor appreciation of physical theory.

Finally, it makes vastly more difference practically whether we disseminate correct ideas among the people at large in the field of human relations than is the case with mechanical problems. For good or ill, we are committed to the policy of democratic control in the former case, and are not likely to resort to it in the latter. As far as material results are concerned, it is relatively unimportant whether people generally believe in their hearts that energy can be manufactured or that a cannon ball will sink part of the way to the bottom of the ocean and remain suspended, or any other fundamental misconception. We have here at least established the tradition that knowledge and training count and have persuaded the ignorant to defer to the judgment of the informed. In the field of natural science the masses can and will gladly take and use and construct appliances in regard to whose scientific basis they are as ignorant as they are indifferent. It is usually possible to demonstrate such things on a moderate scale, and literally to knock men down with "results." In the field of social science, however, fortunately or unfortunately, these things are not true. Our whole established tradition tends to the view that "Tom, Dick, and Harry" know as much about it as any "highbrow"; the ignorant will not in general defer to the opinion of the informed, and in the absence of voluntary deference it is usually impossible to give an objective demonstration. If our social science is to yield fruits in an improved quality of human life, it must for the most part be "sold" to the masses first. The necessity of making its literature not merely accurate and convincing, but as nearly "fool-proof" as possible, is therefore manifest.

Whether or not the use of the method of exact science is as necessary in the field of social phenomena as the present writer believes, it will doubtless be conceded; even by opponents of this view, that it *has been* employed in the great mass of the literature since the modern science of economics was founded. It may also be granted that the terminology, concepts, and modes of thinking in our economic instruction and in general discussion are and for a long time must be largely dominated by the established tradition. And it will certainly not be denied that *if* the method of reasoning from hypothetical or simplified premises is followed, its use must be thoroughly safeguarded by emphasizing the character of the premises and the consequent conditional or approximate validity of the conclusions reached. If, finally, it is admitted that this has not been adequately done hitherto, and that mischief and misunderstanding have followed from the loose use of assumptions and looser application of conclusions, then the call for such a study as the present will be established.

The tendency toward a sharper separation of the theoretical portion of economics from the empirical portion, and toward the clearer formulation of premises, can be traced in the literature of the subject, and notable progress in the right direction has recently been made. The work of the mathematical economists and non-mathematical pure theorists has already been mentioned. A considerable and fairly satisfactory body of consciously and rigidly "theoretical" (i.e., general and approximate) doctrine has been built up. The work of Pareto and Wicksteed seems to the writer especially worthy of note. Unfortunately it has not achieved the recognition and been accorded the fundamental place in the general program of the science which we think it should have; mathematical economics in particular seems likely to remain little more than a cult, a closed book to all except a few of the "initiated." In the great mass of economic literature there is certainly still wanting the evidence of a comprehensive grasp of general principles and even more of the meaning and importance of general principles in a scientific program. There is still a need for thoroughgoing and critical comparison and contrast of theoretical assumptions with the conditions of real life and of theoretical conclusions with concrete facts. The makers and users of economic analysis have in general still to be made to see that deductions from theory are necessary, not because literally true—that in the strict sense they are useful *because not* literally true—but only if they bear a certain relation to literal truth and if all who work with them constantly bear in mind what that relation is. It must be admitted that even the pure theorists have not generally been assiduous in emphasizing the practical significance of their work and its relation to the outside body of the science; they have been too exclusively interested in the construction of their *a priori* systems, and perhaps a little disposed to regard these as a disproportionate part of economic science. Such a bias is natural and even useful, but in a field where the relations between theory and practice do not come instinctively to the minds of the users of both, the supplementation of theory by works of interpretation becomes indispensable.

Indication of progress in this field is furnished especially by the discussion centering around the concept of normality in the work of Marshall in England and the related notion of the static state espoused in particular in this country by J. B. Clark.[8] The meaning and bearings of the fundamental concepts are in the writer's opinion much better worked out by Marshall than by any other writer generally read. But Marshall himself has adopted a cautious, almost antitheoretical attitude toward fundamentals; he refuses to lay down and follow rigidly defined hypotheses, but insists on sticking as closely as possible to concrete reality and discussing "representative" conditions as opposed to limiting tendencies. The gain in concreteness and realism is in our opinion much more than offset by the obscurity, vagueness, and unsystematic character of the discussion, the inevitable consequence of burying fundamentals in an overwhelming mass of qualification and detail. Professor Clark, on the other hand, is frankly theoretical and insistent upon the deliberate use of abstraction. But the writer at least is unable to agree with him on the question of what abstractions should be made and the manner of their use. While the specifications for his theoretical state are more definite and explicit than those of Marshall, they seem to us less correctly drawn up.[9]

The opposition to pure theory in general is based on a failure to understand it, and especially common is the misconception as to the meaning of static or normal hypotheses. It is not recognized that their use is inherent in the methodology of science, is in fact the very essence of scientific procedure; that it is not at all recondite or intellectual in its appeal, but is mere practical common sense. The aim of science is to predict the future for the purpose of making our conduct intelligent.[10] Intelligence predicts, as shown above, through analysis, by isolating the different forces or tendencies in a situation and studying the character and effects of each separately. Static method and reasoning are therefore coextensive. We have no way of discussing a force or change except to describe its effects or results under given conditions.

The "static" method in economics does merely this. It inquires what conditions exist and studies the results which recognizable forces at work (or changes in progress—we know nothing about force;

---

[8]The static state idea is further developed along rigidly theoretical lines by Professor Schumpeter in Austria.

[9]We shall attempt to show that it does not represent, as Professor Clark contends, the assumptions implicit in the classical economic theory. (See chapter II.)

[10]Cf. Dewey's definition of reason as the method of social diagnosis and prognosis.

it is the assumed "cause" of change, which is the only fact) tend to produce under those conditions. It is "unreal" only in the simplification of its problem; i.e., in taking the more conspicuous forces and more important conditions and provisionally neglecting others. This the limitations of our minds compel us to do. We must first discuss one change at a time, assuming the others suspended while that one is working itself out to its final results, and then attempt to combine the tendencies at work, estimate their relative importance, and make actual predictions. This is the way our minds work; we must divide to conquer. Where a complex situation can be dealt with as a whole—if that ever happens—there is no occasion for "thought." *Thought* in the scientific sense, and *analysis*, are the *same thing.*

The reference to *final* results calls for a further word. The concept of *equilibrium* is closely related to that of static method. It is the nature of every change in the universe known to science to have "final" results under any given conditions, and the description of the change is incomplete if it stops short of the statement of these ultimate tendencies. Every movement in the world is and can be clearly seen to be a progress toward an equilibrium. Water seeks its *level*, air moves toward an equality of *pressure*, electricity toward a uniform *potential*, radiation toward a uniform *temperature*, etc. Every change is an equalization of the forces which produce that change, and tends to bring about a condition in which the change will no longer take place. The water continues to flow, the wind to blow, etc., only because the sun's heat—itself a similar but more long-drawn-out redistribution of energy—constantly restores the inequalities which these movements themselves constantly destroy.

So also in economic phenomena. Goods move from the point of lower to one of higher demand or price, and every such movement obliterates the price difference which causes it. The circulation of goods continues because the life activities of man (the production of wealth) keep new supplies forthcoming. The same applies to shifts in productive energy from one use to another. There are really as many static states as there are changes to be studied, sets of given conditions to be assumed. It is arbitrary but convenient to speak of the static state in relation to given conditions of the supply and demand (production and consumption) of consumption goods. We shall see that there are in fact two other fundamental static problems; the first assumes given supplies of consumption goods, and the second, given general conditions under which the creation of production goods and changes in wants take place; the first is the problem of the market or of market price, and the second that of social economic progress, often referred to as economic dynamics.

The argument of the present essay will center around the general idea of normality, viewed as an attempt to isolate for study the essentials or general principles of a competitive social economic organization. The aim will be to bring out the content of the assumptions or hypotheses of the historic body of economic thought, referred to by the classical writers as "natural price" theory. By this is meant, not the assumptions definitely in the minds of the classical economists, but the assumptions necessary to define the conditions of perfect competition, at which the classical thought was aimed, and which are significant as forming the limiting tendency of actual economic processes.[11]

As the title of the essay indicates, our task will be envisaged from the immediate standpoint of the problem of profit in distributive theory. The primary attribute of competition, universally recognized and evident at a glance, is the "tendency" to eliminate profit[12] or loss, and bring the value of economic goods to equality with their cost. Or, since costs are in the large identical with the distributive shares other than profit, we may express the same principle by saying that the tendency is toward a remainderless distribution of products among the agencies contributing to their production. But in actual society, cost and value only "tend" to equality; it is only by an occasional accident that they are precisely equal in fact; they are usually separated by a margin of "profit," positive or negative. Hence the problem of profit is one way of looking at the problem of the contrast between perfect competition and actual competition.

Our preliminary examination of the problem of profit will show, however, that the difficulties in this field have arisen from a confusion of ideas which goes deep down into the foundations of our thinking.

---

[11]We need not here more than mention the obvious fact that the theoretical method is applicable to monopoly as well as competition and has dealt with both. It has been, of course, a theoretically "ideal" monopoly also the real assumption being an exceptional instance of perfect monopoly in a general system of perfect competition. The contrast between theory and reality and the significance of the former is of the same sort in both cases, and we shall also discuss the meaning of perfect monopoly in the proper connection. (Chapter vi.)

[12]It will be perceived that the word "profit" is here used in the sense of "pure profit," a distributive share different from the returns to the productive services of land, labor, and capital.

The key to the whole tangle will be found to lie in the notion of risk or uncertainty and the ambiguities concealed therein. It is around this idea, therefore, that our main argument will finally center. A satisfactory explanation of profit will bring into relief the nature of the distinction between the perfect competition of theory and the remote approach which is made to it by the actual competition of, say, twentieth-century United States; and the answer to this twofold problem is to be found in a thorough examination and criticism of the concept of Uncertainty, and its bearings upon economic processes.

But Uncertainty must be taken in a sense radically distinct from the familiar notion of Risk, from which it has never been properly separated. The term "risk," as loosely used in everyday speech and in economic discussion, really covers two things which, functionally at least, in their causal relations to the phenomena of economic organization, are categorically different. The nature of this confusion will be dealt with at length in chapter VII, but the essence of it may be stated in a few words at this point. The essential fact is that "risk" means in some cases a quantity susceptible of measurement, while at other times it is something distinctly not of this character; and there are far-reaching and crucial differences in the bearings of the phenomenon depending on which of the two is really present and operating. There are other ambiguities in the term "risk" as well, which will be pointed out; but this is the most important. It will appear that a *measurable* uncertainty, or "risk" proper, as we shall use the term, is so far different from an *unmeasurable* one that it is not in effect an uncertainty at all. We shall accordingly restrict the term "uncertainty" to cases of the non-quantitave type. It is this "true" uncertainty, and not risk, as has been argued, which forms the basis of a valid theory of profit and accounts for the divergence between actual and theoretical competition.

As a background for the discussion of the meaning and causal relations of uncertainty, we shall first make a brief survey of previously proposed theories of profit. After a summary glance at the history of the treatment of the subject down to recent decades, it will be necessary to dwell at slightly greater length upon the controversy recently carried on in connection with the explanation of profit in terms of risk. The crucial character of the distinction between measurable risk and unmeasurable uncertainty will become apparent in this discussion.

Part Two (chapters III-VI) will be taken up with an outline study of a theoretical, perfectly competitive society. In the course of the argument it will become increasingly evident that the prime essential to that perfect competition which would secure in fact those results to which actual competition only "tends," is the absence of Uncertainty (in the true, unmeasurable sense). Other presuppositions are mostly included in or subordinate to this, that men must *know what they are doing*, and not merely guess more or less accurately. The "tendency" toward perfect competition is at once explained, since men are creatures endowed with the capacity to learn, and tend to find out the results of their acts, while the cause of the failure ever to reach the goal is equally evident so long as omniscience remains unattainable. Now since risk, in the ordinary sense, does not preclude perfect planning (for reasons which can easily be made clear), such risk cannot prevent the complete realization of the tendencies of competitive forces, or give rise to profit.

At the conclusion of this brief treatment of perfect competition we shall devote a short chapter to limitations of perfect competition other than the imperfection of knowledge, and then take up in Part Three a careful analysis of the concepts of Risk and Uncertainty (chapter VII), proceeding (in the remaining chapters) with a somewhat detailed study of the effects of both, but especially of true or unmeasurable uncertainty upon the economic organization and of its bearings upon economic theory. The economic relations of risk in the narrower sense of a measurable probability have been extensively dealt with in the literature of the subject and do not call for elaborate treatment here. Our main concern will be with the contrast between Risk as a known chance and true Uncertainty, and treatment of the former is incidental to this purpose.

Chapter 2. Theories of Profit;Change and Risk in Relation to Profit

IN VIEW of the facts set forth in the introductory chapter as to the relation of profit to theoretical economics, and the vagueness in the minds of economic writers as to fundamental postulates, it is not surprising that the theory of profit[13] has remained one of the most unsatisfactory and controversial divisions of economic doctrine. Considering, however, the universal recognition of the "tendency" of competition to eliminate profit, it is perhaps somewhat remarkable that the problem of profit itself has not, with one important exception,[14] been attacked from the direct point of view adopted in this essay, of an inquiry into the causes of the failure of ideal competition to be fully realized in fact. It is, indeed, only within comparatively recent years that the existence of profit as a really distinct share has

[13]Excellent histories of profit theory are to be found in the introductory sections of several monographs on profit and make it superfluous to go into this phase of the subject in detail. See especially the following:

Mangoldt, H. v., Die Lehre vom Unternehmergewinn. Leipsig, 1855. Pierstorff, J., Die Lehre vom Unternehmergewinn. Berlin, 1875. Mataja, V., Der Unternehmergewinn. Vienna, 1884. Gross, G., Die Lehre vom Unternehmergewinn. Leipsic, 1884. Porte, M., Entrepreneurs et 'profits industriels. Paris, 1901.

[14]The exception is Professor Clark's theory of perfect competition as equivalent to the "static state" and the corresponding "dynamic theory " of profit as the result of progress. This view will presently be taken up and criticized.

become established and the problem of its explanation given definite status.

As in the case of most sciences whose subject matter is some field of human activity, economic theory has been much influenced by practice, and in particular the loose use of terms in everyday affairs has given rise to serious confusions in terminology. The concept of profit is bound up in a certain type of organization of industry, a type realized in various degrees in different places and times, and always undergoing modification and development.

At the time when the English classical school of economists were writing—i.e., in the later eighteenth and early nineteenth centuries — corporations were relatively unimportant, being practically restricted to a few banks and trading companies. There was, of course, some lending at interest, but in the dominant form of industry men used their own capital, hiring labor, and renting land from others. The managerial function centered in the capitalist. Moreover, English industries were new and rapidly expanding; competition was not highly developed; the possession of capital seemed to be and was the dominant factor in the situation. Only in more recent times has the accumulation of capital, the perfection of financial institutions, and the growth of competition transferred the center of interest to business ability, made it easy or at least generally possible for ability to secure capital when not in possession of it by direct ownership, and made common the carrying-on of business predominantly with borrowed resources.

Under these early conditions it was natural to connect the income of the business manager with the ownership of capital, and in all the classical writings we find the word "profit" used in this sense. A further source of confusion was the indefiniteness of the conception and use of the ideas of natural and market price in the minds of the early writers. It is natural and inevitable that a distinction which goes to the heart of the fundamental problems of the nature and methodology of economic science should be but imperfectly worked out in the initial stages of the speculation. Only recently, again, has the analysis of long-time normal price by Marshall and of the "static state" by Clark and Schumpeter begun to give to economists a clearer notion of what is really involved in "natural" or normal conditions. To the earlier classical writers this obscurity hid the fundamental difference between the total income of the capitalist manager and contract interest. The only separation considered necessary in the explanation of distribution was to restrict the theory of the business manager's income to the explanation of "normal profit," which was regarded as substantially equivalent to contract interest. Another barrier to the formulation of a clear statement of the relations between interest and profit was the lack of an adequate understanding of the productivity of capital, which also these authors did not possess and which has first been worked out in recent years.

The qualification of "near" or "substantial" identification of normal profit and interest is necessary, however, in referring to the classical treatments. Even Adam Smith and his immediate followers recognized that profits even normally contain an element which is not interest on capital. Remuneration for the work and care of supervising the business was always distinguished. Reference was also made to risk, but in the sense of risk of loss of capital, which does not clearly distinguish profit from interest.[15] Adam Smith is explicit in regard to these elements, while Malthus and McCulloch were more so. J. S. Mill pointed out in a somewhat groping way that the wages of management are determined in a different way from other wages, and noted also that profits, so called, include as a third element a payment for risk, as well as wages of management (and interest). The inclusion of interest in profit was opposed by Bagehot, and in the United States by Walker , but the use of the term is still somewhat loose in England, as is seen in Marshall. Even in this country the development of corporation accounting, while separating wages of management from profit, has tended to a new confusion of profit and interest.

The early French writers, beginning with J. B. Say, adopted a different view of profit, or at least a different use of the word, insisting on a separation of profit from interest and defining the former explicitly as a wage. The difference in procedure may have been

[15]For a fuller discussion of the views of the English writers, with citations, see Cannan, Theories of Production and Distribution, chap, vi, sec. 2; also the same author's article on "Profit" in Palgrave's Dictionary of Political Economy. In opposition to the German historians and critics, who take the classical economists very literally, Cannan is sure that they really held, like their French followers, a wage theory of profit. Between the two views this seems the fairer on the whole, but it could hardly be maintained that the difference in expression does not represent some difference in thought. However, much of the contrast is undoubtedly due to differences in the use of terms. Old words used to designate new things necessarily become ambiguous, and "profit" is still correctly used with several different meanings.

due, as v. Mangoldt suggests,[16] to the different character of typical French industry and the greater importance of the manager's personality in it relatively to the capital factor. It is worthy of note that in the fourth edition of his "Traité," Say included in profit the reward for risk-taking; he had in the earlier editions viewed this income as accruing to the capitalist as such, but now transferred it to the entrepreneur. Especial mention should be made of Courcelle-Seneuil, who insisted that profit is not a wage, but is due to the assumption of risk.[17]

The older German economists varied widely in their treatment of profits. Some, of whom Schäffle is perhaps the most notable example, follow the "English" view in classing profit as essentially a return to capital. Others, notably Roscher, adopt the "French"[18] attitude and treat it as a form of wages. Roscher does not even use the term "profit," but substitutes *Unternehmerlohn.* Other writers, such as Hermann and Rau, took a more or less intermediate position.

Still another group, of more importance for our purposes, contended that profit should be recognized as a unique form of income, not susceptible of reduction to remuneration for either capital or la-

---

[16]Op. cit. t p. 19, note.

[17]Article, "Profit," in Coquelin and Guillaumin's Dictionnaire de economie politique, Paris, 1852. It is true that in another work (TraitS d'Sconomie politique, 2d ed., 1867) Courcelle was not so explicit, and also that in the same article he says that profit depends on the intelligence of the entrepreneur and the favorable or unfavorable conditions under which he works. This hesitation may explain Kleinwachter's classifying him with the followers of Say and adherents of the wages theory. (See Das Einkommen und seine Verteilung, p. 278.) It seems more probable, however, that Courcelle glimpsed the fact (which KleinwSchter did not) that the assumption of a "risk" of error in one's own judgment, inherent in the making of a responsible decision, is a phenomenon of a different character from the assumption of "risk" in the insurance sense. We shall build largely upon this distinction later.

[18]These national designations of the two schools hold closely. The only notable exceptions (aside from Courcelle) are on the one side, Rossi, a French (naturalized Italian) writer, who strongly espoused the capitalistic or English view, and on the other Samuel Read, who, while agreeing with the current English treatment in terminology, broke with it in substance and agreed with Say and his followers. Read insisted on identifying "profit" with the return to capital, or interest, and treating the distinctive income of the entrepreneur as a wage. He also emphasized the "compensation for risk" element in his "profit" (really interest), but thought it due to no determinate causes and "outside the pale of science." This last phrase shows at least an insight into the unique character of this sort of risk, since the assertion would certainly not have been made of an insurance premium. See his Political Economy, Edinburgh, 1829, pp. 263 and 269, note.

bor. This position was taken in a somewhat timid way by Hufeland[19] and more definitely by Riedel,[20] but its most notable advocates were Thünen and v. Mangoldt. Thünen's great work, "Der Isolirte Staat,"[21] defines profit as what is left after (a) interest, (b) insurance, and (c) wages of management, are met. This residuum consists of two parts: (1) payment for certain risks, especially changes in values and the chance of failure of the whole enterprise, which cannot be insured against, and (2) the extra productivity of the manager's labor due to the fact that he is working for himself, his "sleepless nights" when he is planning for the business. Thünen called these elements respectively *Industriebelohnung* and *Unternehmergewinn*, and their sum *Gewerbsprofit.*

A most careful and exhaustive analysis of profit is contained in the monograph of H. v. Mangoldt, already referred to. Proceeding on the basis of an elaborate classification of the forms of industrial organization and a discussion of the economic advantages of the entrepreneur form, this writer finds in the income of the business enterpriser a complex group of unique elements. He divides it first into three parts: (1) a premium on those risks which are of such a nature that he cannot shift them by insurance; (2) entrepreneur interest and wages, including only payments for special forms of capital or productive effort which do not admit of exploitation by any other than their owner; (3) entrepreneur rents. These last again fall into four subdivisions: (a) capital rents, (b) wage rents, (c) large enterprise rent, and (d) "entrepreneur rent in the narrower sense." They are all due to the limitation of special capacities or characteristics (the last to special combinations of such) and are called "premiums on scarcity" (*Seltenheits prämeien*). This is, of course, a question-begging term (though many writers have used it) since all incomes depend in the same way on the limitation of the agencies to which they are imputed. It would seem that every imaginable source of income is included in this minute and subtle classification.

A special place in the history of theories of profit should be given to the German socialist school, the so-called "scientific" socialists, Rodbertus, Marx, Engels, Lassalle, and their followers. These writers take the English classical treatment of profit in a narrowly literal

---

[19]Neue Grundlage der Staatsimssenschaft, vol. I. Giessen, 1807.

[20]National Okonomie, 1839.

[21]Appeared 1826. 3d ed., 1876. See 3d ed., vol. n, pp. 83 ff.

(one must say wholly uncritical and superficial) sense as including all income accruing to capital, to which they add land. Combining this with an equally blind reading of the labor theory of value which was the starting-point of Smith and Ricardo, they derive a simple classification of income in which all that is not wages is a profit which represents exploitation of the working classes. Capital is equivalent to property, which is to be regarded as mere power over the economic activities of others due to the strategic position of ownership over the implements of labor. It is analogous to a robber baron's crag, a toll-gate on a natural highway, or a political franchise to exploit. Pierstorff, in the monograph referred to above, follows Rodbertus in the main, after criticizing alternative views.[22]

After the publication in 1871 of Menger's "Grundsätze" had given a new interest and new turn to value theory in Austria and Germany, a notable series of discussions of profit appeared in those countries. Those calling for especial mention are the monographs of Gross[23] and Mataja[24] and the treatments by Mithoff[25] and Kleinwächter[26] in Schönberg's "Handbuch," the last-named elaborated in the author's book already referred to. Gross takes as his starting-point the plain fact that profit is the difference between the cost of goods and their value, and studies the position of the entrepreneur in the two markets in which he buys productive services and raw materials and sells his finished product. He may be said to reduce profit to bargaining power, in which, of course, superior knowledge and foresight are recognized as playing a large part, but Gross does not work out a systematic treatment of the nature and significance of risk or uncertainty. He thinks an income which is a premium for taking risks is inherently impossible, as gains and losses would necessarily

[22]See also the article " Unternehmergewinn," by Pierstorff in Conrad's Handworterbuch der Staatswissenschaften. Dr. Thorstein Veblen's conceptions of capital and profit show strong leanings toward the same views.

[23]Referred to above, p. 22 n.

[24]Ibid

[25]G. Schonberg, Handbuch der Politischen Oeconomie, 2d ed. (Tubingen, 1885), pp. 670 ff.

[26]Ibid., pp. 220 ff. Other works in the same group with the above are:

E. Aug. Schroeder, Das Unternehmen und der Unternehmergewinn. Vienna, 1884. (The same date of publication as Gross and Mataja.) A. Wirminghaus, Das Unternehmergewinn und die Beteiligung

Arbeiter am Unternehmergewinn. Jena, 1886. E. Zuns, Swei Fragen des Unternehmer-Einkommens. Berlin, 1881. A. Korner, Unternehmen und Unternehmergewinn. Vienna, 1893.

balance. Few other writers agree with this proposition. Socially, profit is for Gross the inducement to follow closely the economic law of cheapest possible production and most effective utilization of goods.

Mataja's analysis of profit is a more literal application of Menger's utility theory of value. He seeks to explain price differences by means of the differences between the various uses of "goods of higher order" in making different kinds of "goods of lower order" and ultimately different consumption goods. His discussion does not get beyond a statement of the problem.

Mithoff holds that the entrepreneur's income consists of rents, wages, etc., at market rates for the productive services which he furnishes to the business, plus a "profit" which may be regarded as remuneration for taking the risk of its failure. He contends, however, that this profit is at best a mere abstraction, a complex of a number of indeterminate surpluses, and that the entrepreneur income as a whole alone has definite meaning or practical significance.

Körner is another writer who explains the entrepreneur's income in terms of superior bargaining power. His position is figured as that of a watchman on a tower and is summed up in the expression that his is a wider market than that of the men he buys from and sells to, especially the laborer whom he hires. The essential mystery of why the competition of other watchmen on similar towers does not eliminate his peculiar gain is not touched upon. The nonsocialistic German writers are usually particularly concerned to combat the allegations of the socialists and furnish a social justification of profit.

Kleinwächter views profit from the social standpoint as pay for taking the twofold risk of production—technical and economic, a distinction made by Gross—and for the care of supervision. From the individual point of view it is a speculative gain arising from advantage taken of differences between the prices of economic goods and the prices of the agents necessary to their production. In his fuller treatment in his book on distribution, Kleinwächter devotes most of his energy to a sarcastic polemic against the English classical economic theory, according to which the prices of commodities should equal their costs of production or the sum of the wages, interest, and rent paid the agents employed to produce them. No serious criticism of this theory is attempted, however, nor any sign displayed of a comprehension of its real meaning as a statement of the limits of tendencies. The general conclusion that the existence of profit follows from a divergence between the conditions of theory and those of fact is the starting-point of the present study. It is, of course, a statement of the problem, and not a solution of it; Kleinwächter virtually explains profit by ridiculing the idea that it should be thought to call for explanation.

In other than the German-speaking countries the subject of profit has not been prolific of independent monographs and treatises, but has usually been dealt with as an integral part of the general theory of distribution (though there are some exceptions in France and Italy which would have to be noticed in a fuller historical treatment). It is, of course, impossible to take up even the important theorists in all countries and summarize their views, while any brief treatment by schools or groups would be misleading rather than helpful. The writers already mentioned pretty well cover the fundamental theories and standpoints, with exceptions yet to be noted.[27] A very common procedure is to treat profit as a special case of monopoly gain, or to combine elements of monopoly position with other factors. This method is apt to degenerate into a mere confusion of the two income categories. The common use of the term "monopoly profit" to designate monopoly revenue directly incites to this confusion.

The first notable development in the field of profit theory in America was the work of General Francis A. Walker.[28] Walker effectually emphasized the place and importance of the entrepreneur or "captain of industry," and helped to free economic treatises in English from the careless handling of profit as an element in interest. His own "rent theory," however, in spite of its vogue at the time of its promulgation, need not now detain us. Walker wrote before

[27]A noteworthy innovation in the treatment of profit has been made by a recent French writer, M. B. Lavergne, in his Theorie des Triarchies Socionomiques (Paris, 1910). In his view profit is the remuneration of the idte productrice, which is elevated to the position of an independent productive factor. His book outlines an ingenious and suggestive theory of distribution. See review by Professor A. A. Young, American Economic Review, vol. I, pp. 549 ff.

[28]Political Economy, part iv, chap. iv. See also "The Source of Business Profits and Reply to Mr. Mac vane," Quarterly Journal of Economics, vol. i, pp. 265 ff ., and vol. n, pp. 263 ff. (Macvane held a monopoly theory; cf. Quarterly Journal of Economics, vol. n, pp. 1 ff. and 453 ff.) A view similar to that of Walker has been advocated in France by Leroy-Beau-lieu (Sr.). See Memories de V Academic des sciences morales et politiques, vol. i, pp. 717 ff, and Traits oeiconomie 'politique, part iv, chap. ix.

Marshall, Clark,[29] and Hobson[30] had shown that all incomes are like rent in the mode of their determination, and with that point once made clear the rent theory is reduced to a wage theory merely, and its special significance disappears.

More recently the center of interest in the discussion of profit has shifted from Walker's theory to two other opposed views, the "dynamic theory" and the "risk theory" respectively. The former is the view upheld by Professor J. B. Clark and his followers and the latter is sponsored in particular by Mr. F. B. Hawley.[31] Neither the connection between profit and changes in conditions nor that between profit and risk is an entirely new idea, but hitherto neither had been erected into a definite and ostensibly sufficient principle of explanation of the peculiar income of the entrepreneur. These two theories call for somewhat fuller treatment.

The dynamic theory is a correlate of Professor J. B. Clark's theory of distribution in the profitless "static state."[32] Professor Clark outlines a systematic structure of theoretical economics in three main divisions. The first treats of universal phenomena, and the second of static social phenomena. Starting with those laws of economics which act whether humanity is organized or not, we next study the forces that depend on organization but do not depend on progress. Finally it is necessary to study the forces of progress. To influences that would act if society were in a stationary state, we must add those which act only as society is thrown into a condition

[29] " Distribution as Determined by a Law of Rent," Quarterly Journal of Economics, vol. v, pp. 289 ff.

[30] "The Law of the Three Rents," ibid., vol. v, pp. 263 ff. More exhaustive than either Clark or Hobson is Wicksteed, The Coordination of the Laws of Distribution, London, 1894.

[31] It is not meant that these are the only noteworthy advocates of the views in question, nor that other American writers on distribution have not been in some degree original in their treatment of profit. The discussions by the various authors — Davenport, Ely, Fetter, Fisher, Johnson, Seager, Seligman, Taussig, and others are accessible everywhere. Perhaps especial mention should be made of the chapter on profit in Carver's Distribution of Wealth. Carver's distinction between compensation for risk-taking and the results of successful risk-taking points to the direction in which a solution of the problem is to be sought. Other writers also have seen the importance of a critical dissection of the risk concept, but none have so far carried out the work. Unquestionably the best of these textbook discussions is that of Professor F. M. Taylor in his unpublished Principles of Economics, a work characterized throughout by correctly reasoned and accurately stated theoretical argument.

[32] See The Distribution of Wealth, 1900; and Essentials of Economic Theory, 1907.

of movement and disturbance. This will give us a science of Social Economic Dynamics.[33]

The static state is the state of "natural" adjustments of Ricardo and the early classical writers. What are called "natural" standards of values and "natural" or normal rates of wages, interest, and profits are in reality, static rates. They are identical with those which would be realized, if a society were perfectly organized, but were free from the disturbances that progress causes.... Reduce society to a stationary state, let industry go on with entire freedom, make labor and capital absolutely mobile... and you will have a regime of natural values.[34]

To realize the static state, we should have to eliminate five kinds of change which are constantly in progress: Five generic changes are going on, every one of which reacts on the structure of society, by changing the arrangements of that group system which it is the work of catallactics to study:

1. Population is increasing.
2. Capital is increasing.
3. Methods of production are improving.
4. The forms of industrial establishments are changing, the less efficient shops, etc., are passing from the field, and the more efficient are surviving.
5. The wants of consumers are multiplying[35]

In the static state each factor secures what it produces, and since cost and selling price are always equal there can be no profits beyond wages for the routine work of supervision. The prices of goods are in these older theories said to be "natural" when they equal the cost of producing them;... in reality their "natural prices" were static prices.[36] The prices that conform to the cost of production are, of course, those which give no clear profit to the entrepreneur. A business man whose goods sell at such rates will get wages for whatever amount of labor he may perform, and interest for any capital that he may furnish; but he will have nothing more to show in the way of gain. He will sell his product for what the elements that compose it have really cost him, if his own labor and the use of his capital be counted among the costs. We shall see that this condition of no-

[33]The Distribution of Wealth, pp. 30, 31.

[34]The Distribution of Wealth, p. 29.

[35]Ibid., p. 56.

[36]Ibid., pp. 68-69.

profit prices exactly corresponds to the one that would result from the static adjustment of the producing groups.[37]

Profits are, then, the result exclusively of dynamic change. "Obviously, from all these changes two general results must follow: first, values, wages and interest will differ from the static standards; secondly, the static standards themselves will always be changing."[38] The type of dynamic change is invention; "an invention makes it possible to produce something more cheaply. It first gives a profit to entrepreneurs and then... adds something to wages and interest.... Let another invention be made.... It also creates a profit; and this profit, like the first, is an elusive sum, which entrepreneurs grasp but cannot hold." It "slips through their fingers and bestows itself on all members of society."[39]Thus the effect of any one dynamic change is to produce *temporary* profits. But in actual society such changes constantly occur, and the readjustments are always in process. "As a result, we... have the standard of wages moving continuously upward and actual wages steadily pursuing the standard rate in its upward movement, but always remaining by a certain interval behind it."[40]

In another sense profit is dependent on "friction": "The interval between actual wages and the static standard is the result of friction; for, if competition worked without let or hindrance, pure business profit would be annihilated as fast as it could be created...."[41] "Were it not for that interval, entrepreneurs as such would get nothing, however much they might add to the world's productive power."[42]

---

[37]Ibid. Professor Joseph Schumpeter, who has carried the static analysis farther in some respects than Professor Clark, points out that in the static state there is no entrepreneur, properly speaking. The consumer, he adds, is really the entrepreneur; but it would seem preferable to say that the function is absent and let it go at that. (Theorie der Wirtschaftliche Entwickelung.)

[38]The Distribution of Wealth, p. 404.

[39]Ibid., p. 405.

[40]Ibid., p. 406.

[41]Ibid., p. 410. This is fallacious even under the assumptions, since the profits of change come largely in the form of readjustments of capital values. The difficulty is, of course, avoided if "friction" be so broadly defined that "perfect mobility" means the absence of all resistance to the human will. But in a world where a breath could transform a brick factory building into a railway yard or an ocean greyhound there would be no need for economic activity or economic science.

[42]The Distribution of Wealth, p. 411. At this point Professor Clark makes a statement which if followed out would lead to serious questionings in regard to his analysis: "Profit," he says (p. 411), "is the lure that insures improvement, and improvement is the source of permanent additions to wages. To secure progress,

The fatal criticism of this procedure of taking changes in conditions as the explanation and cause of profit is that it overlooks the fundamental question of the difference between a change that is foreseen a reasonable time in advance and one that is unforeseen. Now, if we merely assume that all the "dynamic changes" which Professor Clark enumerates, and any others which may be named, are foreknown for a sufficient time before they take place, or that they take place continuously in accordance with laws generally and accurately known, so that their course may be predicted as far into the future as occasion may require, then the whole argument based on the effects of change will fall completely to the ground. If the retort is made that this is a supposition contrary to fact and illicit, the answer is that it is only partly contrary to fact. Some changes are foreseen and some are not, the laws of some are tolerably accurately known, of others hardly at all;[43] and the variation in foreknowledge makes it clearly indispensable to separate its effects from those of change as such if any real understanding of the elements of the situation is to be attained. It is evident that a society might be ever so dynamic, as Professor Clark defines the term, and yet have all its prices "natural" or constantly equal to production costs, excluding

---

this lure must be sufficient to make men overcome obstructions and take risks." (My italics.) It would seem that effort and risk have some connection with the income of the "entrepreneur as such," as well as change and friction. Along the same line is the statement in his first chapter (p. 3) that "free competition tends to give to labor what labor creates, to capitalists what capital creates, and to entrepreneurs what the coordinating function creates." When we ask, as we presently shall, whether the "effort" and "risk" connected with making progress, or the income to which they give rise, are essentially different from any other effort and risk and their incomes, we shall find ourselves forced to answer in the negative, and to look outside the fact of change altogether for an explanation of the unique income of the entrepreneur.

[43]It may be objected that in regard to some changes it is an absurdity to imagine their being foreseen, since this would cause them to take place at once. The statement doubtless holds in regard to some discoveries of fact, which to anticipate would be to make them now. But not many of the dynamic economic changes are of this sort. The accumulation of capital and increase in population are in fact relatively predictable and the broader features in the development of wants are known and the knowledge has no effect on the changes themselves. It is possible even to predict discovery of natural resources without saying just where they will be found, and the making of an invention without actually writing the specifications. The probability that inventions will be made and processes improved is in fact very frequently taken into account in making valuations and determining business policies. The assumption that all change might be predictable is contrary to fact, but not self-contradictory, and we leave it to the argument as a whole to justify its usefulness as well as legitimacy.

any chance for the entrepreneur to secure a net profit. It is fallacious to define "natural" conditions as "static" conditions.

No a priori argument is necessary to prove that with general foreknowledge of progressive changes no losses and no chance to make profits will arise out of them. This is the first principle of speculation, and is particularly familiar in the capitalization of the anticipated increase in the value of land. The effect of any change which can be foreseen will be adequately discounted in advance, any "costs" connected with it will be affected in exactly the same way as the corresponding "values" and no separation between the two will take place.

It will be interesting to follow this line of thought somewhat farther, as suggested above in connection with Professor Clark's characterization of profit as the lure that causes men to make the efforts and take the risks involved in progress. It is in fact but a short step from the foreknowledge of change to the fact that change in reality does not usually just happen, but is largely itself the result of human activity. It is evident that if the laws of economically significant changes are known, those human actions which give rise to such changes will be governed by the same motives as the operations productive of immediate utilities, and in the competition of resources for profitable employment returns will be adjusted to equality between the two fields of use. Industrial progress would certainly take place under these conditions quite as readily as where the operations giving rise to it gave highly unpredictable results, but the rewards of making inventions, discovering new natural resources, etc., with the speculative character of the operations once removed, would be in no wise different from wages, interest, and rent in any other line of productive activity. They would be equal in amount, determined in the same way, in the same competitive market, and in short would be wages, interest, and rent merely, and not profit. And this is what does come about to the extent that progress can be foreseen, which is to say in very large measure. Dynamic changes give rise to a peculiar form of income only in so far as the changes and their consequences are unpredictable in character.

It cannot, then, be change, which is the cause of profit, since if the law of the change is known, as in fact is largely the case, no profits can arise. The connection between change and profit is uncertain and always indirect. Change may cause a situation out of which profit will be made, *if* it brings about ignorance of the future. Without change of some sort there would, it is true, be no profits, for if everything moved along in an absolutely uniform way, the future would be completely foreknown in the present and competition would certainly adjust things to the ideal state where all prices would equal costs. It is this fact that change is a necessary condition of our being ignorant of the future (though ignorance need not follow from the fact of change and only to a limited extent does so) that has given rise to the error that change is the cause of profit.

Not only may change take place without occasioning profit, but profit may also arise in the entire absence of any "dynamic" or progressive changes of the kind enumerated by Professor Clark. If conditions are subject to unpredictable fluctuations,[44] ignorance of the future will result in the same way and inaccuracies in the competitive adjustment and profits will be the inevitable consequence. And the failure of an anticipated change to occur is the same in effect as the occurrence of an unanticipated one. It is not dynamic change, nor any change, as such, which causes profit, but the divergence of actual conditions from those which have been expected and on the basis of which business arrangements have been made. For a satisfactory explanation of profit we seem to be thrown back from the "dynamic" theory to the Uncertainty of the Future, a condition of affairs loosely designated by the term "risk" in ordinary language and in business parlance.

Except for one or two passing references, Professor Clark does not take up the subject of risk in the treatise from which we have quoted. In a short article on "Insurance and Profits"[45] (written in refutation of Mr. Hawley) he takes the position that risk-taking gives rise to a special category of income, but that it accrues to the capitalist, and cannot go to the entrepreneur, as such. How he would treat this income, what relation it would bear to interest, he does not tell us. But it is no part of profit, which is defined as "the excess of the price of goods over their cost."[46] "It goes without saying that the hazard of business falls on the capitalist. The entrepreneur, as such, is empty-handed. No man can carry risk who has nothing to lose."[47] In his later work, the "Essentials of Economic Theory,"

[44]It is necessary to stipulate that the fluctuations must be of sufficient extent and irregularity that they do not cancel out and reduce to uniformity or regular periodicity in a time-interval short in comparison with the length of human life.

[45]Quarterly Journal of Economics, vol. vn, pp. 40-54.

[46]Ibid., p. 41.

[47]Ibid., p. 46.

the subject of risk again receives scant attention.[48] Risks are simply ruled out of the discussion, since "the greater part of them arise from dynamic causes," and the "unavoidable remainder" of static risk can be taken care of by setting aside "a small percentage of the annual gains [of each establishment, which]... will make good these losses as they occur and leave the businesses in a condition in which they can yield as a steady return to owners of stock, to lenders of... capital, and to laborers all of their real product."

It is clear that Professor Clark admits that his perfectly competitive state implies substantially perfect knowledge on the part of all members of society of present and future facts significant for the ordering of their business conduct. Dr. A. H. Willett[49] has supplemented the theory of the static state in this field, and Dr. A. S. Johnson has some discussion of it in his study of rent.[50] Willett recognizes that the disturbing effects of progress do not constitute the sole cause of divergence between actual society and the theoretical ideal; "the conception of the static state is reached by a process of abstraction," which "cannot stop" with the elimination of the five dynamic changes: If all dynamic changes were to cease, the ideal static state would never be realized in human society. There are other assumptions which have to be made, such as a high degree of mobility of capital and labor, the universal prevalence of the economic motive, and the power of accurately foreseeing the future.... It is the influence of the last of these disturbing factors on static rates of wages and interest that we are to seek to determine. The ideal adjustment could be realized only on the condition that there were *no discrepancies between the anticipated and the actual results of economic activity.* Production and consumption must go on either with absolute uniformity or with a regular periodicity.[51]

From the above admission that the static state is not an adequate formulation of the conditions of ideal competition, it would be an easy inference in line with static theory as a whole that some modification in the treatment of profit would be called for. But

---

[48] Footnote, pp. 122-23.

[49] The Economic Theory of Risk and Insurance, Columbia University Studies in Political Science, vol. xiv, no. 2.

[50] Rent in Modern Economic Theory. Publications of the American Economic Association, 3d Series, vol. in, no. 4. See chapter vi: "Rent, Profit, and Monopoly Return." (Both these monographs are doctoral dissertations written under Professor Clark's supervision.)

[51] Willett, op. cit. t pp. 13-14. (My italics.)

this inference is not drawn by the author quoted. He is not looking for and does not find any connection between profit and risk. He agrees explicitly with Clark that the entrepreneur takes risk only as a capitalist, and that the income resulting is therefore not profit. In his discussion of the reward for risk-taking, Willett states even more emphatically than Clark had done the contention that only the capitalist as such can take risk or get the reward of risk-assumption. To him this "seems to be a self-evident proposition,"[52] but he fails to take account of the familiar fact that men may secure their obligations in other ways than through pledging material resources already owned and invested, as for example by mortgaging their current income from all sources and their future earning power.

In his discussion of profits referred to above, Dr. Johnson makes some reference to risk, but he also makes no attempt to find in it an explanation of profit. He discovers four elements in "the income of a fortunate and capable entrepreneur."

(1) A gain due to chance, offset by a smaller loss (borne, however, by some other entrepreneur);

(2) a gain due to his own power of combining labor and capital in ways more effective than those usually employed in the community;

(3) a certain share in the first fruits of economic improvements;

(4) a part of the gains which entrepreneurs as a class secure through the fact that their services are limited in proportion to the demand for them.

We need not stop to criticize this analysis in detail; it might be pointed out that shares (2) and (4) are identical, and that neither formulation would distinguish profit from wages (and (4) not from any other income, as we have remarked above); (3) is a reference to the "dynamic" explanation of profit and is unclear without further elaboration; (1) seems to point to a connection between profit and risk, but this is not worked out. It is clear that these discussions of risk, as emendations of the dynamic theory, make no pretense of explaining the connection between profit and uncertainty which our discussion of Professor Clark's treatment showed to be necessary. Both writers are, indeed, opposed to and attempt to refute the doctrine that profit is the result of assuming risk.

---

[52]Ibid., p. 72.

The doctrine that profit is to be explained exclusively in terms of risk has been vigorously upheld by Mr. F. B. Hawley,[53] who finds in risk-taking the essential function of the entrepreneur and therefore the basis of his peculiar income. In Mr. Hawley's distributive theory the entrepreneur, or "enterpriser" as he is called, plays a role of unique importance. Enterprise is the only really productive factor, strictly speaking, land, labor, and capital being relegated to the position of "means" of production. In regard to profit, the reward of enterprise, Hawley says:[54] ...the profit of an undertaking, or the residue of the product after the claims of land, capital, and labor (furnished by others or by the undertaker himself) are satisfied, is not the reward of management or coordination, but of the risks and responsibilities that the undertaker... subjects himself to. And as no one, as a matter of business, subjects himself to risk for what he believes the actuarial value of the risk amounts to—in the calculation of which he is on the average correct—a net income accrues to Enterprise, as a whole, equal to the difference between the gains derived from undertakings and the actual losses incurred in them. This net income, being manifestly an unpredetermined residue, must be a profit, and as there cannot be two unpredetermined residues in the same undertaking, profit is identified with the reward for the

[53]The most complete exposition of Hawley's theory is in his book. Enterprise and the Productive Process (1907). Articles of earlier date in the Quarterly Journal of Economics contain briefer statements.

[54]An earlier attempt by Mr. Hawley to present the essentials of his theory in the most compact form is superior in some respects and is worth quoting:

"The final consumer is forced to include in the price he pays for any product not only enough to cover all the items of cost to the entrepreneur, among which items is a sum sufficient to cover the actuarial or average losses incidental to the various risks of all kinds necessarily assumed by the entrepreneur and his insurers, but a further sum, without which, as an inducement, the entrepreneur, or enterpriser, and his insurers will not undergo or suffer the irksomeness of being exposed to risk.

"This surplus of consumer's cost over entrepreneur's cost, universally regarded as profit, and, from the nature of the case, an unpredetermined residue, is the inducement for the assumption by the entrepreneur, or enterpriser, of all the risks, whatever their nature, necessitated by the process of production. As the inducement to any given action and the reward for that action are the same thing, — the difference being not in the thing itself, but only in the point of time from which it is looked upon, — the unpredetermined residue, which served as the inducement to risk at the commencement of any industrial transaction must necessarily, when determined and realized at its close, be regarded as the result, reward, of the risks undergone." {Quarterly Journal of Economics, vol. xv, pp. 603-20.) (In the original the portion quoted is all in italics.)

assumption of responsibility, especially, though not exclusively, that involved in ownership.[55]

Mr. Hawley is in agreement with Professor Clark and his followers in defining profit as "residual income," and as to the nature and basis of the special income connected with the assumption of risk as an excess of payment above the actuarial value of the risk, demanded because exposure to risk is "irksome"; but Hawley insists that residual income and uncertain income are interchangeable concepts,[56] while Clark is equally sure that the reward of risk-taking necessarily goes to the capitalist as such and that the pure profit of the entrepreneur is a species of monopoly gain arising in connection with dynamic disturbances, and that his only income under static conditions would be wages of management or coordination. Hawley contends that such income is wages merely, and not profit, and does not distinguish between "static" and "dynamic" conditions. Coordination, however, is in his view distinguished from labor by the fact of proprietorship, "which is the very essence of the matter in dispute."[57] Profit cannot be the reward of management, for this can be performed by hired labor if the manager takes no risk, but this individual is no longer an entrepreneur.

It is admitted that the entrepreneur may get rid of risk in some cases for a fixed cost, by means of insurance. But by the act of insurance the business man abdicates so much of his entrepreneurship, "for it is manifest that an entrepreneur who should eliminate all his risks by means of insurance would have left no income at all which was not resolvable into wages of management and monopoly gains" (i.e., no profit).[58] To the extent to which the business man insures, he restricts the exercise of his peculiar function, but the risk is merely transferred to the insurer, who by accepting it becomes himself an enterpriser and the recipient of an unpredetermined residue or profit." The reward of an insurer is not the premium he receives, but the difference between that premium and the loss he eventually

[55] Op. cit, pp. 106-07.

[56] Quarterly Journal of Economics, vol. vn, p. 465; vol. xv, p. 88.

[57] "Enterprise and Profit," Quarterly Journal of Economics, vol. xv, p. 86.

[58] Quarterly Journal of Economics, vol. vii, p. 464. It should be explained that "monopoly gain" for Mr. Hawley includes all income due to limitation, and he finds that it forms a considerable portion of wages and interest, all of rent, and a large part of profit. We have repeatedly observed examples of this fallacy and remarked that there is no income which is not due to the "scarcity" of the agent securing it.

suffers."[59]

The clue to the disagreement and to the straightening-out of the facts as well is to be found in a confusion fallen into by those on both sides of the controversy, in assuming that the "actuarial value" of the risks taken is known to the entrepreneur. There is a fundamental distinction between the reward for taking a known risk and that for assuming a risk whose value itself is not known. It is so fundamental, indeed, that, as we shall see, a known risk will not lead to any reward or special payment at all. Though Willett distinguishes between "uncertainty" and "risk" and the mathematical probability of loss,[60] he still treats uncertainty throughout his study as a known quantity.[61] The same applies to Johnson; he also implicitly recognizes at various points that the true chance or actuarial value of the risk may not be known, and devotes some space[62] to Thünen's emphasis on the distinction between insurable and uninsurable risks; but he also fails entirely to take account in his discussion of profit of the fact that the risk involved in entrepreneurship is not and cannot be a known quantity.

In a similar way Hawley repeatedly refers to the fact of uninsurable risk as well as to "pure luck" and to "changes that no one could have foreseen," but he fails to inquire into its meaning or to recognize its theoretical import.[63] Once he goes so far as to say that "the great source of monopoly profit is to be found in the fact that the actuarial risk of any given undertaking is not the same for dif-

[59]Enterprise and the Productive Process, p. 111.

[60]Op. cit., pp. 27 ff.

[61]Risk is defined as "the objective correlative of the subjective uncertainty" (p. 29), which varies with the mathematical chance of loss in such a way as to be at a maximum when the chances for and against the event are exactly even. But it is still to be regarded as a known quantity, since the mathematical chance is assumed to be known. Willett nowhere makes an explicit statement on this point, as Hawley does (see quotation in text on p. 42 above), but his discussion clearly shows that it is viewed as a known quantity. He takes his illustrations from games of chance or from the field of insurance, speaks of the influence of "a given degree of risk" (p. 65) on investors, etc. He does recognize the fact that the degree of risk is not always known in fact, and discusses methods of estimating the degree of risk; but (pp. 66 and 76) he expressly eliminates from the discussion the consequences of error in estimating the true value of the risk.

[62]Op. cit. t p. 112.

[63]The reader will recall that many of the early discussions of profit (discussed in the early pages of this chapter), notably those of v. Man-goldt and v. Thunen, recognized the fact that some risks are insurable and others are not. No explanation of the fact, however, has been given, beyond phrases such as "in the nature of the case," which imply that it does not call for explanation.

ferent entrepreneurs, owing to differences among them in ability and environment";[64] and again, that "profit is the result of risks wisely selected."[65] Even here, however, he fails to develop the point and draw the consequences from the fact that the actuarial value of the risk undergone by any venturer is not known, either to himself or to his competitors.

In a sense Mr. Hawley comes still nearer to the crux of the matter in his insistence on the responsibility and risk of proprietorship as the essential attributes of entrepreneurship. The entrepreneur is the owner of all real wealth, and ownership involves risk; the coordinator "makes decisions," but it is the entrepreneur who "accepts the consequences of decisions."[66] He admits that others than the recognized entrepreneur are subject to risk; the landlord is also a proprietor, and his land may change in value; the capitalist especially requires payment for the large risks he runs, and a part of both rent and interest is accordingly profit. A person who invests his own capital in any form of opportunity necessarily combines the two functions of capitalist and enterpriser. The same should apparently apply to the laborer, who is also admitted to run risks.

Mr. Hawley does not regard the term "risk" as calling for special definition, but it is clear that, like the other writers, he treats it as a known quantity; he says this much explicitly.[67] He and his opponents alike have failed to appreciate the fundamental difference between a determinate uncertainty or risk and an indeterminate, unmeasurable one. The only practical bearing of the question as to whether the value of the risk is known which is recognized by Hawley is to determine whether it is likely to be insured, which is to say merely who will get the "profit" for assuming it; even this point is not very explicitly made. Now a little consideration will show that there can be no considerable "irksomeness" attached to exposure to

[64]"The Risk Theory of Profit," Quarterly Journal of Economics, vol. Vii, p. 468.

[65]Enterprise and the Productive Process, p. 108. Cf. Carver, "Risk Theory of Profits," Quarterly Journal of Economics, vol. xv, pp. 456 ff., and The Distribution of Wealth, chap. vii. Also A. A. Young in Ely's Outlines of Economics, 3d ed., chap. xxv. The phrase "successful risk-taking," used by both Carver and Young, like Hawley's "risks wisely selected," is certainly descriptive of the origin of profits. What is wanted is an examination of the meaning of risk-taking which will elucidate the conditions under which it will be successful and show the significant differences between cases of success and cases of failure.

[66]"Enterprise and Profit," Quarterly Journal of Economics, vol. xv, p. 88.

[67]See above, p. 42.

an insurable risk, for if there is it will be insured; hence there can be no peculiar income arising out of this alleged indisposition. If risk were exclusively of the nature of a known chance or mathematical probability, there could be no reward of risk-taking; the fact of risk could exert no considerable influence on the distribution of income in any way. For if the actuarial chance of gain or loss in any transaction is ascertainable, either by calculation a priori or by the application of statistical methods to past experience, the burden of bearing the risk can be avoided by the payment of a small fixed cost limited to the administrative expense of providing insurance.

The fact is that while a single situation involving a known risk may be regarded as "uncertain," this uncertainty is easily converted into effective certainty; for in a considerable number of such cases the results become predictable in accordance with the laws of chance, and the error in such prediction approaches zero as the number of cases is increased. Hence it is simply a matter of an elementary development of business organization to combine a sufficient number of cases to reduce the uncertainty to any desired limits. This is, of course, what is accomplished by the institution of insurance.

It is true that the person subject to such a risk may voluntarily choose not to insure, but it is hard to distinguish such a course from deliberate gambling, and economists have not felt constrained to recognize gambling gains in general as a special income category in the theory of distribution. If it is objected that practical difficulties may prevent insurance even where the risk is determinate, the reply is that insurance, in the technical sense, is only one method of applying the same principle. We shall show at length in our general discussion of risk and uncertainty that if the risk is measurable, but the "moral factor" or some other consideration makes ordinary insurance inapplicable, some other method of securing the same result will be developed and employed. When the technique of business organization has reached a fairly high stage of development a known degree of uncertainty is practically no uncertainty at all, for such risks will be borne in groups large enough to reduce the uncertainty to substantially negligible proportions.

The result of the foregoing analysis should be to show the inadequacy of the two opposed theories of profit and to indicate the reasons for it and the direction in which a tenable solution of the problem of profit is to be sought. It has been seen, first, that change as such cannot upset the competitive adjustment if the law of the change is known; and now, secondly, that an unpredictable change will be similarly ineffective if the *chance* of its occurrence can be measured in any way. In a well-organized society, if business men know either (1) what actual changes are impending or (2) the "risks" they run—i.e., what is the probability of any particular occurrence,—the effect in the long run is the same; the only result of such changes will be a certain redistribution of productive energy which will take place continuously and without any disturbance of perfect competitive conditions.[68] The fact that prediction may involve costs, and likewise the organization for grouping risks and eliminating their uncertainty, does not negate the truth of the proposition, so long as these costs are given elements in the competitive situation.

Yet it is equally evident that there is a principle of truth in both the "dynamic" and the "risk" theories, and the true theory must to a considerable degree reconcile the two views. On the one hand, profit is in fact bound up in economic change (but because change is the condition of uncertainty), and on the other, it is clearly the result of risk, or what good usage calls such, but only of a unique kind of risk, which is not susceptible of measurement. The Clark school has confused change with a common but not universal or necessary implication of change, and both schools have followed everyday speech into the fallacy of treating risk as a substantially homogeneous category, where a fundamental difference in kinds of risk is in fact the key to the whole mystery.

The meaning of "uncertainty," and of the different kinds of uncertainties, and their significance in competitive economic relations, will therefore constitute the principal subject which we have finally to investigate in the present study. The next step in the progress of the argument will be to lay a comparative basis for this investigation by attempting to gain a clear view of the mechanism of competitive valuation and distribution as they would be if uncertainty and its correlative profit were entirely absent. The next three chapters will therefore be taken up with an examination of the conditions and workings of a perfectly competitive society; of these conditions the crucial one will constantly appear as the possession of accurate and certain knowledge of the whole economic situation by all the competitors.

[68]It must be understood that by laws and chances being "known," we mean that they are generally known, known to all to whom they are of any concern.

Part II. Perfect Competition

Chapter 3. The Theory of Choice and Exchange

We turn now from historical and critical considerations to the real work of construction. We have seen that the historic body of economic theory rests upon the assumption of perfect competition, but that the precise character of this assumption has been partially implicit and never adequately formulated. We do not criticize the older economists for making abstract assumptions in order to simplify and analyze their problem, but contend that the assumptions actually made and their implications need to be brought to the surface and emphasized. To display these implicit premises of theoretical reasoning is, we have argued, to explain the problem of profit, the absence of which is the essential distinction between theoretical and actual economic society. This explanation will immediately take the form of a general inquiry into "Uncertainty," the presence or absence of which will appear as the most important underlying difference[69] between the conditions which theory is compelled to assume and those which exist in fact. The present chapter and the two next following will be taken up with the attempt to define and analyze perfect competition. The argument is to be regarded as a condensed summary of classical economic theory, with especial reference to and emphasis upon those premises and implications which have not been adequately emphasized in the theory itself and have been liable to escape the observation of its readers. Aside from this special emphasis the argument will differ not a great deal from that of J. S. Mill and very little from Marshall's "Principles."

[69]Outside of monopoly considerations. But see chapter VI.

Economics is a human science; its foundations are laid in the principles of human behavior, and consequently we must begin with some observations on the psychology of human conduct which controls economic life. Economic analysis may be truly said to deal with "conduct," in the Spencerian sense, of acts adapted to ends, or of the adaptation of acts to ends, in contrast with the broader category of "behavior" in general. It assumes that men's acts are ruled by conscious motives; that, as it is more ordinarily expressed, they are directed toward the "satisfaction of wants."[70] At the very outset the science is thus subjected to notable restrictions, since it is only to a limited extent that our behavior, even our economic behavior, is of this character. Much of it is more or less impulsive and capricious. The conclusions of economic theory must in general be admitted subject to the qualification, in so far as men's economic activities are rational or planned.

This limitation is far more sweeping in its scope and import than is easily imagined. It raises the fundamental question of how far human behavior is inherently subject to scientific treatment. In his views on this point the writer is very much of an irrationalist. In this view the whole interpretation of life as activity directed toward securing anything considered as really wanted, is highly artificial and unreal. To be sure, this characterization seems to hold good for an individual at a given time and place, if the time is short enough. It is the way we think of ourselves as acting, not for the sake of the action or experience itself, but in order to some ulterior object. If, however, the object is merely accidental and temporary, such "wants"

[70]This is intended as a statement of historic fact, not a dogma of necessity or desirability. To the extent that in behavior of any other sort principles may be discovered of a sufficiently general applicability to enable useful conclusions to be drawn from them, there is no reason why such principles should not be incorporated in the premises of pure theory. On the other hand, it is indisputably legitimate to begin, as an early approximation to reality, with the assumption that all the behavior of which we treat is of the character which certainly belongs to a great part of it. In any case we have to separate fundamental tendencies by such a process of analysis (i.e., abstraction) if we are to know anything about them individually. Here we are not concerned to inquire into the possibilities of an economics of instinct and reflex, much less to build up the science; we rest on the fact that the historic body of speculation has dealt with that section of behavior which we call "conduct," and, in line with our leading aim, point out the corresponding limitations of the conclusions from the reasoning. It would be futile to insist further (for those who have not grasped the point already) that limitations are no valid objection to a theory, — may even be a condition of its having any worth, — but the limitations must be recognized and appreciated.

are of little service in interpreting an economic process which must look far forward. It is the writer's belief that this view of behavior, even though it is the view taken by the subject himself, is superficial at best. It appears that a relatively small fraction of the activities of civilized man are devoted to the gratification of needs or desires having any foundation beyond the mere fact that an impulse exists at the moment in the mind of the subject.

Most human motives tend on scrutiny to assimilate themselves to the game spirit. It is little matter, if any, what we set ourselves to do; it is imperative to have some objective in view, and we seize upon and set up for ourselves objectives more or less at random—getting an education, acquiring skill at some art, making money, or what-not. But once having set ourselves to achieve some goal it becomes an absolute value, weaving itself into and absorbing life itself. It is just as in a game where the concrete objective—capturing our opponents' pieces, carrying a ball across a mark, or whatever it may be—is a matter of accident, but to achieve it is for the moment the end and aim of being. And, as in a game again, so with life generally, the social situation furnishes much of the driving power, though again there are many who can become intensely interested in solitaire.

The basis of a *science* of conduct must be fixed principles of action, enduring and stable motives. It is doubtful, however, whether this is fundamentally the character of human life. What men want is not so much to get things that they want as it is to have interesting experiences. And the fact seems to be that an important condition of our interest in things is an element of the unanticipated, of novelty, of surprise. We must beware of the temptation to judge the nature of our conduct by the way in which we think about it. To think about it is, of course, to rationalize it, at least to "think" in the scientific sense, which has pretty well preempted the word. Logical thought is instrumental in character, a device for controlling and using the environment. It is, perhaps, a vice of Western civilization that the habits of thought which condition our wonderful material achievements tend to be carried over into the sphere of our personal lives. The writer ventures to surmise that this sort of thing is approaching, if it has not already reached, a climax. The fever of achievement in an external sense which now dominates our attitude toward life may be expected to give place to a saner, more epicurean view. Men will think more in terms of thought, beauty, and joy for their own sakes and less in terms of what things are good for, what can be done or gotten with them.[71]

Economics, as we have observed before, is the science of a certain form of organization of human activities. The fact of organization still further limits the scope of the discussion to the rationalistic view of activity as directed to the satisfaction of wants conceived as given and permanent entities. Conduct itself is necessarily forward-looking, but organized conduct is still more so. Any machinery of organization implies relatively much taking thought, since it requires time for its development and time for its operation. A most essential feature of economic organization as it exists is its anticipation of the wants of the consumer over a long and ever longer period of production; and this anticipation implies stability in the character of the wants themselves.

A clear view of what we are doing demands special emphasis on this character of economic theory as the science of a system of organization. Human activity might be relatively unorganized or it might be organized in many different ways. History, and especially modern history, is largely the story of progressive organization and its changes in form. Organization is nearly synonymous with division of labor. In organized activity individuals perform different tasks, and each enjoys the fruits of the labor of others. The two fundamental problems of organization are the assignment of tasks and the apportionment of rewards. In unorganized action each person performs all the tasks by whose performance he benefits, and his reward is the immediate, physical benefit of his own work. But when men work together some machinery must be provided to give each his special work and to determine the amount of the results of others' effort which he shall obtain and the amount of his own product which he shall give up to others.

---

[71]It is impossible to follow out this line of thought to the length that its importance really justifies. Considerations somewhat along the line suggested are ably put forward in a lecture on John Rushin as an Economist, by Patrick Geddes (The Round Table Series); also by Professor H. W. Stuart in his essay on "The Phases of the Economic Interest," in the volume by Dewey and others entitled Creative Intelligence. Cf. also Wesley C. Mitchell, "Human Behaviour and Economics," Quarterly Journal of Economics, vol. xxix, pp. 1 ff.

At the opposite extreme a presentation of economics uncritically rationalized and devitalized to the point of approximate chemical purity may be found in the writings of Professor T. N. Carver. The old economists employed the concept of an economic man deliberately and intelligently; for Carver he is literally the man in the street.

Modern industrial society, the "existing economic order," performs this twofold task chiefly through free agreement and voluntary exchange between individuals themselves. Economic theory is the analysis of this mechanism, viewed for the scientific purpose of simplification as the only form of human relation. Going back to medieval times or to the American frontier, we find relatively little joint activity, except for the division of labor between the sexes and in the family. Such organization as existed for war, religion, etc., was not along free exchange lines. But there was always some commerce with different regions, and this has always been worked out largely through exchange. As time passes we find that the greatest change is in the development of organization, and especially of the voluntary, free exchange type, though, to be sure, the functions of the political state develop also. We can imagine that industrial progress might have taken a very different form. The problems of the apportionment, of tasks and rewards might be solved for a complicated, technical civilization by an autocratic, theocratic, or militaristic giving of orders and rationing of produce in which the individual would have no voice in the least detail either of his work or his enjoyment.[72] Or, again, we might have any one of numerous forms of democratic socialism. Some (the anarchists) have imagined that organization might be carried out without either exchange relations or a centralization of authority, simply by general consent. But it has been and is done principally through competitive free agreement, and our task is to study this mechanism and not any other.

The first essential of the existing system is that it solves its two fundamental problems together, as one. It is individualistic; it apportions tasks through the apportionment of rewards; it is an automatic system, in which the interrelations of individuals are determined by self-seeking on the part of each. The foundation of the process is the private ownership of productive resources—a synonym for individual freedom. There is (as we shall see more at length as we proceed) no difference in principle between the ownership of one's own powers and the ownership of other productive resources. The essence of ownership is the association or union of these two facts: (1) control of the agency, and (2) the right of disposition over its product. Modern society (on the economic side) is organized on the theory that the owners of productive resources will find their best

[72]The extinct civilizations of Mexico, and especially of Peru, are alleged to have been largely of this character.

use and place them in it, because in that way they can procure the largest returns for themselves. This system, therefore, involves the assumption that even in a complex organization the separate contribution of each separate productive agency can be identified, and that free competitive relations tend to impute to each agency its specific contribution as its reward for participation in productive activity. And to the extent that the system works at all, that we have an economic order and not chaos, this assumption must be justified.

From another point of view we may envisage the task of organization in three steps or stages:

1. Society as an organized entity must decide the relative importance of different lines of consumption as a basis for the guidance of production. Closely connected with this task, and worked out together with it, is the apportionment of existing stocks of goods, the product of past industry, in the satisfaction of existing wants. This twofold problem is worked out in the consumption goods market from day to day. The study of the process constitutes the first main division of economic science, the theory of market price.

2. Society must actually organize production. Every available productive agency is, so far as the system is successful, to be assigned to that task, and grouped with others in that way which will enable it to make the greatest possible contribution to the social dividend (of goods equated quantitatively according to the value scale established in the consumption goods market). The machinery for the direction of productive resources to their different uses is organized in the market for productive resources. The study of its workings is the second fundamental division of the science. It falls into two subdivisions, short-time distribution theory and long-time value theory.[73] For the purpose of this study the supplies of productive resources must be taken as fixed, as well as the demand which they are to satisfy. Both the prices of consumption goods and the distributive shares are in fact much affected by the third general problem cutting across both the others.

3. At the same time that society is employing existing resources to satisfy existing wants it is also setting aside a portion of its existing resources to increase the supplies of those resources themselves, to improve the effectiveness of their use by working out better methods of production, and to increase its own membership in numbers and quality by providing for an excess of births over deaths and

[73] For fuller statement see below, chapter v.

through education and refinement. There is thus another aspect to the problems of relative importances and of organization. Decision must be made as to how much of society's income is to be diverted from present consumption and to be used for the purpose of furthering social progress, and the diverted income must be applied to this purpose as effectively as may be. The first part of the problem is solved in the market by competition between present goods and the prospective fruits of their investment, giving rise to a rate of capitalization or of interest; and the second part is solved by competition for savings between different opportunities for their use.[74]

The fact that theoretical reasoning must take a large, long-run view of life leads to a difficulty in the treatment of wants which has been the source of much confusion. Our wants have the character of intermittence and recurrence; in any short period of time they are satisfied with a relatively small amount of what the want calls for, and we turn to the satisfaction of some other want. But if it is a true fundamental want it comes back again, and from a long-run point of view they all, with their satisfactions, take on the character of *continuity.* The periodicity, alternation between desire and satisfaction in the case of any one and dominance of different wants in succession, drops out if we look ahead a considerable distance so as to include a number of "complete cycles," so to speak. This long-run point of view is the one necessarily taken by a planned program of satisfying wants; it is evident that our activities at a moment are not predominantly affected by the thing we happen to be "hungry" for at that moment. When we go into a store to make our purchases we do not consult the momentary state of appetite or satiety in respect of any particular need, but its long-run importance in our existence viewed as a continuous process.

The problem of want-satisfaction is, therefore, a problem in *proportions*, or *relative rates*. The question is not how much absolutely of this or that, but how much—i.e., how large a share—of our time or income is to be devoted to each need or line of activity, how much

---

[74]We must by no means be understood to assert or assume that these things are done ideally or even in the best practicable manner by the free exchange system of organization. In the first and third problems in particular, the formation of the social value scale and the use of resources in furthering progress, its methods and results, are open to severe criticism. But again we do not assert that there is any better method or solution practically available. It is our business simply to analyze and describe the workings of a purely voluntary, individualistic, competitive system in relation to the fundamental tasks of organization.

per year or some other period long enough to get rid of the fluctuations. We can get the point of view by imagining that we had to plan our lives for a year on the first of January and live out the plan in detail. Economic discussion in terms of "quantities" of effort or satisfaction or choice between alternatives, under the influence of motives as immediate desires, is therefore elliptical, and more or less dangerous. The quantities of economics are properly *rates*, the motives not desires immediately present to consciousness, but detached judgments of need or value.

A fundamental fact about wants is their habit of conflicting among themselves. In fact, conflict seems to be essential to the very nature of conscious desire. It is questionable whether wants, as conscious motives to conduct, ever exist unless we are in a position of having to choose, to adopt one line of conduct and renounce another. Wants must be distinguished from needs which do not enter into our planful ordering of life. We "need" iodides and vitamines, and an infinite number of things of whose existence the race at large has been blissfully ignorant; but we do not "want" them, because they give rise to no conflicts and hence no "conduct." The common basis of conflict, and we may say of the existence of wants at all, is the limitation in the means of gratifying some impulse or need. When some means of satisfaction is limited in amount so that we have to plan its use and plan to increase its supply, then it enters into the field of conduct and we have a want. The most common and fundamental conflicts are between claims for our own time and energy, and after these upon some limited material agency or means employed as an aid in satisfying ourselves. Our personal powers are, of course, limited absolutely, and limited in fact still further, conditionally, by the tendency of exertion to become disagreeable, giving rise to a "want" to avoid it.[75] The confusion to be avoided is that

[75]It is outside our purpose to attempt a detailed classification of wants. We may notice in passing the difficulty of distinguishing between really different wants and different means of satisfying the same want. For example, we may speak of the want for food, or wants for different foods; one can supply the place of another within limits, but only within limits, and finally the desire for variety itself becomes a want. In our view wants must be classified for the purposes of economic science in accordance with the actual market classification of goods. Nor shall we pretend to go into the psychological problem of the basis of desire. Our discussion deals with things in relation to conduct, and it is a matter of no concern whether we want the things or the conscious states we expect to derive from them, or what, so long as the relation between the acts themselves and the material changes toward which they are directed is clear.

between a want, proper, as related to consciously planned action, the weighing of alternatives, and such things as supposed needs or metaphysical explanations of the immediate fact.

The power of things to satisfy conscious wants, or quality of being wanted, is *utility* in the economic sense, which is equivalent to "power over conduct." Utility, of course, must have the same fundamental properties or dimensions as want; it is not, therefore, a quantity in any simple sense, but a quality having intensity, or a rate. We speak of the utility of a given amount of a thing, but this again is elliptical; the psychological variable is in fact a degree of utility of a certain rate of consumption of the good. And as want is a correlate of conflict, utility is a correlate of limitation; intensity of want and rate of supply of means of satisfying it are strictly connected, each varying inversely as the other; that is to say, as a good is supplied for the satisfaction of any want at higher rates it loses degree or intensity of utility in that use and gains (degree of) utility in the conflicting employment.[76] The confusion between a want and a need or hypothetical reason for having the want is manifest in the field of utility in ascribing economic utility to "free" goods, goods that exist in superabundance. This is a pernicious error. Such goods have no causal relation to conduct and no place in a science of conduct. The confusion has doubtless arisen from the fact that there are many things like air and water which under some circumstances do come to have power over conduct, or utility, though ordinarily they do not. This fact brings home to our consciousness their "potential" utility, the fact that they would have great utility if cut off or subject to limitation; but they have utility only when not free.

Diminishing utility is the scientific designation for the general fact that as any want is satisfied relatively to others[77] it diminishes

[76]There seem to be and perhaps are exceptional cases where this description does not fit the facts; there seem to be, that is, absolute wants, based on absolute limitation and not on limitation due to conflicting demand for the means of satisfaction. These are certainly of negligible importance in economics, however, and on scrutiny they have a tendency to lose the character of "wants" altogether. It is hard to see how a science can deal fruitfully in a constructive way with utterly capricious phenomena; of course it must deal with them in the sense of recognizing that they exist and form a limitation on the completeness of theory, but they can hardly be taken account of in the theory itself.

[77]We carry some wants to complete satiety because it takes less effort than would be required to calculate accurately the most desirable place to stop when this point would be near the absolute satiety limit, as in the case of eating bread, for example. The fact may serve to illustrate the fundamental "irrationality" of

in intensity, or, from the point of view of the means of satisfaction, that the one loses in utility and the other gains. The essential relation of conflict and relativity of utilities is somewhat obscured by the existence of intermediate "means" of satisfaction, and even of series of such. But the further course of the analysis will show that without significant exception there is always in question a *diversion* of the *ultimate means* from one use to another; it is a matter of *alternatives*, and the ground of one want or satisfaction being alternative to another is the dependence on a *common*, *limited* means of satisfaction.

The intermittence of wants, with wave-like alternation of desire and satisfaction, tends to give a false conception of diminishing utility. It is beside the point to talk of boys eating successive oranges or other "dinner-table" illustrations as is so commonly done. The serious error resulting from this method is that it gives the impression that there is a difference between the utilities of different portions of supply. This also is fatal to clear thinking, as will be seen if the contrast between such a situation and that of laying in supplies for a long time in advance (or even an ordinary shopping trip) is considered for a moment. The utility of any one unit is, in its effect on conduct, which is the only relevant consideration, exactly like that of any other; the essential fact is that as there are more units relatively, the utility per unit or utility of any unit is relatively less.

The fact of relativity is important, because easily and commonly lost sight of. Every valuation *is* a comparison; we have no conception of an absolute utility or an absolute standard of utility. The notion of value is meaningless except in relation to alternatives of choice. Not only is utility measured by another utility,—all things are measured by things of their own kind as standards, but its existence is conditioned by that of the alternative; it is like a force in the physical world; action and reaction are equal, a force cannot be imagined separate from an equal and opposite force or resistance.

The case of conflict of utilities most crucial in economic analysis is the familiar alternative of enjoying utilities at the expense of effort *vs.* sacrificing the utility for the sake of freedom from the exertion. "Labor" is usually thought of in an inverted, positive sense as a *disu-*

---

a perfectly "rational" attitude to life. One of our most significant "wants" is freedom from the bother of calculating things or making close estimates. Cf . J. M. Clark, " Economics and Modern Psychology," Journal of Political Economy, vol. 26, nos. 1 and 2.

tility. It is important to see that there is sufficient practical reason for this usage, but also that there is really no exception to the general principle of alternatives without distinction of kind. The point is that "labor" is really the sacrifice of some desirable alternative use of one's time and strength. If there is no alternative there is no sacrifice, nor any motivation, valuation, or "problem" of any kind. In truth, there is no distinction for conduct between a pain and the absence of a pleasure; it is all a matter of choice between alternatives, of "preference." The pleasure-pain question belongs exclusively in the field of the inner consciousness, and has no bearing on problems such as those of economics.[78] The valid reason for the distinction between kinds of alternatives, for fixing our attention on something chosen in one case and something avoided in another, is, as will be shown more at length later on, that we are interested in measuring the alternatives, and we can come nearer a satisfactory quantitative determination of time and effort than we can of the indeterminate uses that would have been made of them if the labor of producing the (measurable quantity of) goods had not been performed.

The whole theory of conduct may now be summed up, as far as it is relevant for our purposes, in a comprehensive "Law of Choice": *When confronted with alternative, quantitatively variable lines of action or experience, we tend to combine them in such proportions that the physically correlated amounts or degrees of each are of equal utility to the person choosing.*[79]

[78]Even "for consciousness" the difference between pleasure and the absence of pain and conversely, though real, is of an "accidental" and very elusive character; we cannot formulate a difference between the two series or classify experiences between them. It is too obvious to call for discussion that the same event will be a pleasure to one person and a pain to another, and even pleasurable to the same person at one time and painful at another, according to circumstances, and, especially, expectations. The difference fades out on scrutiny. An inheritance of a hundred thousand, which is a pleasure to one to whom it is a surprise, may be an intense grief if he has expected and made his plans for ten million. A prison sentence is undoubtedly a source of joy to a man who counted on being hanged, and it is ridiculous to say that it is "really" only an escape from a worse pain, or the inheritance a deprivation of a greater pleasure. The comparison of alternatives and fact of preference is the real thing; pleasure and pain are accidental and arbitrary matters.

[79]The general method of taking the principle of choice as the starting-point of economic reasoning and treating "diminishing utility" in a comparative sense has been used with especial clearness and force by Wick-steed {Common Sense of Political Economy), and is also adopted by Fetter in his recent work {Economic Principles). Economists generally have been coming to recognize that the psy-

A somewhat different statement of the principle of choice may better emphasize the basis of the alternative character of the alternative lines of conduct, the fact that not only must one give up more of the one to get more of the other, but, that this is true in a quantitative sense, that a definite amount of one is given up in return for a definite amount of the other. The reason for this fact we have found in the circumstance that the two kinds of satisfaction are both dependent on some common "means" or "resource." Accordingly we may restate the fundamental law of conduct in this way: In the utilization of limited resources in competing fields of employment, which is the form of all rational activity in conduct, we tend to apportion our resources among the alternative uses that are open in such a way that equal amounts of resource yield equivalent returns in all the fields.

This formulation makes it possibly a little more obvious that the principle is a true statement of the goal of rational planning. For, clearly, if a given unit of a given resource is yielding in one use a want satisfaction preferable to that which a similar unit is yielding in another, the yield of that resource can be increased by transferring some of it from the second use to the first until the importance of the one is increased and of the other decreased to the point of equivalence.[80]

It will be apparent that utility curves, as commonly drawn, rep-

chology of the subject is properly behavioristic; that an economist need not be a hedonist (Jevons and Edge-worth notwithstanding), and that he does not need even to consider the issue between rival psychologies of choice. See Mitchell, "The Role of Money in Economic Theory," Proceedings, Twenty-Eighth Annual Meeting of the American Economic Association. The principle of relativity of utility and value holds in the same way under any theory of motivation.

[80]Close scrutiny makes it appear doubtful just how much real explanatory value the viewpoint of the utilization of resources adds to the bare principle of combining alternatives. It seems that what we call a "resource" is such, not on its own account, but solely because of the uses to which it can be put, and its quantitative aspect, how much resource there is, is still more evidently determinable only in terms of the use. But at least the resource idea helps us to mediate in thought the fact of the quantitatively alternative character of the opposed lines of utilization, as is shown by the fact that we habitually make use of it. The form of the unsophisticated psychosis in regard to sacrifices or "costs" is in fact a bit puzzling. If we ask what a thing has cost, we seem inclined to answer first in terms of money or effort, etc., i.e., of "resources " ; but when pressed, we are likely to go back of the latter and evaluate the resource in turn in terms of some other utility which might have been had for it. The "ontologizing" of the notion of resources seems to be an illustration of an "instrumental concept," but one which it would be difficult to get along without.

resenting diminishing utility and increasing sacrifice as absolute and independent magnitudes, and ascribing varying utility to successive units of commodities (and of disutility of exertion), require considerable modification or reinterpretation if the foregoing reasoning is valid. If utility is relative and in its essence a comparison, such a curve can only represent one variable measured in terms of the other, or each curve presupposes the other already drawn. The role of money in the process tends to complicate and confuse the exposition still further.

The principles above stated in general terms can be brought into relation with current treatments of the subject and with concrete fact if we begin by taking up a simple case of choice between alternatives such as is constantly dealt with in economic analysis. Let us take Marshall's[81] example of a boy gathering and eating berries, but with the stipulation that some re-wording would be necessary to make the exposition accurately fit the case of choice between (i.e., combination of) alternatives in a comprehensive, long-time, plan of conduct. We can hardly suppose that the boy goes through such mental operations as drawing curves or making estimates of utility and disutility scales. What he does, in so far as he deliberates between the alternatives at all,[82] is to consider together, with reference to successive amounts of his "commodity," the utility of each increment against its "cost in effort," and evaluate the net result as either positive or negative, either of a character to prompt the combined action of production and consumption of that unit, or not of this character. The "cost in effort" is evidently in fact the sacrifice of some alternative use or uses of the effort. Even that nondescript conduct called merely idling is still conduct, an alternative motive, and subject to the law of diminishing utility or relative proportions

[81]Principles of Economics, book v, chap, II, sec. 1.

[82]Which, to be sure, is not very far. Nor is this any criticism of the boy. Quite the contrary ! It is evident that the rational thing to do is to be irrational, where deliberation and estimation cost more than they are worth. That this is very often true, and that men still oftener (perhaps) behave as if it were, does not vitiate economic reasoning to the extent that might be supposed. For these irrationalities (whether rational or irrational!) tend to offset each other. The applicability of the general "theory" of conduct to a particular individual in a particular case is likely to give results bordering on the grotesque, but en masse and in the long run it is not so. The market behaves as if men were wont to calculate with the utmost precision in making their choices. We live largely, of necessity, by rule and blindly; but the results approximate rationality fairly well on an average.

like any other. However, while to the eye of critical scrutiny there is no "logical" distinction between an increasing disutility experienced and an increasing utility foregone, a "psychological" difference must be admitted; there is no difference for conduct, but there is one for consciousness, to our pecuniarily sophisticated consciousness at least.

If it is desired to represent the situation graphically without the misleading implications of a comparison of separate absolute variables, it can be done by omitting the commodity axis as in the accompanying figure. The line 0Y is merely directed in space to show that "preference" increases in a vertical direction. Quantities of commodity are measured by a scale as shown, but the "utilities" are not fitted to any scale at all.

If we call the curve U which represents the desirability of the commodity, and the other E for exertion, the one will show a (relative) fall in value and the other a (relative) rise as the production and consumption of the commodity increases. It is a matter of indifference whether the ascending curve is thought of as a sacrifice or a positive pain, whether the growing motive to divert energy from the use in question is imaged as an attraction or a repulsion. The intersection shows that at a certain point (on the commodity scale) the diversion will take place.

Figure 1:

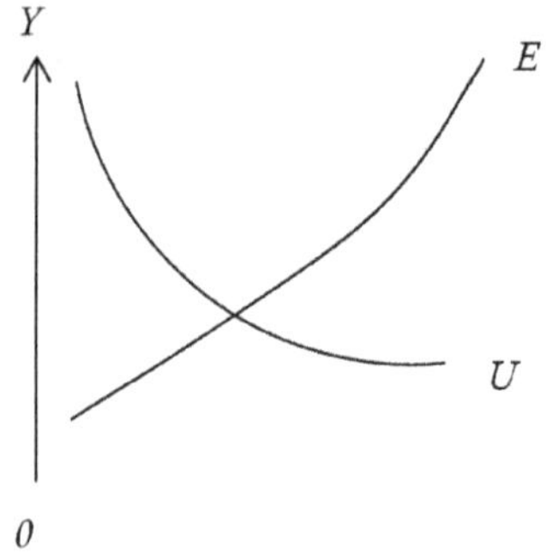

Beyond this point the curves have still less meaning for the reason that the E curve really represents nothing definite, but merely any alternative whatever; as drawn they indicate a rapidly increasing pressure against this particular line of activity. The curves indicate no absolute values of any sort; the vertical distance between them alone has meaning, each being the "base" for the other; this distance shows what might be called the "net utility" of picking and eating the successive increments of berries, as compared with all possible alternatives of conduct.

A still simpler and less ambiguous way to represent the facts would be to draw on a Cartesian plane a single curve of "net utility," as in the accompanying sketch. This curve will cut the X or commodity axis at the point where some other alternative becomes preferable, and then fall away rapidly into the "negative utility" field. It will be seen that the Y values of the curve have only the vaguest quantitative character. The boy not only does not ask how much sacrifice is how many berries worth, but merely, are these berries worth the sacrifice; he does not even ask, "by how much" are these berries worth "the" sacrifice.

Figure 2:

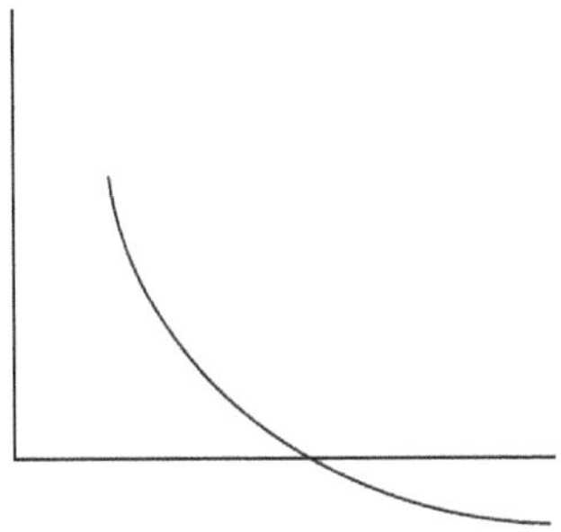

There is no true psychic quantity involved; only the commodity is measured or measurable. Still, there is a certain feeling of quantitative variability in the degree of preference, and such a curve is not utterly false to the facts of consciousness. The only point of clearly determinate locus on the curve is the zero point, and it is questionable whether that is to be interpreted as a quantitative equality between opposite incentives to action or merely the absence of incentive altogether.[83]

[83]The discussion assumes that the quantitative relation between the alternatives themselves remains unchanged, that one is sacrificed for the other in the same ratio throughout, or "resources" converted into both at the same rate. In practice this is only exceptionally possible; in general not only the relative importance of given quantities of alternative goods will change as the supply changes, but in addition the amount of one which must be sacrificed to obtain a given amount of the other will increase as the supply of the first increases; i.e., a "law of diminishing productivity" (likewise a law of proportions merely) becomes operative in addition to the law of diminishing utility (and works in the same direction).

Professor Patten has raised the objection to the utility analysis that consumption also requires time, which must be saved out of the productive operations. (See Annals, Amer. Acad. 1892-93, pp. 726-28. Cf. also Edgeworth, Mathematical Psychics, p. 68, where the energy as well as time required for consumption is considered.) It seems logically more accurate, however, to include in production everything except the actual experience of satisfaction, and if this is done the objection loses its force. In our method of approach to the problem, viewing it as a matter of choice between (i.e., combination of) alternatives, and taking the alternatives simply for whatever they may be in the facts of the case, the whole

It follows at once from the non-quantitative or indefinitely quantitative character of the psychic variables[84] that the "surpluses" which have cut so much figure in economic discussion are very shadowy and elusive things, if not altogether unreal. If the ordinates of the curves discussed above mean nothing definite, of course the areas under the curves mean no more. The fallacious notion of the surplus follows naturally from the confusion between momentary satiety and the correct standpoint, the estimation of relative importance of things in planning ahead, commented on above. The illicit use of "dinner-table " illustrations in the exposition of diminishing utility shows the same error. We cannot insist too strongly upon the point that men do not determine the expenditure of their income, generally speaking, on the basis of a comparison of momentary cravings for things for instantaneous consumption. A child in a candy store would not do that. From such a viewpoint there is a psychic difference in different units of a commodity, and it might be possible to substantiate a surplus doctrine. But this is not the viewpoint of economic reasoning, because in so far as men plan at all, they do not expend their incomes and so fix the prices of things and determine the utilization of social resources and the whole structure of the competitive economic system, on the basis of that sort of calculation.[85]

---

issue loses its relevance.

[84]This may be expressed in technical phrase by saying that they are " ordinal" rather than "quantitative"; they are variable, but not measurable, can be ranked, but not added. The nature of this attribute will lose its mystery if any simple sensation, as a sensation, is considered for a moment. It is easy to tell when one light is brighter than another, impossible to tell how much brighter. The intensity of light is indeed "measured" by science, but it is done by a method analogous in principle to the discussion of utility above. One light is removed to such a distance that it becomes equal in intensity to the standard, and the distance is measured. Obviously this does not involve the measurement of sensation at all. Similarly, a thermometer does not measure the sensation of heat, or a balance that of weight. A better illustration of "ordinal" variables is furnished by the field of aesthetics (another form of "value," of course). We can tell that one poem or picture is better than another, but no one would seriously propose measuring the superiority. To be sure, in school and in contests we may go through the motion of "grading" such things (even deportment !) on a percentage scale, but no one whose opinion is entitled to respect attaches any particular weight to the results of this make-believe.

[85]That to a considerable extent purchases are based on momentary impulse and not on an estimation of relative long-time significance, is, of course, true, and perhaps increasingly so with the development of the "anti-social" arts of window-dressing, display advertising, and salesmanship. This is one of the important "allowances" that has to be made in applying economic theory to actual fact,

If we take a rational attitude toward the problem of value—as, for example, by the device, previously suggested, of placing ourselves in the position of one who had to determine the apportionment of his resources for a year or five years in advance—we shall get a different view of it. Then the earlier units are no different from the later ones, on either side of the balance; up to a certain point the balance is positive, then it suddenly becomes negative, and when the balance is struck the debits and credits are equal. There is a sort of Emersonian principle of Compensation applicable to every item; each is worth what it costs, but also costs what it is worth.

It does not at all follow that we have proved the pleasures of life just equal to its pains. That question is irrelevant to our problems, and our analysis has nothing to say about it. It is not the province of economics to determine the value of life in "hedonic units" or any other units, but to work out, on the basis of the general principles of conduct and the fundamental facts of the social situation, the laws which determine the prices of commodities and the direction of the social economic process.[86] It is therefore not quantities, nor even intensities, of satisfaction with which we are concerned (though the limitations of language compel the use of these terms at times), or any absolute magnitude whatever, but the purely relative judgment of comparative significance of alternatives open to choice. Now, for conduct, it is self-evident that the importance of anything is the effort or sacrifice necessary to get it. Two things, each of which can

---

until the progress of the science reduces the phenomena to general laws and incorporates them into the deductive system. (Cf. above, p. 52, and note; also p. 61, note.) Effects balance out to approximate rationality under the law of large numbers.

[86]The doctrine of the surplus is one of the few points where the writer is compelled to disagree with Marshall on a fundamental matter of doctrine. (See Principles, 6th ed., pp. 125-33, esp. p. 129, note.) The question relates to "scope and method," however, rather than to fact or logic. I simply cannot see any use for the notion in understanding human conduct or explaining economic phenomena, and am convinced that the confusion of viewpoint which underlies putting it to the fore has led to serious error and the drawing of wholly irrelevant conclusions from economic reasoning. Moreover, an appeal to "unsophisticated common sense" seems to fail utterly to substantiate the existence of the phenomenon, A man might pay, say, a thousand dollars for the "first" loaf of bread (whichever one that is) rather than do without it, but it does not follow and is not true that when he gets it for a dime he gets $999.90 worth of free satisfaction. Various thinkers have perceived the mythical character of these alleged surpluses; it is hoped that the argument above will suggest the source of the error and so render it more easily identified and avoided.

be obtained at will by the sacrifice of the other, cannot conceivably have any other than equal importance from this point of view, and it is meaningless to speak of a surplus. The situation is especially clear in an exchange system which fixed prices where things can be converted at will at known rates by purchase and sale. We submit that it is clearly impossible, in such a situation, to conceive of things serving as motives to action in any other than the established ratios of conversion or substitution.

For understanding the psychology of valuation, the two points are equally important: (1) that, logically, choice is a matter of comparing alternatives and combining them according, to the law of rational procedure above formulated,[87] and (2) that there is none the less a practical difference between two kinds of alternatives in an ordinary situation. This difference is perhaps connected with the distinction between our feelings of painfulness and pleasantness, but in its essence it relates to the quantitative character of the alternatives (in their physical aspects, not the psychic states involved). In the case just considered, of the boy and berries, the difference is evident from the fact that we use the berry alternative to measure the leisure alternative. We speak of a certain quantity of berries and the sacrificed alternatives corresponding to them, not of a certain quantity of alternative independently determined. The "trouble," "exertion," or what-not is not quantitative on its own account, it is measured by the berries; it is "the" amount of exertion, etc., connected with a specified amount of the measurable commodity. This result is inevitable because, as remarked above, "the" alternative is not in fact some particular alternative, but any alternative; it is not merely not measurable, but is heterogeneous and wholly indeterminate. It is this fact which throws us back on the conception of "resources" for rationalizing the deliberative process, making of it a quantitative comparison; it is this fact which gives its great importance to the "time" measure of effort. Time does not in any true sense measure the alternative or sacrifice, and, as we have seen, its employment in any use is a sacrifice in the first place only because there are other uses for it, which are the real sacrifice; but it is measurable, and our intelligence, forced to have something quantitative to feed upon, like the proverbial drowning man catches at any straw.

In spite, therefore, of the purely relative character of pain and pleasure and of the essential parity as motives of all alternatives

[87]Pages 64, 65.

of conduct, it is pragmatically necessary to distinguish in productive activity between the incoming "economic" utility and the sacrificed (resources, representing) non-economic, unspecified alternatives in general, between utility and disutility, or commodity and cost. "Cost," in this sense, is "pain cost," or "opportunity cost," as one prefers; there is no real difference in meaning between the two.

From this long but apparently necessary discussion of the fundamentals of valuation of psychology, we may proceed to consider a somewhat more complicated situation, as an approach to the study of the principles as manifested in the field of exchange relations. We will suppose an individual choosing between the production and consumption of a large number of "commodities," in addition to the alternative of not producing any of them, but of putting his time, etc., to "noneconomic" uses. This is the situation of Crusoe on his island, of which many economists have made use. The same law of choice will hold as before; between any two alternatives or among all that are open, the man will choose such amounts, or divide his time and "resources" among them in such proportions, that the physically alternative or correlated quantities of all are to him equally desirable. The only difference is that the alternatives are more complicated than in the case of the boy and his berries, and of a somewhat different character; in particular, the presence of a number of economic alternatives, involving concrete, measurable sources of satisfaction, is important.

In Crusoe's mind there would undoubtedly be built up something of the nature of a price system or value scale, if he seriously attempted to get the maximum of satisfaction out of the conditions of his environment. For an "intelligent" use of his opportunities can be arrived at in no other way. He must ascertain the ratios in which different goods are to be obtained for subjectively equivalent sacrifices in "effort," and similarly form judgments of their relative subjective importance to him, and attempt to bring the two sets of ratios into coincidence. But a set of equivalence ratios or scale of equivalent amounts of things is the essence of a price system. Exchange is a means by which things may be conveniently converted into or sacrificed for each other in determinate amounts, and substantially the same result follows from choosing between different lines of production in a Crusoe economy. It is sufficiently evident that the quantities involved in such a calculation are quantities of things and not of satisfaction or any psychic magnitude.

The rile of the "resource" idea and the concept of "cost" will also take on characteristic form in the Crusoe case. The mental labor of evaluating everything in terms of everything else must force recourse to a crude measurement of "effort" as the common standard of value or "medium of exchange" (it is almost like that) for mediating the comparisons. It is clear that this is an "instrumental" but none the less very important device. "Really," it is purely a question of combining alternatives, among which are those indefinite, "non-economic" occupations, exploring the island, chatting with the parrot, sport or recreation of any appealing kind, or "loafing and inviting the soul." But the indefinite, heterogeneous, and uncertain character of these last, and the convenience of "time" as a rough basis for an approximate evaluation of the stuff they are made of, make it a matter of economy to resort to its use as a common denominator of alternatives. It will not be true that all things produced in equal times will be equated, for there are elements of "irksomeness," etc., which have to be taken account of. Crusoe's value scale will probably be based on time as a "first approximation" with mental allowances for the other factors to be considered.

Measurement relations will be reciprocal, in this case as always. The use of effort to measure other things amounts to an evaluation of effort in terms of other things. Thus we get the concept of a quantitative outlay cost meaning something more than merely any sacrificed alternative. As pointed out before, in stating in terms of "resources" the general law of choice among alternatives, this concept of cost has no very substantial independent meaning; "when pressed" we reformulate our resource or effort (or money) costs in terms of positive alternatives we might have had; but as a mediating, instrumental idea, it is none the less a useful and universally used notion. There is, however, no occasion to speak of a possible divergence between outlay cost and value return, of anything like a "profit" from operations.

There are many intermediate stages in the successive complication of alternatives which might be discussed, and which would shed light on various phases of economic relations; but for present purposes it is best to pass at once to the case of a group of people producing goods for exchange in a free market. The relations among the want-satisfying activities of a plurality of persons are based upon another "conflict," the conflict between similar wants of different individuals, to a large extent dependent on common, immediate means of satisfaction, while these immediate goods are almost entirely dependent upon a common fund of ultimate productive resources. The effect of the possibility of exchange is vastly to multiply and complicate the alternatives open to any individual. He is now free, not merely to make any possible combination of commodities for production and consumption, but to combine the production of some with the consumption of any combination—on terms afforded by an established set of exchange ratios, the investigation of which is the principal problem before us. In order to study first the most essential features of exchange relations, it will be necessary to simplify the situation as far as possible by a process of "heroic" abstraction. We therefore explicitly make the following assumptions as to the characteristics of our imaginary society:

1. The members of the society are supposed to be normal human beings in essential respects as to inherited and acquired dispositions, differing among themselves in the ways and to the degrees familiar in a modern Western nation—a "random sample" of the population of the industrial nations of to-day.

2. We assume that the members of the society act with complete "rationality." By this we do not mean that they are to be "as angels, knowing good from evil"; we assume ordinary human motives (with the reservations noted in the following paragraphs); but they are supposed to "know what they want" and to seek it "intelligently." Their behavior, that is, is all "conduct," as we have previously defined the term; all their acts take place in response to real, conscious, and stable and consistent motives, dispositions, or desires; nothing is capricious or experimental, everything deliberate. They are supposed to know absolutely the consequences of their acts when they are performed, and to perform them in the light of the consequences.

3. The people are formally free to act as their motives prompt in the production, exchange, and consumption of goods. They "own themselves"; there is no exercise of constraint over any individual by another individual or by "society"; each controls his own activities with a view to results which accrue to him individually. Every person is the final and absolute judge of his own welfare and interests.[88]

[88]Dependent members of the society must be completely dependent on some particular individual in it. The wants of any dependent person will then operate only through wants on his behalf felt by his sponsor, and we need not consider them at all. We need simply regard the independent members of the society as having normal solicitudes in regard to families, etc., but each person enters into economic life on an absolute equality with others or not at all.

4. We must also assume complete absence of physical obstacles to the making, execution, and changing of plans at will; that is, there must be "perfect mobility" in all economic adjustments, no cost involved in movements or changes. To realize this ideal all the elements entering into economic calculations—effort, commodities, etc.—must be continuously variable, divisible without limit. Productive operations must not form habits, preferences, or aversions, or develop or reduce the capacity to perform them. In addition, the production process must be constantly and continuously complete; there is no time cycle of operations to be broken into or left incomplete by sudden readjustments. Each person continuously produces a complete commodity which is consumed as fast as produced. The exchange of commodities mint be virtually instantaneous and costless.

5. It follows as a corollary from number 4 that there is perfect competition. There must be perfect, continuous, costless intercommunication between all individual members of the society.[89] Every potential buyer of a good constantly knows and chooses among the offers of all potential sellers, and conversely. Every commodity, it will be recalled, is divisible into an indefinite number of units which must be separately owned and compete effectually with each other.

6. Every member of the society is to act as an individual only, in entire independence of all other persons. To complete his independence he must be free from social wants, prejudices, preferences, or repulsions, or any values which are not completely manifested in market dealing. Exchange of finished goods is the only form of relation between individuals, or at least there is no other form which influences economic conduct. And in exchanges between individuals, no interests of persons not parties to the exchange are to be concerned, either for good or for ill. Individual independence in action excludes all forms of collusion, all degrees of monopoly or tendency to monopoly.

7. We formally exclude all preying of individuals upon each other. There must be no way of acquiring goods except through production

---

The meaning of the above assumptions is not necessarily that they form a complete description of the people and their relations. This is but an emphatic way of saying that we here consider only their market behavior, which is assumed to conform to these specifications.

[89]It goes without saying that our imaginary society is "isolated." Every individual who has anything at all to do with it is in it and of it on a par with all the rest.

and free exchange in the open market. This specification is really a corollary from numbers 2 and 3, which exclude fraud or deceit and theft or brigandage respectively, but it deserves explicit mention.

8. The motives for division of labor and exchange must be present and operative. These have never been adequately treated in the literature of economics in spite of the fact that the subject has been discussed more or less by countless writers on social problems from Plato down. The principal condition is diversification of wants associated with specialization of productive capacities or dispositions, or with physical restrictions on the range of productive activity. An important fact in this connection in the real world is the space distribution of the different resources of the earth and the limitations on human mobility. In addition the physical nature of the production process frequently calls for the simultaneous prosecution of a number of operations. For simplicity we shall assume that the first two conditions alone are sufficient to restrict each individual to the production of one single commodity at any given time. (Cf. number 11.)

9. All given factors and conditions are for the purposes of this and the following chapter and until notice to the contrary is expressly given, to remain absolutely unchanged. They must be free from periodic or progressive modification as well as irregular fluctuation. The connection between this specification and number 2 (perfect knowledge) is clear. Under static conditions every person would soon find out, if he did not already know, everything in his situation and surroundings which affected his conduct.

The above assumptions, especially the first eight, are idealizations or purifications of tendencies which hold good more or less in reality. They are the conditions necessary to perfect competition. The ninth, as we shall see, is on a somewhat different footing. Only its corollary of perfect knowledge (specification number 2) which may be present even when change takes place, is necessary for perfect competition. In addition to these differences in degree only from actual life, we must lay down for the special purpose of the immediate analysis two further suppositions quite contrary to the facts.

10. The first is that for the present there is to be no productive property in the ordinary sense in the society. Every productive agency or capacity is an inseparable part of the personal endowment of some member of the society. Material implements of production

may be used provided they are either superabundant, and consequently free goods, or else are absolutely joined to their owners (not subject to lease or sale) and not subject to increase or decrease. The last characteristic, if not that of inseparability, is, of course, really implied in the specification of static conditions. We must also observe explicitly that personal powers themselves are similarly fixed in amount and character. The social consequences of the transfer of productive goods between individuals, and especially of their increase by "investment," will call for extended discussion later, and must be isolated by a preliminary study of a society in which they are absent.

11. The second "analytic" assumption is also contained in the preceding "idealizing" group. Under number 8 we declared that division of labor was to be carried to the point where each individual produced a single commodity. In modern industrial life it is, of course, carried vastly farther. But it is important to study separately a society where production is organized through the exchange of finished products only.[90] At a later stage we can then discuss the special problems of that further stage of organization called secondary division of labor.

This isolation is of especial importance in view of the fact that the distribution of products is very much complicated when the agencies of production cooperate in the production of a single commodity, the product of a single agent being then no longer immediately identifiable. The problem of isolating the product of a single agency, where a number work jointly, is, of course, the familiar problem of "imputation" or distribution in the technical sense, which has been the greatest single center of controversy in economic discussion.

The above list of assumptions and artificial abstractions is indeed rather a formidable array. The intention has been to make the list no longer than really necessary or useful, but in no way to minimize its degree of artificiality, the amount of divergence of the hypothetical conditions from those of actual economic life about us. For the most part these same assumptions, especially the first eight, and to a considerable extent the ninth, are really involved at one point or another in a large part of the discussion of economic literature. If

[90]We might characterize such a society as a "handicraft" system in contrast with "enterprise," in which the operative has lost his responsible status and lives, not by the production and sale of a commodity, but by the sale of productive services to an entrepreneur.

they are present, and necessary, and when present whether necessary or not, there will be no disparaging the importance of having their abstract and unreal character brought conspicuously to the surface.

Our next task is to form a picture of such a society in action, and to discover the conditions of equilibrium or natural results of the operation of the forces and tendencies at work in it. We are therefore to imagine such a population, set down in such an environment as described, starting out de novo in the business of satisfying their wants. Each person, on taking in the situation in its essential outlines, will enter upon the production of some commodity, with a view, through exchange with others, of securing the means of satisfying his varied wants. After a brief interval of time has elapsed, each will have accumulated a small stock of his particular good, and we may think of them all as meeting in a central market to exchange their wares.

The situation now presented is the familiar one in economic discussion, of a group of individuals with given stocks of goods which have to be disposed of,[91] and we need not dwell upon the process by which fixed rates of exchange among all commodities will be established.[92] When the process is finished the whole mass of commodities will have been reduced to a single homogeneous fund of exchange equivalence or value. Nor do we need to concern ourselves with the mode of expressing and handling this fund; in practice it would be inevitable that some sort of standard exchange medium would be set apart; but it is immaterial for present purposes whether there is some one kind of money or as many kinds as there are different commodities.

If intercommunication is actually perfect, exchanges can take

[91]We treat the entire stock as for sale without reserve. The demands of present owners for their own goods, which underlie any possible reservation prices, are in fact no different from the demand of other persons, and the situation as a whole is most truthfully and significantly represented as given quantities of goods over against given dispositions to own them, since the question of whose disposition it is has nothing to do with the price that will be established. We must, of course, include the demand of present owners in the demand for every good; that it is "backed up" by the good itself instead of some other good in hand has nothing to do with the result. (Cf . Davenport, Economics of Enterprise, chap, v, pp. 48 ff .)

[92]The problem of a perfect market is best treated mathematically (i.e., symbolically) and has been well handled by mathematical economists. See Edgeworth, Mathematical Psychics, pp. 40 ff., and Marshall, Principles, Appendix F, and Mathematical Appendix, note xii bis.

place at only one price.[93] We may imagine it to be determined all around what the ratios are to be through the medium of inquiries. Every individual, knowing the worth of the thing he possesses in terms of everything else, is in substantially the same position as a person spending a given money income in a market where selling prices are fixed by the seller and placarded. The good in his hands represents exchange power, a "resource," and he will apportion it among the possible uses according to the law of choice, so that each unit of it purchases equivalent utilities, want satisfactions, or "importances."

To show just how the price scale itself results from the fact that individuals act according to the law of choice in apportioning their purchasing power in a situation where the prices are given, is the task of that branch of economics known as the theory of market price. At any given price (ratio of sacrificing one good for the other) the more purchasing good is expended for any one commodity the less becomes the amount of want satisfaction purchased with each unit (relatively to the want-satisfying capacity either of the good given up or of any other good for which it might have been exchanged). From this it follows that the higher the price of any good (relative to others, including the purchase good), the less of it will be purchased by any individual.[94] It is therefore theoretically possible to construct a schedule, or curve, of the amounts of any good that will be taken by any individual at every price in terms of other goods, and by adding

[93] Easily proved by disproving the contrary. If exchanges be thought of as taking place at different prices the buyer at the higher price and seller at the lower will get together at an intermediate figure.

[94] These two propositions are often treated as equivalent in economic discussion, but the relation between them is not so simple as that. To prove the second from the first, suppose that at any given price the individual has determined upon the proper amount to purchase. (For the sake of similarity with the pecuniary situation let us leave the purchase good out of account and think of a comparison between two commodities being bought with money which has no commodity value.) Now let the price of one commodity rise, relatively to that of another. If the commodity which has risen in value is a very important one, it is probable that the individual will spend as much of his resources for it as before, quite possibly even more. But he will not buy as much of the commodity, measured in physical units. For to do so he would have to spend correspondingly less resources for the alternative good, and buy less of it. But if he buys the same amount of one good as before, and less of the other, the utility ratio between the two is upset (since it was in equilibrium), and a given amount of resources is buying less utility in the good of which relatively more is purchased; resources will therefore be diverted from this good to the other. That is, he will buy less of the good which has risen (relatively) in price. Q. E. D.

these amounts for all individuals, to construct a similar schedule for the society as a whole. But there is a fixed amount of each good available in any given short space of time to be disposed of, and it must all be sold at one price. Therefore, in a perfect market each commodity will command a definite price, which is the highest uniform price at which the entire existing stock can be disposed of (including taking out of the market by present owners).

The diagrammatic representation of the market-price equilibrium is simple and obvious. The utility relations involved in the figures and analysis for the boy-and-berries situation above[95] are applicable. The exchange situation is shown in the accompanying sketch. The horizontal base line is a scale of prices.

The "demand" curve D shows the potential purchases at each price, for any individual or for the society as a whole, according to the scale used. The amount for sale is independent of price, a fixed physical quantity, and is represented by a horizontal line cutting the vertical or commodity axis at the proper point. The horizontal value of the intersection point gives the market price under the conditions.[96]

Figure 3:

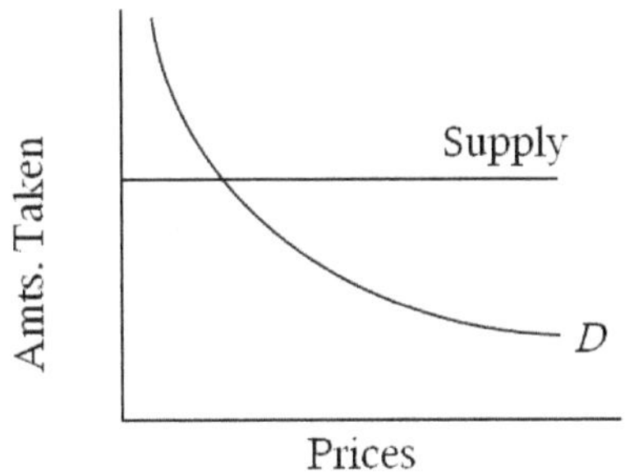

It is especially to be observed that all the quantities involved in this whole analysis are physical and not psychic. If utility in the individual consciousness is not a true, measurable magnitude, as argued, it is still more evident that utility in any social sense, involving a sublimation of individual utilities into a "social" estimate is a wholly inadmissible supposition. The concept of social utility is in fact a mere substitute for analysis. The whole problem is pre-

[95]Pages 66 ff.

[96]It is also possible, but complicates matters needlessly, to plot the demand of others than present owners of the good, only, in the demand curve, and draw an ascending curve to represent the sales at different prices, taking account of the present holders' reservation prices. The same data will give the same price point whichever method is used, and the one described in the text is the more significant description of the situation, since there is no practical difference in the causes or motives back of reservation prices and demand prices.

cisely this of showing how an objective and uniform price results from palpably subjective and variable individual preferences. This must be done by exhibiting the interactions of individual offers and bids in the actual market.[97] We in fact know nothing about any absolute utility to any individual or about absolute amounts purchased by any one. All that can be said about the adjustment which results from perfect competition is comprised in three statements: (1) Under the conditions (the price alternatives as they are fixed) each individual achieves the goal of rational action, maximizing the want satisfaction procurable with his given resources (whatever they are) in purchasing power, by distributing them among the alternatives according to the law of choice; (2) the conditions themselves, the prices or exchange ratios being the same for all individuals, and the relative utilities adjusted to equality with these, it follows that the relative utilities of all goods (which any individual purchases at all) are the same to every individual; (3) the exchange ratios will be so adjusted that at those ratios no individual will wish to exchange anything in his possession for anything in the possession of any one else.

The emphasized expressions are so treated because of current ambiguous or actually confused conclusions in regard to the beneficence of the results of ideal competition. To call this result socially ideal or the best possible, involves assuming in addition to all the theoretical conditions as to the workings of the process itself[98] that the initial situation, the distribution of goods before the exchanges commenced, was the best possible (i.e., either absolutely ideal or absolutely beyond human power to modify). All that is true (and stated baldly it is little better than a truism) is that free exchange tends toward that redistribution of goods which is the most satisfactory all around of any that can be obtained by voluntary consent all around.

[97]Seligman's treatment (Principles of Economics, pp. 179 ff. and 192 ff.) is a particularly glaring instance of the organism fallacy. B. M. Anderson, Jr.'s Social Value involves the same error. Anderson palpably confuses social influences back of individual judgments and preferences with social judgments and preferences in any proper sense. Of course the individual is a social product, but consciousness is still an individual phenomenon, and the conduct with which economists are concerned no less so. It is individual purchases and sales which fix prices, not social, unless in a socialistic state or one organized in some other way than through free exchange between individuals, the kind economics deals with.

[98]See above, pp. 76-80.

It is self-evident that in ideal exchange the quantities exchanged are equal in value terms, and there is no chance for anything like a "profit" to arise.

The main condition of perfect exchange not realized in real life is that of "perfect intercommunication," which is to say perfect knowledge of what they are doing on the part of all exchangers.[99]

In our actual system middlemen fix a price which in the absence of monopoly is their best estimate of the theoretical price—which would just enable the visible supply to be disposed of—and change it from time to time as the rate of sales indicates it to be too high or too low. It is a familiar fact that in consequence of imperfect intercommunication appreciably different prices for the same commodity may obtain at different points in the general market area. Certain factors aggravate the effect of uncertainty in disturbing the theoretical adjustment: (1) Inertia or inflexibility of prices, due to habit, indifference, rounding off of figures, etc.; (2) variations in the "commodity" (and fraudulent representations of variations which do not exist); and this both in the crude physical ware, and still more in by-perquisite utilities, convenience or fashionableness of place of sale, ornamental containers, trade names, personality of vendor, etc.; (3) consumers' speculation; consumers do not buy continuously for their current needs, but lay in supplies or hold off, according to their prognostications of the market.

When terms are properly defined and allowances made for real commodity differences (which include all the factors under number 2 above) the tendency toward a definite and uniform price for similar goods is strong and conspicuous, and a fair approximation to this result is generally reached. There is, of course, the greatest difference in commodities in respect of this standardization, from wheat and cotton at one extreme to artistic products at the other.

When in our imaginary perfectly competitive society the exchanges are finished and the goods consumed, everybody will again start out to engage in production. But occupations will not be chosen as before; there will now be an established scale of prices of every good in terms of every other, and in accordance with this price scale every one will direct his effort and gauge its intensity, conforming, of course, to the Law of Choice in making his decision. The commodities produced will be thought of simply as purchasing power

[99]The use of money does not affect the theory at all, and the use of circulating credit not in any way that vitiates the argument, if it does not change in value.

over goods in general, and the immediate alternatives are simply producing "wealth" and not producing it, which means doing something, or nothing (which is also doing "something") entirely outside the scale of quantitative comparisons, and this now means outside the market sphere. Every man will, therefore, like Crusoe, or the boy in the berry patch, carry his exertions to the point where utility and disutility—"really" sacrificed utility, but of an unspecified and non-quantitative sort—are of equal importance in the amounts which are alternative to each other.

As production goes on and goods accumulate in the hands of our "homines œconomici," they will be exchanged as before, distributed among the exchange possibilities in accordance with the Law of Choice; and the exchange possibilities will continuously be modified by the same process so as to be kept constantly at that point where momentarily the utility ratios of every one can be brought to equality with the price ratios. But this process of adjustment and readjustment also tends toward an equilibrium; the investigation of this tendency toward a condition in which production and consumption of all commodities would go forward at unvarying rates falls in the province of the second grand division of economic theory, one branch of which is the theory of normal price.[100]

In a situation such as we have described, with the production, exchange, and consumption of commodities going on continuously, the value scale or system of quantitative equivalences of commodities, becomes much more objective and definite than it could ever be in the economy of an individual Crusoe. The constant presence of the published scale of exchange ratios and the working-out of the whole organization in terms of it must have a tremendous influence in "rationalizing" the economic activity, in impressing its quantitative features on men's minds, and enforcing precise calculations and comparisons. The result is that all goods are reduced to a homogeneous aggregate or fund of value units. This fund of value, as the medium of solving the problems of alternatives, naturally divides the economic process for each individual into two parts or stages fairly distinct in his thought. The goods he produces being thought of merely as so much value in exchange, the problems of combining alternatives in production is separated and simplified by the neces-

[100]The other branch is the theory of distribution under static conditions, but under our present assumptions there is no such problem since joint production is absent.

sity of considering but two alternatives, as we have noted above. Similarly, the problem of consumption is considered independently, taking the form of the problem of expending value in exchange, which is worked out on its own account in accordance with the principle of rational choice or distribution of resources among competing uses. Thus value in exchange on the expenditure side, becomes like the concept of exertion to Crusoe; it is an instrumental idea, with no ontological content, but extremely useful in solving the problem of choice. The separation of the two halves of the economic problem is much heightened in real life by the storing-up of value in exchange, and the production of it for the purpose of storing it up, against unknown contingencies, with no thought of any particular use to be made of it. The separation is still further heightened by the tendency of the production of wealth to lose all connection with the notion of consuming utilities and take on the form of a competitive contest in which value in exchange becomes a mere measure of success, a counter in the game.

The further establishment and objectification of the value-system will also involve a more definite evaluation of productive sacrifices or "exertion," really the "non-economic" alternative occupations given up to perform productive labor. This evaluation being in terms of value in exchange, productive labor is in this sense brought into the general value fund, though under the conditions we are now discussing (independent individual production only) it would not actually come into the market and be exchanged. The evaluation of productive effort, i.e., its measurement in terms of an established scale of equivalences of economic alternatives, furnishes a correspondingly substantial content for the notion of "outlay cost" in a quantitative or value sense, and men's minds would undoubtedly work largely in terms of this concept.

Now it is especially important to note that at this point in the hypothetical construction we have first arrived at a set of conditions where the outlay cost of a particular good is not necessarily and axiomatically equal to the value of the good itself. For, while the readjustment toward normal price or equilibrium conditions is taking place, the "value" of the labor will be determined in the market price situation at one moment, while the value of the good which it yields will be determined at a slightly later time, and there will typically be some difference between the two. The value of the productive effort is that which the good it produces has previously had, while the value of the good it does actually produce will when it comes on the market be something else. The difference, positive or negative, between the value of a good and the (value of) its cost is analogous to "profit." Its occurrence is manifestly due to the fact that men must base their acts on past conditions, or on uncertain inferences as to the future based upon past conditions, and not on the actual future conditions to which they really relate. As soon as men find out accurately what goods are going to be worth after they are produced, they will employ their productive energy accordingly, and the profit differential will disappear. And since this is what they constantly strive to do, with some measure of success, the system will tend toward that equilibrium adjustment in which no profit exists.

The theory of the normal price adjustment is precisely analogous to that of market price, since there is no difference in principle (but only one in complication) between the purchase of a good by the sacrifice of another in exchange and its"purchase" by the sacrifice of the production of another good in its production. Both normal price and market price theories are little more than corollaries from the single fundamental Law of Choice.

On the production side of the twofold alternative, the utility or importance of any good is its purchasing power, and the higher the price the more of it will be produced, for the same reason that Crusoe would produce more of a more wanted good or an individual in a market purchase more of a similar one. But the higher the price of any good the less of it can be disposed of. Now since the amounts produced and disposed of are axiomatically the same, the price will move toward the point at which the natural amounts of production and sales at that price are the same. Diagrammatically, taking again a scale of prices as a horizontal basis, an ascending curve will represent the (rate of) production or supply at different prices (in terms of other goods), while a descending curve will represent the (rate of) sales or demand. The intersection of the curves gives the price point.

Figure 4:

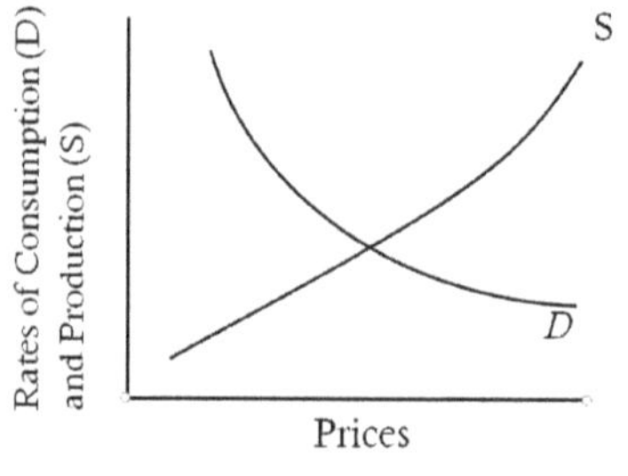

A slightly different way of viewing exactly the same facts will make clearer the individual motivation and show the bearings of the idea of value-cost. The demand curve, viewed from the other direction, or with the axes interchanged, is in fact a cost of production curve. The amount produced (in unit time, the rate of production) at any price is the amount that can be produced at that price without either profit or loss. For if any given price yields a profit, resources will be diverted to, and if a loss, from the production of that good; the real meaning of profit is simply that resources being used to produce other goods (and valued in the other uses) will yield more in the production of the good in question; while similarly, loss means that resources producing the good in question are worth more in other uses (their value being determined by that of the best use). From the present point of view the demand curve shows the possible selling prices of different sizes of supply, and the condition of equilibrium is that cost and selling price shall be equal. The intersection of the curves then shows on one axis the equilibrium rate of production and consumption, and on the other the equilibrium price. The character of the whole analysis as an easy deduction from the Law of Choice is clear enough without further elaboration.[101]

Space does not permit us to give more consideration to these first fundamentals, and we must allow the above brief and perhaps somewhat dogmatic treatment of controverted issues to stand. It is difficult in the light of such an analysis to see any real meaning in such questions as the causal relation between cost and value, and others about which controversy has raged. Under competitive conditions a value involves an equal cost and a cost an equal value, so directly and obviously (since it is all a purely relative matter of choosing between alternatives in such a way as to equate them) that the two are but little more than different words for the same phenomenon viewed from different standpoints. Cost is the value

[101]It will be noticed that our cost curve is one of increasing costs. This is the only case to be considered from the present point of view. The question of decreasing costs comes in at a later stage of the analysis under more complicated conditions. It is obvious that to increase the production of any good involves the diversion of resources from producing other goods, which will raise their value while lowering that of the good first considered, and since resources are valued according to the best available use, this means increasing cost with increased output. At the present stage of the argument there is no problem as to the cost of any unit of commodity or yield of any unit of productive agency, since only one kind of agency is used in making any one good.

of the resources embodied in a thing, which is to say the value of some use for them; it may be an "economic" or a "non-economic" (measurable and marketable or the opposite) use, but if there is not a competing attraction of some sort the "resources" will not be "resources" at all, just as if the thing itself is not wanted somewhere else it will not have (exchange) value, and we should say not even utility if the word is properly defined.

The whole argument is merely an elaboration of the Law of Choice (the correct form of the principle of utility), that preference ratios between alternatives will by combining the alternatives in the requisite proportions be made equal to the externally given physical equivalence ratios, first in the market and then in production. That "goods" are largely alternative to each other in production (involving the use of the same ultimate resources) is the condition of our having an economic order, an organization of want-satisfying activities based on free production and exchange. We turn now to consider the further complications of the competitive situation arising from the organization of a plurality of productive agents in the making of a single commodity.

Chapter 4. Joint Production and Capitalization

THE PRESENT chapter will bring a greater semblance of reality into the imaginary, highly simplified economic system partially constructed above. Many of the features of everyday life abstracted for simplification can now be introduced in succession and their relations and bearings separately studied. In this way we shall ultimately determine what is necessary to perfect competition and what is not. It will be found that most of the simplifying assumptions hitherto made can be dropped without destroying the conditions necessary to a perfect equilibrium in which costs and values are identical throughout. So long as we adhere to the fundamental condition already emphasized, that men know exactly what they are doing, that no uncertainty is present, other elements of reality hitherto abstracted merely complicate the process of adjustment without changing the character of the result. Their elimination has served the necessary end of simplifying the study of the fundamentals of economic behavior and made possible the separate study of these complicating considerations themselves, which we shall now undertake.

The first step in this further development of the imaginary social structure is to examine the nature and bearings of organized production. Hitherto our society has been arbitrarily restricted to the unorganized or individual creation of goods; there has been only "primary" division of labor, through the exchange of products. We now turn to consider "secondary" division of labor, or division of occupations within the separate industries, the cooperation of a large number of persons in the making of a single product. This added element in the situation gives us two serious new problems, though closely related; first, the mechanism of the actual organization of productive groups through free contract alone, and, second, the division of a joint product among the individuals making different kinds of contributions to its production. The latter is the familiar problem of "imputation" (Zurechnung) or "distribution" in the technical sense.

Practically speaking, we are now turning to the second general problem of economics as it is met with in the real world. For methodological reasons we have, indeed, found it necessary to discuss a society in which specialized production takes place, but not joint production. In reality, of course, production is joint, practically without exception. The subject for discussion now is, therefore, the general principles of social organization under free exchange where given resources are used (in the production of goods) for the satisfaction of given wants (and under given conditions as to available methods of technical organization, etc.). It is the problem of the "static state." In order to keep the problems of the organization of production and the division of the product as simple as possible and to introduce complicating factors one at a time, no other changes are now to be made in the arbitrary specifications of the system we are studying. In regard to production particularly, we assume the absolutely continuous creation of the complete article and its immediate exchange and consumption when complete, and the absence of productive "property" in the ordinary sense.[102] That is, there are to be no material productive agents which are not either superabundant, and therefore free, or else rigidly attached to the persons of their owners, and no way is to be open either to increase the productive efficiency of person or thing or to decrease it through use. The only change now introduced in the conditions of our problem is that at least a large part of the commodities produced and consumed in our society are to be made by groups of individuals, performing a number of different kinds of productive work. It is not necessary that every individual perform a unique function; rather let it be typically true that considerable numbers perform the same sort of work and that there are gradations of similarity in the different tasks.[103]

---

[102]See above, chapter III, pp. 76-80, for the assumptions under which we are working.

[103]See note above, p. 86 n., on indifference as to the presence and use of money.

The possibility of an automatic organization of production through free agreements between individuals depends upon a technological principle governing joint production and not hitherto introduced. This new axiom is as fundamental to economic thought and process as the principle of choice or diminishing utility, and very similar to it in statement. It is the principle of the variation of proportions in the factors of production, already long famous .Sunder the name of "diminishing returns," though its clear and approximately accurate formulation in general terms is a relatively recent achievement. This new law is a generalization from the facts of physical nature as the former is a generalization from the facts of human nature. Like the other, and all other "laws," it is an approximation, and its approximateness must be kept in mind in making practical applications of conclusions resting on it as a premise. Like the other great axioms in economics, it is purely a principle of relativity, dealing with proportions only.' In this respect the current statements of the principle are generally less misleading than in the case of diminishing utility, there being less temptation to give it an absolutistic interpretation. It does seem strange, however, that it took economists so long (nearly a century) to recognize the inherent reversibility of a change in proportions and to draw the obvious inferences from the fact. We may observe finally that the new principle is much"truer"; i.e., more universally and accurately in conformity with the facts, more dependable, than its psychological counterpart.

In many other respects, also, there is similarity between the two fundamental principles of proportionality, the psychological law of diminishing utility and the technological one of diminishing returns. A formal and accurate statement of either presupposes continuous divisibility of the variable element, which is not true to fact in a particular case, but which does hold good with practical accuracy in a large market. In both cases divisibility breaks down completely (in an individual case) for minimum amounts. As there is a definite minimum quantity of any consumption good required to give it any significance, so there are limits to the proportions of productivity agencies which will yield any effect at all. As to minima in the case of consumption goods in the different sense of minimum amounts necessary to life, this, though commonly assumed, is ordinarily not true. It is only under very special circumstances that any particular commodity, as the market defines and differentiates commodities (and this is the only sound or relevant method), is indispensable.

In the case of both the law of diminishing utility and that of diminishing returns, also, there are maxima to be taken into account beyond which the good or agency ceases to enter into problems of conduct at all, becoming a "free good" — better called a potential good, as we have seen. The correct procedure is of course to treat superabundant elements in production as we did those in consumption; i.e., to take them absolutely for granted and ignore them completely. Only the "possibility" of a situation arising in which a thing would not be superabundant can give it significance or lead to its being consciously considered in any way.

In discussing the principle of diminishing returns a special difficulty arises in the confusion of varying proportions in a combination with changes in the absolute size of the combination as a whole. These things must imperatively be kept separate; in the writer's opinion more error has arisen over this point than any other single matter in distributive theory. If the amounts of all elements in a combination were freely variable without limit and the product also continuously divisible, it is evident that one size of combination would be precisely similar in its workings to any other similarly composed. But under this condition the tendency to monopoly in the production of every good would be unimpeded. For the competitive system to work, it is necessary to postulate that the conditions as to divisibility of factors are such that the bargaining unit of any one factor is quite small in relation to the total stock of agencies which more or less effectively compete with that unit, and also that an establishment of relatively small size in proportion to the industry as a whole is more efficient than a larger one. Under these conditions the first effect of competition must be to bring all the plants within an industry to the most economical size, and leave a sufficient number in operation to compete effectively for the productive agencies which all use.[104]

[104]Competitive relations between similar establishments are much complicated in real life by the fact that practically every business enjoys a certain degree of partial monopoly. It does not turn out exactly the same product (bundle of utilities) as its competitors. An extreme example is the case of railroads where a part of the output, the through traffic, is competitive while the other part, the local traffic, is monopolistic. This whole question of the relation between the size of an industry and the size of an establishment seems to the writer badly mixed up in the literature. Professor Bullock has distinguished between the three principles of diminishing returns with varying proportions between the factors, diminishing costs in an industry as a whole and decreasing costs in the single establishment, or economy of large-scale production. (Cf. Quarterly Journal of

The principle of diminishing returns in its now current form runs somewhat as follows: As successive increments of any one agency are added to fixed amounts of other agencies in a combination, the physical product of the combination will increase, but after a certain point the output will increase in less proportion than that of the agency in question and will ultimately decrease absolutely.[105] A more general formulation, emphasizing the reference to proportionality in contrast with absolute size, and the reversibility of the law, might run as follows: When the proportion of agencies in a combination is continuously varied over a very wide range, there is generally a first stage in which the product per unit of either agency increases; then a stage in which the product per unit of the relatively increased agency decreases and the product per unit of the relatively decreased agency increases; and finally a third stage in which the product relative to either agency decreases. Since either agency may be the increasing and the other the decreasing one, the first and third stages are identical in meaning. [106]

Economics, vol. xvr, pp. 473 ff.) But no one, so far as I know, has worked out these cost laws adequately. (Cf. also Davenport, Economics of Enterprise, chap. xxiv). Davenport does not go as far as Bullock in the analysis of the problem.

[105]See F. M. Taylor, Principles of Economics, chap, iv, for a very thorough and sound non-mathematical discussion of the whole question of variable proportions and diminishing returns. I must remark, however, that Taylor's treatment of the economy of large-scale production seems to me to be based on fallacy.

[106]The second statement of the law is deducible from the first. All that is involved in the law of diminishing returns is properly to be regarded as a deduction from the following self-evident premises:

1. The proportions of agencies in a combination may be varied without destroying its productivity.

2. If to a certain amount of one agency (say, labor) another agency (say, land) is added in amounts varying continuously from zero to infinity, a definite amount or range of amounts of this second agency (neither zero nor infinity) will yield a larger total product than will larger or smaller amounts. In other words, if the proportion of one agency to another is increased without limit, the product per unit of the decreasing agency will first increase and then decrease; i.e., there is a maximum point, or range, beyond which in either direction the product (per unit of the increasing agency) will decrease.

3. It is demonstrably true, and is necessary to the theory of distribution that extreme variation (short of infinity) in either direction will yield a zero product.

It is most essential in regard to this law that it relate to any variation in proportions irrespective of the absolute amount of any factor present and of the direction of the change. But the conventional case of the application of labor to land, or rather of land to labor, is easy to visualize and suitable for illustration. Let us imagine a group of new settlers on a virgin continent faced with the problem of how much of the unlimited supply of land to use with their limited

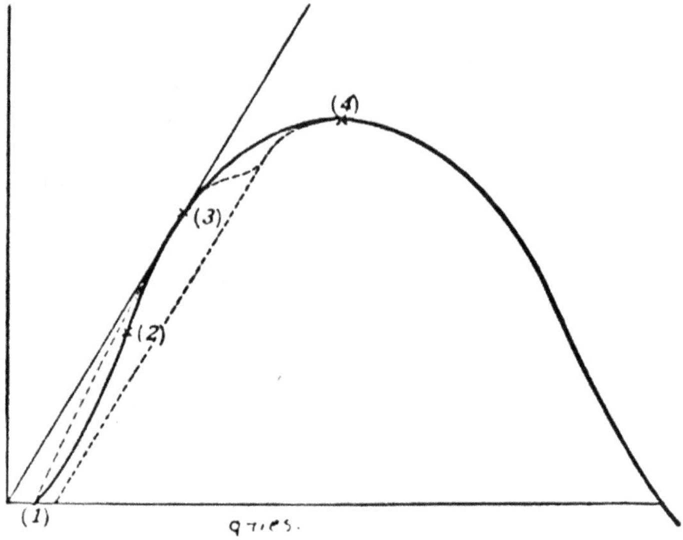

Figure 5:

It is requisite for an intelligent organization of production and a determinate division of the produce among the factors by competitive price forces that not merely the product increase in less ratio than the factor, but that equal arithmetic increments of factor yield decreasing increments of product. These two principles have entirely different meanings, of course, but they are badly confused in many statements of the theory of diminishing returns. The second can, however, be deduced from the first, which follows from the very nature of an economic situation, as shown below. The relations of the various elements in the problem can best be shown by reference to a graph. In the accompanying figure, the horizontal or X distances represent quantities of the single variable productive factor in a combination, and the vertical or Y distances, the corresponding total physical output of the group. In graphic terms the point where diminishing returns begin is the point (3) where this curve becomes tangent to a straight line through the origin. Less than this proportion of the variable agent cannot intelligently be employed even if it

supply of labor. It is surely evident: (1) that they can use different amounts and still get some product (Ax. 1) ; (2) that they can use too little or too much to get the largest amount of product (Ax. 2) ; (3) that they might conceivably try to use so little or so much land that no product at all would be secured (Ax. 3).

is free, for the output could be increased by discarding a portion of the other factors, if no more of the variable one could be obtained at a uniform price. It is true, necessarily and a priori, that there is such a point on the curve, that for less amounts the product increases in greater ratio than the factor. That is, for any point on the curve between this point (3) and the intersection of the curve with the X axis the tangent must cut the X axis positively. Now, if below this point (3) the tangent to the curve cuts the positive X axis, if at this point it passes through the origin and beyond this point it cuts the positive Y axis, then manifestly the curve is concave downward at the point in question. And this is the graphic condition representing decreasing increments of product. It seems reasonable to assume that the same condition (concavity downward) holds from point 3 to the maximum point (4), but this is not demonstrable a priori. If it is untrue for a certain stage in this interval between points 3 and 4 over the whole field of industry, as represented by the dotted line in the figure, there is indeterminateness in the competitive situation in that interval and to that extent, but this is a rather incredible supposition.

It is immaterial what shape the curve has below point 3 so long as its tangent always cuts the X axis. No doubt in any one industry the curve will show stages of increasing returns interspersed with stages of decreasing returns, and various proportions of combination of the factors are wise and stable.[107]

If men are supposed to know what they are doing there is no occasion for discussing the first and third stages at all. The boundaries of the second stage represent extreme limits where one agency or the other becomes a free good and passes out of consideration altogether. Beyond this point the product is absolutely diminished by increasing one agency or the other, as the case may be, which is an absurdity. The identity in meaning of the first and the third stages is evident; the first stage when passing in one direction is the third when reading the data in the opposite order. It is a mere matter of

[107]It is to be noted that we must assume the size of individual establishments to be nearly a matter of indifference. The above reasoning proves also that the curve itself cuts the X axis positively as drawn in our figure, and does not pass through the origin. It follows further from the symmetry of the relation between factors that the curve will cut the X axis again beyond the maximum point and not become asymptotic, as it should do if it passed through the origin. Professor Taylor's curve was incorrectly drawn in this detail as it should either become asymptotic or else not pass through the origin.

the arrangement of results, not of the results themselves. Beyond the limits of the stage of "decreasing returns," therefore, or under circumstances where the law did not hold, there could not exist an "economic" situation. Unless the return per unit of any agency does decrease it is not productive at all; its use adds nothing to the output of the combination. If we imagine increasing returns the agency is negatively productive. This fact has been recognized in the case of land in the common statement that additional land would never be taken up until diminishing returns set in on that[108] already in use.

The facts of variability in the proportions of agencies in the productive organization, and of the variation of the yield relative to the different agencies in accordance with the principle of diminishing returns not merely make possible the economic organization of society through free contract, but in their absence the whole question of organization would be meaningless; there would be no such problem. Unless there were open for use various combinations of various productivities, with the possibility of comparing them, there would be no question of using any one arrangement rather than any other. Organization is called for, is possible, and is carried out only through the fact that the separate contributions of separate agencies to a joint product can be identified. The organization through free contract under competition is possible and real and effective in so far as such a system tends to give to the owner of each agency the separate contribution of that agency. Modern society is organized through the association of control over productive agencies with the right to their yield. Only because the income is greater where the product is larger is such organization possible at all. In the absence of a law connecting distributive share with effective contribution our social system would be no system, but chaos. It is, therefore, inappropriate for economists to argue as to whether the separation of contributions to a joint product can or cannot be made; it is made; it is our business to explain the mechanism by which it is accomplished.

[108]Really on the other agencies applied to the land, but we follow the usual formulation. The assumption must be borne in mind that men know what they are doing and are motivated by the desire to maximize production. In fact, the results are much distorted by ignorance, the effect of tradition carried over from a place where land is scarce to new countries where it is abundant, ingrained land hunger, etc., and in the United States by the conditions of land settlement and preemption.

The business man does find out how much different agencies or units of productive power are worth to the productive process or he could not carry on his business. It is obvious that the business man, in bidding for the use of separate agencies, must think in terms of the added contributions of added units, — in technical economic parlance the "marginal" product, — and it is demonstrable that when the units are sufficiently small the sum of the separate, specific contribution of all the agencies exhausts the total joint product.[109]

It is to be observed that when a new productive unit is added to a productive combination the technical law of diminishing returns does not fully describe the variation in the output. In consequence of this law alone, the added physical product of similar agencies will rise in the position from which the one in question is withdrawn and fall in that into which it moves.[110] But in addition, since the transfer decreases the total output of the commodity from whose production the agency is withdrawn, and increases the output of the industry into which it is moved, the price of the former will rise and of the latter fall relatively. In an organized free exchange society, producers naturally estimate product in terms of its exchange value and not of its physical magnitude. The variations in physical contribution and in the value of that contribution when an addition of any kind of agency is made, work in the same direction and must be added to give the total decrease in the value product. We shall call the aggregate variation by the name of diminishing value productivity or simply diminishing productivity, which must always be distinguished from the diminishing physical returns.[111]

---

[109]Cf. below, p. 108 and note.

[110]The fall in specific or marginal contribution is an easy inference from the law of the variation of product per unit.. For a detailed demonstration see Taylor, loc cit. especially pp. 101, 102. The "added product" of a unit in the text above is what Taylor and most writers call "the marginal product" of the "factor." For reasons which will presently appear I prefer to avoid the misleading terminology of factors and margins altogether.

[111]This terminology is more or less arbitrary, but is one way of straightening out the current confusion and giving different names to different things. Taylor (loc. cit.) uses both expressions "diminishing returns" and "diminishing productivity," in connection with the instrumental law; in fact in virtually the same sense, and does not bring out the contrast between the variation of physical product and that of value product. Strange to say, he does not use the principle of diminishing returns which he so well formulates in his discussion of distribution, but adopts a different line of reasoning through different proportions of factors in different industries without variability of proportions in single industries. That this same principle is involved is recognized by Taylor, who thus

It is unnecessary to introduce into our society any factors or agencies other than labor in order to study the mechanism of imputation. Groups of individuals more or less specialized to and specializing in different productive functions in the making of the same commodity represent in principle all that is involved in the cooperation of agencies of whatever difference in nature. We may, therefore, refer to these different functionaries as types of agencies, or indeed as "factors" of production, though we shall presently find reasons for avoiding this term, on account of its misleading connotations. When the conditions of a "static" society — i.e., given conditions of the production and consumption of goods — are correctly laid down, there is, as we have seen, no room for property in any sense which differentiates it from productive capacities inherent in the person of the owner.[112]

This matter will be discussed at greater length as we proceed. Let it merely be understood at this point that any class or group of agencies, or "factor" of production to which we refer, is formed on the basis of the physical facts and includes those things which are actually interchangeable one with another in the production process. If we speak of "factors" at all, there will thus be not three, but a quite indefinitely large number of them.[113]

As a matter of fact, a great deal of unnecessary mystification has been thrown around the problem of imputation. It is merely a case of joint demand, and the same situation is common in the case of consumption goods. There is really no more mystery or special difficulty about separating the demand for labor or any particular kind of labor, due to the fact that it is not employed alone, than there is about constructing a separate demand curve for butter, which is always consumed along with other commodities. The principle of variable proportions is the key to the solution in both cases. Commodities always used together and always in the same proportions would not be separate commodities, as far as consumption is concerned, but parts of one commodity, though they might still be valued separately if the conditions of production were distinct.

---

shows a considerable advance over Wieser. This author, it will be recalled, uses the same theory of imputation which Taylor uses, but advances it in place of the specific productivity theory, applied to industries independently, which he repudiates. (See below, p. 110.)

[112]Cf. above, chapter III.

[113]As Davenport has remarked. (Cf. Economics of Enterprise, chap. xxii.) But Davenport's position will come up for criticism later on. (Below, p. 124.)

Keeping in mind the above facts and the simplified conditions under which we are working, it is not difficult to picture the actual mechanism of the organization. Let us begin as in the last chapter with a random adjustment and follow through the successive readjustments to the equilibrium condition. Suppose that groups of producers are formed by guess in any chance way, the product of each group as a whole being determined in the manner already described and its division among the members of the group arranged on any basis whatever. It is evident that the desire of every individual to better himself will lead at once to three sorts of inquiries. First, each person will endeavor to ascertain his own value to the group of which he is a member and compare it with the share which he is receiving; and second, he will similarly inquire what he might be worth to other groups. Third, as a member of a group each individual will interest himself in the value to the group of other individuals in it and in the value which individuals outside it would have if they could be procured for his group. As a result, (1) remunerations will rapidly be readjusted toward the values which the individuals contribute to the output of the groups with which they work, and (2) all individuals will gravitate toward those groups in which they can make the largest contributions to output. Any individual receiving from his group more than he is worth will be released or have his remuneration reduced. Any individual receiving less than he is worth will be able to secure his full value,[114] since we have specified conditions under which perfect competition will exist between the groups.

All productive groups would thus compete among themselves for

[114]The mode of internal organization of the groups need not trouble us here. It might take any form which would produce effective common action and responsibility. In life, it is, of course, generally worked out through a responsible entrepreneur as intermediary, but it is necessary to exclude such a functionary at this point in the argument, and in fact his services would be superfluous, except, perhaps, temporarily while the adjustment was being worked out. Greater violence is done to reality by the specification of perfect competition among organizations for members. This assumption involves, in the first place, perfect knowledge and intercommunication throughout the society. In addition it calls for a large number of groups exploiting every sort of service, and entire absence of collusive action among them. The number of establishments in any line of production depends upon the size of each, which in turn depends on the divisibility of the factors being combined. Hence the principle laid down above (p. 98) that competition depends on a degree of divisibility in productive factors. That division of labor is limited by the scope of the market is true, but commodities sold in different markets do not represent the same aggregations of utilities, and are different commodities.

the services of actual and potential members, and the individuals in the society would compete for positions in the group in a manner quite analogous to the existing order of things. The standard of what a group could afford to pay for a man is clearly the amount which he enables it to produce more than it would produce without him. In the final adjustment the individual's contribution to the income of the group is his contribution to the income of society as a whole, which he is under pressure to make as large as possible by placing himself in the position where he is really most effective.[115] The tendency of a competitive organization is, therefore, toward that ideal adjustment familiar in the literature of laissez-faire. In the final adjustment the organization could not be changed without bringing uncompensated losses, and the total produce would be divided among all claimants by giving each his added product.[116]

The conditions precedent to this theoretical result are indeed abstract; but they are the conditions of perfect competition, and they are the conditions which actual society more or less closely approaches. It is important both to understand free competition because society does approach it more or less closely as an ideal, and to be fully aware of the artificiality of the conditions necessary to realize it perfectly.

Another way of formulating the condition of equilibrium is to view the adjustment as a continual repricing of productive services.

---

[115]There is a difficulty in regard to the meaning of the value contribution to a social total. Exchange values being essentially ratios, an aggregate of exchange value has very little meaning. We cannot be sure that the value income of society as measured by the market, in terms, say, of a particular commodity, would be larger when the final adjustment was reached than under any other arrangement, and, of course, it will not do to say that the individual gets the physical commodities which he enables the society to produce. The answer is that he will get the value of the physical contribution which he makes, enough value income to buy it. The actual physical contribution should theoretically consist of infinitesimal increments of practically all the commodities produced in the society, perhaps including an increment of "leisure.".

[116]For a full discussion and demonstration of the theoretical exhaustiveness of the distributive process as described above (though in a somewhat different setting), see Wicksteed, Common Sense of Political Economy, book ii, chap, vi, and The Coordination of the Laws of Distribution, Pflssim. The reader will notice that the lines along which the adjustment is supposed to be worked out above are very different from the "dosing method" familiar in American economic literature. (Cf. especially J. B. Clark, The Distribution of Wealth, chap, xii.) This latter procedure seems to the writer unnecessarily abstract and unreal and more difficult to follow than the realistic method of tracing out the effect of competition among establishments.

This process would be more closely analogous to the process by which the prices of consumption goods are determined. We can think of each producer or group as being in the market with a certain amount of money to spend for productive power in the abstract. At the price level established at any moment those productive agencies will, of course, be purchased which make the largest price contribution to product for a given price outlay. But since the amounts of all agencies in existence are fixed, competition will quickly force a readjustment of prices to that point at which equal price amounts of all agencies make equal price contributions to product, just as in the former case equal price amounts of all goods must represent "equal utilities" to all consumers. The organization of the productive system as a whole is in fact quite analogous to that of the expenditure of income. Productive agencies are now the given resources of which the best use is to be made by distributing them so as to secure equality of remuneration for similar units in all employments. In the organization as a whole, the two principles combine. The money income may be omitted, as an instrumental intermediary, and the result stated by saying that the real resources of society tend to be so distributed among all employments that similar physical units everywhere make contributions psychically equivalent to all persons in the system in a position to choose between them.

It will now be in order to notice the more important objections which have been made to the productivity theory of distribution, though many or all of them have already been answered and probably would not be made against the form of the theory presented above. To begin with, let us insist on the complete separation of the theory of distribution proper from certain sweeping moral and social dogmas, which have been deduced from it. Professor J. B. Clark, the leading American exponent of the theory, is partly responsible for this confusion, through a few unguarded paragraphs in "The Distribution of Wealth."[117] The illegitimacy of these ethical deductions has been well argued, however, by Professor Carver,[118] another expositor of the theory, as well as by Professor J. M. Clark in defending the theory itself.[119] We may, therefore, pass over the strictures of those writers who do not like social implications which the theory does not have, which include a considerable part of the

[117]See especially pp. 8, 9.

[118]Quarterly Journal of Economics, August, 1901.

[119]Political Science Quarterly, June, 1915.

criticism of Professors Davenport[120] and Adriance;[121] we shall take up briefly the question of the ethical aspects of the competitive system in chapter VI.

Against the productivity theory itself an old and common criticism is that well stated by Wieser,[122] who attempts to refute Menger's presentation of it, and substantially the same line of attack has been followed more recently by Hobson,[123] who refers especially to Wicksteed. The contention is that specific or marginal productivity cannot afford a theoretically adequate method of distribution, for the reason that the sum of the products of the separate agencies, as defined by the theory, will be not equal to the total joint product, but considerably larger. The amount subtracted from the total product when "one unit" is withdrawn will, it is argued, be much greater than can be imputed to that agent alone, since the loss of any agent will more or less dislocate the organization. It, therefore, becomes impossible by this method to divide the total accurately into parts ascribable to the separate "factors" individually as the specific contribution of each. Wieser proposes an alternative method, which is identical with Professor F. M. Taylor's exposition of the productivity theory itself.[124] Hobson dogmatically declares the problem impossible.

The error in this line of reasoning lies in fixing the attention upon a comparatively small organization and comparatively large blocks or units of productive service. When account is taken of the actual size of industrial society and of the ordinary unit of most agencies, it will be seen that the "dislocation" is negligible; theoretically, to be sure, the units would have to be of infinitesimal size, separately owned and effectively competing; i.e., the proportions must be con-

[120]The Economics of Enterprise, chap. x.

[121]"Specific Productivity," Quarterly Journal of Economics, vol. xxix, pp. 149 ff., esp. pp. 159 and 160.

[122]Der Naturliche Werth, 3. Abschnitt, "Die Nattirliche Zurenchnung des Productiven Ertrages," § 22

[123]The Industrial System, chap, v, appendix, pp. 112-20. A somewhat different (quasi-mathematical) line of argument to the same end is put forth by R. S. Padan, Journal of Political Economy, March, 1901 (vol. ix, pp. 161 ff.).

[124]Cf. above, p. 104, note. Taylor is right in the contention that specific productivity can be imputed through differences in the proportions of agencies in different industries alone without variability of proportions in the industries individually. In fact, both elements come into play. We have mentioned and shall presently discuss further the fallacy involved in the concept of the "factor" of production.

tinuously variable, in the mathematical sense. But in the typical case the error resulting from this assumption is not large in comparison with other inaccuracies in the competitive adjustment. It is true that there are exceptional cases where agencies are not highly divisible, or even not divisible at all, and competition gives place to a greater or less degree of monopoly. These exceptions are relatively infrequent in the mass of industry as a whole, but are of considerable absolute importance, and we shall have something to say later on in regard to unique and indivisible agencies.[125]

Padan, in the article referred to, further attacks Professor Clark's exposition of the productivity theory on the express ground that the amount received by any factor would depend on the arbitrary size assigned to the marginal unit. This point also is hypothetically sound, but irrelevant. The size of the unit is not an arbitrary matter of methodology, but a question of fact, and Professor Clark may be open to criticism only for seeming to imply the contrary. The soundness of the theory, the possibility of competitive distribution at all, in fact, depends on the actual division of productive agencies into bargaining units of small size.[126] We should hold that it is an error to say that "labor" or any "factor" gets or tends to get its product. This holds good only for the actual individual men or other agencies.

A third, somewhat philosophical, criticism is also advanced by Davenport and Adriance. It is contended that the "marginal" product of labor, for example, is as much a joint product as that of any other than the marginal unit. The laborer who uses no-rent land still has to use it, can produce nothing without it, and hence the product cannot be ascribed to the labor alone. Professor Taussig also, though like Davenport somewhat guardedly, asserts that all product is joint product and cannot be divided into parcels attributable to separate

---

[125]See chapter vi.

[126]We may notice here another point raised by Padan, the bearing of increasing returns upon the theory. It is generally recognized that in the earlier stages of a hypothetical dosing process, increasing returns will be secured, up to a certain point. By "supposing" this stage of increasing returns to last throughout the process, Padan easily makes the application of the method appear absurd. This line of reasoning is still more arbitrary than his earlier point, however, and need not detain us. We have shown at sufficient length that increasing returns is an absurdity; that an agency worked under such conditions is negatively productive and had better not be used at all. Professor A. Landry, in criticizing Professor Carver, has also overworked this supposition. (See Quarterly Journal of Economics, vol. xxm, pp. 557 ff.)

agencies, though at the same time he inclines to regard all income as the "product" of labor.[127] An examination of this reasoning would carry us into the question of the meaning of production and causality, which will be taken up presently. For the present it must suffice to point out that it involves a confusion between mechanical and economic productivity. The land used by marginal labor may be necessary to the operations in the former sense, but is not in the latter, since by hypothesis if it is withheld from use it can at once be replaced by other land equally good; otherwise it would not be free land. The fallacy is parallel to the confusion between "utility" (as usually defined) and economic value. Free goods, like air, may be necessary to life, but no particular portion being necessary, the good cannot have economic value (nor, as we have argued above, should it be said to have utility if this term is to be used to connote any sort of economic significance).

We must notice, finally, another objection raised by Hobson to the general doctrine of "marginalism."[128] With Hobson's fundamental position, that marginalism is the necessary form of a rational treatment of choice, and that the rational view of life is subject to drastic limitations, the writer is in hearty accord. It is not clear that Hobson intends his strictures to apply specifically to the productivity theory of distribution, but it may not be out of place to remark that such an application would be an error. In general we submit that there is much more deliberate, quantitative balancing of alternatives in economic conduct than the discussion under notice would have us believe, but this is a large issue which cannot be threshed out here. It does not seem to us that the composition of life is closely analogous to Hobson's painting or cake in which the proportion of the ingredients is rigidly determined by a recipe or a preconceived ideal of the whole. In any case, the production of goods by industry is very emphatically a rational process, an adjustment worked out by the producer in terms of these very separable effects of separate agencies. Nor is it true, as Hobson does argue elsewhere,[129] that technical conditions prescribe the proportions in which agencies are

[127] Proceedings, Twenty-Second Annual Meeting of the American Economic Association, p. 143. Taussig's statement that labor produces all wealth, but is not entitled to all of it, would better, it seems to me, be reversed. Labor cannot claim to be the only causal source of goods, but may put forth a superficial claim to a right to consume them all.

[128] Work and Wealth, chap: XXII.

[129] The Industrial System, cited above.

to be used. The proportions of labor to land and of capital to either, and to a large extent of various sorts of each among themselves, are open to variation through a range almost without technical limit, in the fundamental industries at least. Again, the final appeal is to fact. It is the value to the producer as an addition to his organization as a whole which determines the amount which he will bid in the market for the use of any unit of labor, land, or capital, or the amount of any one which he will purchase at an established price. Hence it is this "specific product" which rules the apportionment of income at large among productive agencies at large.

As remarked above, most of the objections to the productivity theory relate to the meaning of production and of product, and come down in fine to the propriety of using the word, rather than to any fundamental disagreement as to how the distributive mechanism actually works. We wish now to point out that in calling the addition made by any agency to the total output of a large organization its specific or separate product, we are using the word "product" in the same meaning and the only meaning which the. words "cause" and "effect" or equivalent terms ever have. It is never true in an absolute sense that one event is the cause of another. The whole state of the universe at one moment may perhaps be said to cause its whole state at the next moment, but when we say that " A " is the "cause" of "B" we always assume that other things are equal; we never mean that if the rest of the universe were removed "A" alone would produce "B." And the imputation of any single event to another as cause or effect is always largely arbitrary. Every event has an infinite number of causes, and it depends upon circumstances, the point of view, the problem in hand, which of these we single out for designation as "The" cause. "The" cause of a phenomenon is merely that one of its necessary conditions which is for some practical reason crucial, generally from the standpoint of control. It is the one about which we must concern ourselves, the circumstances enabling us to take the others for granted. It may be quite correct to name a dozen different antecedents as "the" cause of a particular occurrence, according to the point of view. The fact that other agencies, even the whole social system, may be concerned in the production of a certain good does not therefore argue against its being the (specific) product of the particular agency upon whose activity its creation actually hinges under the actual circumstances of the case.[130]

[130] In the writer's opinion, the hostility to the productivity theory is due mainly

A general analytic statement of the principles of static organization, in price terms and on the basis of supply and demand, will consist of two main parts. We have to consider two valuation problems relating respectively to consumption goods and productive services. The problems, are usually designated as "value" and "distribution." It will be convenient to take up the second of these problems first. We have already seen that the effective form of the law of variation of proportions of factors is the law of diminishing value productivity. It is obvious that all readjustments involve transfers of productive resources and that every such transfer implies a price change, raising the prices of goods produced by the organization from which resources are taken and lowering the prices of goods to whose production resources are diverted. And the effect of this price change coincides in direction with the effect of diminishing physical returns. We may content ourselves for the present with this superficial view of the price reactions on the side of consumption goods and proceed to work out the price conditions of equilibrium of the system in terms of the distributive shares. After which the viewpoint will be shifted to regard these shares, not as the remunerations of agencies, but as costs of the goods into which their services enter. When the adjustment and its equilibrium have been studied as a relation between prices and costs of consumption goods, we can bring the two analyses together and see the relations of the three sets of price facts — values of goods, costs of goods, and values of productive services. It is obvious that as aggregates the three concepts are identical, all being in fact the social income looked at from different points of view.

From the standpoint of the present problem of the "static state"

to the notion that the productivity of labor and capital represents their moral desert in distribution, joined to the conviction that the existing order is not morally ideal. The theorists who treat a productivity remuneration as synonymous with ideal justice are merely uncritically voicing the popular view. It is this popular dogma which is the seat of the difficulty, and which represents a confusion of the most egregious sort and leads to equally muddled reasoning on the question of causality in order to avoid a repugnant conclusion as to the justice of things as they are. The question cannot be gone into here, but a little consideration will show that there is almost no case at all for an identification or close assimilation of causal contribution to production with moral desert in distribution. The inequalities in inherited property and opportunity in several senses are obvious, but it must also be recognized that natural differences in personal capacity are equally powerless to create a valid moral claim to favored treatment.

the supplies of all productive agencies are rigidly fixed, and the theory of the valuation of their services is closely parallel to the market price theory as given in the last chapter for consumption goods. The facts of demand and supply for any particular kind of agency can be presented in the form of schedules or graphs showing the respective amounts that will be forthcoming and that can be sold at each price, and the equilibrium point would be manifest in such a presentation. The facts on both the supply and demand sides of the relation are more complicated than in the case of consumption goods. On the supply side we cannot take the amount in existence even at a moment as a given physical datum. For we are dealing with the services of a particular kind of agency, not the agency as such. The amount of the agency is fixed, but the amount of marketable service forthcoming from it may well vary with the price offered. Two courses are open. We may define and classify services on the basis of the physical characteristics of the agencies which render them or in terms of the physical result produced.[131] Let us take first agencies as physically defined. In this case the effect of the substitution of more or less similar agencies is to be taken into account in plotting the demand curve; supply means the supply of the services of a particular kind of physical agent, things which are perfectly homogeneous and universally interchangeable alone being grouped together.

It is usual, because superficially "natural" to assume that a man will work more — i.e., work harder or more hours per day — for a higher wage than for a lower one. But a little examination will show that this assumption is for rational behavior incorrect. In so far as men act rationally — i.e., from fixed motives subject to the law of diminishing utility — they will at a higher rate divide their time between wage-earning and non-industrial uses in such a way as to earn more money, indeed, but to work fewer hours. Just where the balance will be struck depends upon the shape of the curve of comparison between money (representing the group of things purchasable with money) and leisure (representing all non-pecuniary, alternative uses of time). We therefore draw our momentary supply line in terms of price with some downward slope.[132]

[131]It seems to me a manifest absurdity to define them in price terms as does Professor J. B. Clark. (The Distribution of Wealth, chap, vi.) There would be only one factor if measured in price terms, and the theory of distribution would be a pure petitio principii.

[132]If this conclusion is not evident after a little reflection it may be demonstrated by reasoning as follows. Suppose that at a higher rate per hour or per

The second alternative is to define agencies or factors in terms of the physical results which they produce. When this is done the shape of the supply curve at a moment will depend simply on the degree of specialization of the service under discussion. At one extreme we would have an unspecialized service, such as unskilled labor in a certain employment. For such a service there would be no supply at all below the established competitive price in all uses, and a virtually unlimited supply above that price. That is, the supply curve as a function of price would be a vertical line. At the other extreme would be absolutely specialized services, such as diamond cutters or aviators. For these there would be no supply below a certain minimum price, what such men can earn in other lines of work, and as the price rose the supply would rapidly increase until the men trained for the service were all employed in it, beyond which the curve would merge into the supply curve previously discussed of services from given agencies. (See accompanying graphs, which show supply as a function of price.)

---

piece, a man previously at the perfect equilibrium adjustment works as before and earns a proportionally larger income. When, now, he goes to spend the extra money, he will naturally want to increase his expenditures for many commodities consumed and to take on some new ones. To divide his resources in such a way as to preserve equal importance of equal expenditures in .all fields he must evidently lay out part of his new funds for increased leisure; i.e., buy back some of his working time or spend some of his money by the process of not earning it. The conclusion is enforced by the important practical consideration that the expenditure of money also requires time and energy which must be saved from the work period if the best results are to be secured.

The facts as to the shape of the supply curve of labor from given laborers are well known to employers of native workmen in backward countries, especially the tropics. White men in the advanced industrial nations have not always behaved so rationally; their traditions give them a higher preference for the kinds of satisfactions purchasable with money in comparison with the more inward and spiritual enjoyments. But the effect which was to be anticipated was very conspicuous after the outbreak of the World War, when the wages for certain kinds of work rose to unprecedented heights and produced increased loafing and dissipation instead of increased production. (It is important to bear in mind that we are speaking of a permanent change; it would be in keeping with rationality to work harder at a temporarily higher rate in order to purchase more leisure later on.)

While on the subject we may observe that it is also an error to assume that in this respect land or other property services will be different from labor. These agencies also have alternative non-pecuniary uses, and if, say, the rent on land were to rise, landowners could afford to use more of it for lawns, flower gardens, athletic grounds, game preserves, pleasure parks, etc., and less for cultivation and marketable crops; and if they calculated closely they would do so.

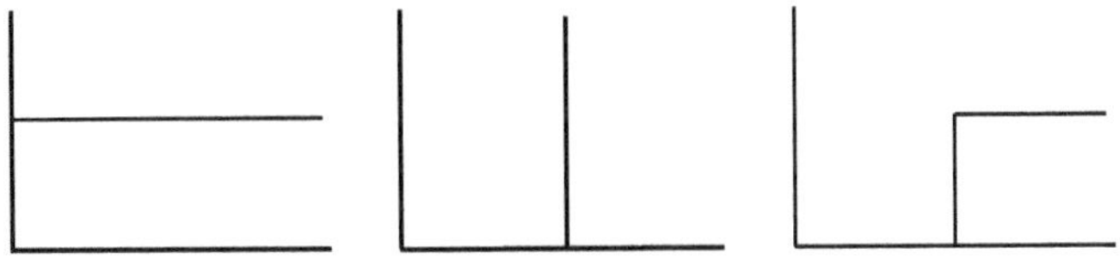

Figure 6: Services from given agencies — An unspecialized service — A specialized service

In regard to demand, also, the case of productive services is less simple than that of consumptive goods; demand is (a) always indirect or derived, a reflection of the demand for the products of the agency, and (b) always joint in character. In connection with the first fact, the demand is also highly composite; identical productive agencies minister alternately to a vast range of wants and widely different agencies to the same wants. These complexities in the use of productive services make a really logical classification of them a difficult if not impossible problem. The fact of joint demand, as we have seen, differentiates producer's goods from consumer's goods in degree only, and to a relatively limited degree.

The shape of the demand curve showing possible sales of the services of any physically defined type of agency as a function of price is similar to that of the consumption goods demand curve. It is the curve of diminishing value productivity already described, descending in consequence both of decreasing physical productivity and decreasing price. That is, if the supply of any productive agency be increased the proportion of that agency in combinations in which it is employed will be raised all along the line, and at the same time there will be a relative increase in the production of those commodities in which its use is relatively important with a consequent decline in their relative price. The equilibrium price point under static conditions is practically the specific productivity of the given supply of the agency (though we must remember that there is some variation in supply of service as price varies even at a moment). In the equilibrium condition, that is to say, the value of each service is equal to the value of its contribution to the total product, and the contributions of physically similar agencies are of equal value throughout the system. It is evident that this adjustment fixes the prices of consumption goods at the same time with those of productive services, and we may apply the supply and demand analysis to consumption goods also, giving the theory of normal price in contrast with the theory of market price studied in the last chapter.

At a moment, the theoretical price of any good is the ("marginal") demand price of the existing supply, the highest uniform price that will take the supply out of the market. The supply is a given physical fact, not an economic variable, but a constant in the equation. The equilibrium price of a good over a long period is a different problem. Here it is not the amount of the good that is constant (together with the facts of demand), but (under "static" conditions) the conditions of production of goods in general (and of demand). The supply of any particular good may change freely and will do so as its price varies, other things being equal. The price must be adjusted not to dispose of a fixed supply, but to equate a rate[133] of production with a rate of consumption, both variable with or "functions of" the price.

No particular reinterpretation of the demand curve is called for, however, the only new problem being on the supply side. Assuming for the moment that the rate of supply as well as the rate of demand is in fact a function of price, it is evident that the price must move toward an equilibrium point equating the two rates; for goods cannot be consumed more rapidly than they are produced and will not be produced more rapidly than they are consumed. Any difference either way will at once react on the price and the price will react on the production and consumption rates in accordance with the assumed functional relations, and so on until the demand and supply both correspond to the existing priced c

To investigate the basis and character of the relation between supply and price, we must consider the motives which control production. The productive group or establishment, however organized, must pay its members (the owners of productive services) enough to retain them; i.e., it must meet competition. When any group can hire a new member at a profit it will do so, and clearly it can get any new member by raising ever so little the remuneration he is receiving elsewhere. Clearly, also, it will dispense with any member who must be employed at a loss; i.e., any to whom competing groups can afford to pay more than it can afford to pay. The amount of any commodity that will be produced at any price, therefore, tends

[133]Marshall correctly treats long-time demand and supply as time rates, but does not sharply contrast this form of the variable with the absolute amounts dealt with in market price.

quickly toward the amount that will yield neither profit nor loss, for when production yields ever so little profit it will increase, and vice versa. For the study of this adjustment it is convenient to interchange the axes of our previous graph and view cost and selling price as functions of the size of supply.

It is usually assumed that cost may either increase, remain constant or decrease as supply is increased.[134] (Selling price, of course, practically always decreases.) The question is really one of the most difficult and perhaps one of the worst muddled in economic theory and cannot be adequately treated here. But examination seems to show that under the conditions necessary to perfect competition, costs must always increase as supply increases. If there is to be competition, conditions must be such that an establishment of relatively small size in comparison with the industry as a whole is more efficient than a large one; otherwise monopoly will result. New supply will then come through an increase in the number of similar establishments, not through an increase in the size of any of them, and no economies of large-scale production will be realized.

On the contrary, the increased supply must mean a diversion of productive resources from other uses, which will raise their price in those uses through the decreased output and consequent rise in price of the competing product. Of course, if competition exists the price will go up uniformly to all producers, and it goes without saying that the cost of all units of the supply is the same.[135]

The precise form of the cost function will depend on the importance of the particular good in the demand for the productive services which enter into it. If its production constitutes a negligible fraction of the demand for all these services, we shall have practically constant cost; if a considerable fraction, a more rapidly rising cost. It will also vary with the character of the function representing the law of decreasing returns in the given technological situation; for as production is increased the proportions of more abundant agencies will be increased relatively to those more limited in supply. The graph

[134]Cf. Taussig, Principles of Economics, chaps. 12, 13, 14.

[135]Economic literature is full of the contrary assumption, but it is a definite error, in dealing with long-time normal price. The existence of differences in costs in different establishments in an industry is proof, when not due to differences in accounting practice, that the competitive adjustment is imperfect. The current conception of marginal cost necessarily falls away through the same reasoning. The producer's calculations are made in terms of cost per unit and selling price per unit.

on p. 91 shows the character of the functions and the meaning of equilibrium, and is applicable also to conditions of joint production.

The equilibrium condition or long-run tendency for the static state has now been formulated in three ways from as many different standpoints. From the standpoint of distribution, every agency must be in the situation where it can make the greatest possible value contribution to the social income and be valued by the contribution which it makes. From the standpoint of consumption goods, prices must be such that rates of production and consumption are equal or that costs and selling prices per unit are everywhere the same. It is important to see clearly that these statements are logically equivalent, presenting different aspects of the same phenomena. It is self-evident that costs of goods are identical in the aggregate with distributive shares, and both with prices of goods; all three are in fact different names for the total income of the society.

Hitherto we have dealt only with different sorts of human services as giving rise to the phenomena of competitive imputation. The meaning and role of property in the problem of economic organization next call for notice. We have seen that material productive goods do not modify the principles of organization so long as they are not subject to increase or decrease and not separable from the persons of their owners, to whose personal capacities the same restrictions must apply.

The conventional classification of productive agencies under the three categories of land, labor, and capital has several times in the foregoing pages been referred to adversely, and it is appropriate at this point to take up for somewhat more detailed notice the difficult problem of correct definition and classification. It is evident that all these classes are anything but homogeneous, that different human beings, different machines, and different natural agents show the greatest diversity in characteristics and in the services which they perform. Cairnes's attempt to reduce labor to more approximately homogeneous bodies gave us the famous "non-competing groups." Still more obtrusive are the dissimilarities of different natural agents — wheat land vs. pineapple land, arable vs. grazing or timber, and all contrasted with mineral-bearing and the multitudinous kinds of the latter. Capital is somewhat peculiar in this respect, its "fluidity" depending on the length of time taken into view.

On the other hand, it is if possible a more important fact that agencies from different classes and of the most divergent physical properties may be equivalent and interchangeable with respect to the results which they achieve. As Carver Thas observed, a (human) ditch-digger is economically as closely akin to a steam shovel as he is to a bookkeeper.[136] Indeed, the possibility of a competitive organization of society depends on the fact of varying proportions, that no particular agency is indispensable, but that within limits they may be substituted for each other and therefore each must compete with others of different kinds for its place. It is evident that otherwise producers would not be in the market for the agencies separately and they could not be separately evaluated through competitive bidding. The existence of a problem of distribution depends on the cooperation of different kinds of agencies performing physically different operations in the creation of product, and the possibility of solving the problem depends on the equivalence of determinate amounts of the several services in contributing to the value result. It follows at once that, as already observed, no classification or measurement of productive services on the basis of their contributions has any meaning for the distribution problem. According to such a standard they all form one vast homogeneous fund.[137]

[136]The Distribution of Wealth, p. 85; cf. also Davenport, Economics of Enterprise, chaps, xi and xxii.

[137]Reference has been made to the absurdity of the two-factor analysis, as exemplified particularly in the work of Professor J. B. Clark. The same author falls into the closely related fallacy of measuring separate agencies by their productive contributions. He recognizes and clearly states the difficulty {The Distribution of Wealth, p. 374, note) and ostensibly gets around it by setting up an absolute subjective standard of measurement. It is very difficult for the present writer to criticize this reasoning, and out of the question in the space available; I can see nothing in it but a complete failure to make connections, a palpable non sequitur. It is to be observed that the fallacy is equally involved in all other distribution theory which makes use of " factors " at all — the number is immaterial and this includes most of the literature of the subject.

A conspicuous exception is Davenport's discussion (Economics of Enterprise, chaps, xi and xxii) already mentioned, which is excellent for this phase of the question. Where it falls short is in failing adequately to separate the long and short period problems of distribution. It is this failure which in the writer's view explains most of the controversial differences between economists in so far as they relate to the scientific explanation of distribution, and not to questions of propriety or policy. It is essential to take account of the fact that from the long-time point of view the question of classification takes on a different aspect, becoming a question of the conditions of supply of different types of agents. The case for the conventional tripartite division (or more especially the separation of land and capital) is argued at length in A. S. Johnson's Rent in Modern Economic Theory. (See especially pp. 35 ff.) This phase of the problem will presently come up for discussion, and it will be pointed out that there is danger

The problem is really a difficult one, and cannot be passed over, since we cannot discuss the valuation of things without knowing what it is that is being evaluated. Much the same difficulty, however, was met with, as will be recalled, in the sphere of consumption goods, and the answer must come from the same source in the two cases — an appeal to the unsophisticated facts of the market. Things quoted under the same name and identically priced may be taken as identical, and vice versa. Some special features of the present case may be mentioned, however. In the first place, interchangeability of productive agents depends on the use; two things may be equivalent for one purpose, entirely dissimilar for another. This is not nearly so true of consumption goods, which, indeed, are not generally open to such a complex variety of uses. Interchangeability is also a matter of time. The problem of changing the form of productive agencies and adapting them to new uses carries us into long-time considerations, and especially the meaning of capital, which will come up in the next chapter. It will be seen that examination tends to widen the capital category greatly; most productive services ultimately represent a previous investment of resources of some sort.

The variation in interchangeability in different uses introduces a special complication which has caused confusion. The consideration which finally determines is not interchangeability in creating any particular physical product, but a certain amount of value. The former variety of interchangeability is not in fact a necessary condition for the operation of competitive distribution. If agencies are combined in different uses, effective substitution is secured through relative growth or decay of the different industries. We have previously remarked that Wieser, who repudiates the productivity theory of distribution as based on variation in proportions, puts forth the really equivalent theory, based on different proportions in different combinations. Taylor, however, takes the latter method for his ex-

---

of over-simplification here also. (See below, chapter v.

It may strike the attention of the reader that while the tripartite classification is emphatically repudiated, the factors are still commonly referred to in the present essay as "land, labor, and capital." If explanation is called for, it is to be found in the necessity, for mere expository purposes, of some expression which explicitly covers the whole group. The significance is the opposite of classificatory; "animal, vegetable, and mineral," or "solid, liquid, and gaseous agencies" could have been used but for their unfamiliarity in this connection. Also the familiar terms have social and ethical significance if none of a strictly economic sort.

planation of the productivity theory, but points out that the two are equivalent. Both sorts of variations in proportion are, of course, concerned in the actual working of the market for productive services, and systematically occur together, as explained in our exposition of distribution theory just given.[138]

To conclude this brief discussion of the productive services, we may merely notice the invalidity of four commonly assumed grounds of distinction between labor and property services: (1) Activity vs. passivity. It is characteristic of the enterprise organization that labor is directed by its employer, not its owner, in a way analogous to material equipment. Certainly there is in this respect no sharp difference between a free laborer and a horse, not to mention a slave, who would, of course, be property. Closely related is (2) the question of preference in the agency itself as to (a) the kind and (b) the amount of service to be performed. But here also there is at most a vague difference in degree; the owner of property quite commonly does have moral or sentimental reasons for restricting the field of its employment. We must not confuse the agency actually performing work with the personality of its owner, and it appears that a tool or a building or a piece of land is in this regard similar to a man's hand or brain. Similarly as to (b) the amount of work done. It may be urged that material agents do not care whether they work or not. But the ground for restricting hours of labor or taking a vacation is a possible alternative use for one's personal resources or the desire to conserve them unimpaired, and the same considerations apply to property resources.[139]

---

[138]See above, p. 119.

[139]The notion of sacrifice has been overworked in economics. Economists as well as employers have been too prone to assume that subjective willingness is the principal limitation on the amount of labor obtained from given persons or for a given outlay. And employers as well as economists are waking up to the efficiency of well-paid labor. There is no doubt that employers as a class have lost much money (not to mention the higher considerations involved) through working their employees beyond, and feeding, clothing, and amusing them below, the point of maximum physical efficiency. This would not be done with a dumb animal! Of course it may be profitable to the individual employer to pay a wage below what is necessary to maintain maximum efficiency and an adequate supply of labor from generation to generation (if the working class maintains the labor supply partly at its own cost) ; what is meant is that they have paid uneconomically low wages even from the standpoint of the short periods for which they have to deal with the same individual laborer. The presence of idle equipment is a great temptation to an employer, and the debit side of overworked help is less conspicuous to view. Of course the ignorance and imprudence of the

(3) Another superficial difference which similarly dissolves under scrutiny relates to "sub-marginal" agencies — too poor in quality to be employed. It may be urged that there is no wageless labor analogous to free land. As a matter of fact, however, marginal and sub-marginal human beings are nearly as common and significant a phenomenon as in the case of land, and far surpass capital in this respect. Every man is a sub-marginal laborer for a considerable fraction of his life at each end of it, and institutions are full of sub-marginal men. And there are thousands and millions of other idle man-hours in a year which would be devoted to anything that brought in the least return above the competitive pay which would have to be given to the equipment necessary to employ them. On the other hand, the same fallacious reasoning noted in connection with overwork undoubtedly leads to the employment of large numbers who use equipment which would yield more product if employed in the "more intensive exploitation" of more competent workers.[140]

(4) The most important alleged difference between property and. personal powers, the moral aspect, is not strictly within the scope of a purely descriptive discussion such as the present, but it may be in place to observe that it also is largely unreal. The contrast between personal service income as "earned" and property income as "unearned," of which much is made by "reformers," is distinctly misleading; it is difficult if not impossible to find grounds for a moral distinction of any general validity between the two. "Some are born great, some achieve greatness, and some have greatness thrust upon them"; and the same applies quite as well to wealth. And the task of separating the portion of product or capacity to produce which is due to conscientious effort from that which goes back to inherited advantage or pure luck is about as impossible — and the evil results

---

workers are as much in point as those of the employer. It is of interest that Lord Leverhulme has recently put forth the contention that a six-hour day, without decreased pay, would be profitable to British employers in many industries, if the men would consent to two shifts during each twenty-four hours.

[140]This is being recognized in the case of child labor by many employers who refuse to employ children simply on the ground that it does not pay in the business sense. This whole problem becomes more important as the amount of capital per worker increases. It is also true that the increasing use of machinery provides tasks which a lower and lower grade of. human capacities are required to perform. The net result is difficult to estimate. The social problem of the "unemployable" — how to identify him and what to do with him — is surely forbidding enough. Like most of our new troubles, it is partly a product of the disintegration of the family as well as of industrial changes directly.

of making a false separation perhaps about as great — in one case as in the other. There is a difference of some significance in the practical possibility of effecting a redistribution in the two cases, which brings us back to the one specification which we found it necessary to lay down in regard to property in order to exclude it as a complicating fact; it is separable from the person of its owner, and labor generally is not, or is so to nothing like the same degree. The only conclusion as to social policy which we shall insert here is the insistence that "society" must get rid of the idea that because income is "earned" it is "deserved "and not otherwise. We are already far from this view in practice, as is shown by the indiscriminate taxation of large "service" incomes and assistance of the unfortunate and incapable. If we are to have organized society and maintain human standards of life, we must either radically eliminate weakness or impose upon strength the burdens which weakness cannot bear. (And even then there are limits to the possible toleration of weakness, and the luck element would still remain!)

Turning again now to consider the causal relations to economic organization of the one causally significant distinguishing attribute of property, let us first suppose that in our society some property is separable by lease, though not by sale, from the person of its owner. The only difference will be that the owner of such property may belong to more than one productive group and contribute more than one kind of service at the same time. The principles of organization of the system as a whole are in no wise affected by this change in the conditions of competitive arrangements.

The possibility of the permanent transfer of property by exchange, even though not subject to increase or decrease, does introduce some new factors into our problem. These results are closely related to the bearings of another abstraction hitherto made, the continuity and timelessness of the production-consumption process. Consequently, we must first get rid of this simplification and consider the effect of the abstracted element. What then will happen in a society such as we have studied when conditions are so modified in the direction of reality that, while perfect knowledge and static conditions in other respects are maintained, the production process is protracted over a considerable period of time and split up into complicated stages and subdivisions, and when, moreover, goods need no longer be consumed at once when finished, but may be stored for future use, or exchanged?

The division of the productive process into stages carried on in different groups or plants is a detail connected with the time length of the process, but which we can pass over with brief notice. It is in fact a relatively accidental matter of organization, and under the "frictionless" conditions here assumed it would make no practical difference whether successive processes in the making of an article were integrated through the internal organization of a single group or through the external mechanism of market dealings between groups. Under these conditions there will be in existence at any time a complex aggregate of partial products, goods in process, which of course will have value. We must separate that element in the value of the partial products which is due merely to the stored-up productive energy which they contain from any modification of this value due to the direct psychical influence of the time which must elapse before they are ready for consumption.

The relation of time to the production and consumption of goods is a complicated and controversial question; while only a very brief discussion can be attempted here, it is necessary to make a superficial survey. The assumption of a general preference in human nature for present over future goods is so commonly and confidently made that some courage is required to call in question the foundations of the entire body of doctrine on the subject; yet it must be done. Most discussion of the subject is, in the writer's view, vitiated by a false conception of the nature of the problem. The fact of the existence of interest in society is wrongly taken as proving that men discount the future. The relation between interest and time preference is, in fact, inverted in this view. In a free market where interest can be obtained it is natural that men should esteem a present dollar equally with its amount at the current interest rate at a future date, since one can be freely exchanged for the other. Nor does the fact that men do not postpone all consumption of goods indefinitely into the future argue an ingrained abstract preference of present to future consumption. Neither do they wish to compress all the satisfactions of a lifetime into the present moment and fast forever after,[141] which act by the same reasoning would prove a disposition to discount the

[141]The point may be illustrated by the anecdote of a tramp who, finding a hundred-dollar bill, made a bee-line to the nearest quick lunch and excitedly ordered a hundred dollars' worth of ham and eggs. That men do not behave after this fashion does not prove that, other things equal, they prefer a future satisfaction to a present one of the same magnitude.

present in favor of the future.

The error in the current reasoning is a wrong choice of a zero point from which to measure time preference. The correct basis is not everything to-day and nothing in the future; a more sensible form of question would be this: If one had to choose between enjoyment to-day with abstinence to-morrow on the one hand, and abstinence to-day with enjoyment to-morrow, on the other, which would be more desirable, all other things being equal? Or better still, if a man were given his entire income for a year in a lump-sum payment on January first, how would he distribute its expenditure through the year? There would clearly be no question either of eating it all up the first day or saving it all till the last day; a zero time preference obviously means a uniform distribution in time. Any piling-up of consumption at an earlier date to be compensated by reduced consumption later on would be a real discount of the future, while to skimp now for the sake of plenty or luxury in the future would be to discount the present. Of course, we abstract from the element of uncertainty as to the future. We seem justified in pronouncing either tendency irrational if other things are really reduced to equality in the alternatives.[142]

As to the facts of human nature it is safe to assume that different individuals would give the most varied forms of distribution. Doubtless few, if any, of these would conform to straight lines or smooth curves of any sort, ascending, descending, or level. Most would go in waves of greater or less period and amplitude, intervals of moderation or even abstemiousness alternating with "blow-outs" of various sorts and degrees. Irregularity seems in fact to be a virtue on its

[142]H. Sidgwick similarly takes the view that a preference on the ground of time alone is irrational, criticizing Bentham for including "propinquity" as a basis of preference between otherwise similar enjoyments. See History of Ethics, p. 241, note. Cf. also Jevons's discussion, Theory of Political Economy, pp. 72 ff., where the same position is taken. Jevons's illustrative problem of the consumption of provisions on a vessel at sea is very effective in bringing out the issue.

It will be noted that the effect of the uncertainty of the future is very complex. Against the chance of loss of future enjoyment through death or incapacitation must be set the danger of future privation due to other contingencies. We are more likely to suffer loss of earning power than of power to enjoy, and the consequences of need without ability to gratify need are very unpleasant. Perhaps the perfectly rational homo oeconomicus would discount the present up to the point of making provision for the more urgent necessities as far ahead as he was at all likely to live and discount the future beyond this point in increasing degree. The point is significant chiefly as showing the absurdity of hedonistic rationalism as a theory of actual behavior.

own account, at least to the spirited individual.[143] Whether there would be an upward or downward trend would depend also upon the individual. To many, a bird in the hand is worth two or more in the bush, while others take much thought for the morrow. Some children, as Marshall remarks, pick the plums out of the pudding to eat first, while others save them until the last, and many do not pick them out at all; and adults differ in the same way. The improvidence of savages is proverbial. Of course, the physical conditions of life set limits to the discounting process in both directions; we cannot enjoy to-morrow unless we live to-day, and many have learned at a cost that too high a rate of living in the present may have a similar effect upon the capacity for future enjoyment. No generalization in regard to the human race at large seems to be worth making, especially in view of the unreality of any simple assumptions as to the conditions surrounding the choice. The facts of mere prodigality on the one hand and mere miserliness on the other are indisputable and may be studied without attempting to strike any precise balance.

It is perhaps even more important at this point to insist that the mere question of time preference in consumption is relatively unimportant at best as an explanation of the phenomenon of saving. The disposition to spend or to save, to consume income in the present or to store up wealth, is much more influenced, in fact, by other motives.[144] Like human conduct in other respects it is mostly a matter of social standards, of what is "good form," "the thing" or not the thing to do. The fact of possessing an accumulation of goods confers social prestige and in addition vast power over one's fellows. Even where, as we are now assuming, productive employment is not

---

[143]Cf. Spencer, First Principles, chap, x, "The Rhythm of Motion."

[144]It is fundamental to the actual phenomenon of capital accumulation, that the principal, once saved, never is consumed; if it is consumed later, there is no net addition to the capital supply of society. Men save in large measure with no thought of ever consuming the capital, or even the income which it yields. For this reason the older term "abstinence"! seems to me far more descriptive than its modern substitute "waiting." [To be sure, an income of five dollars a year in perpetuity represents more consumption than one hundred dollars now; but no one consumes an income in perpetuity or expects to do so. Even if the saver consumes the entire income from his investment as long as he lives, he may or may not consume a total amount equal to the principal saved. Capital formation is the result of abstinence rather than waiting.

In fact, the term "saving" itself is misleading. Men do not generally produce wealth to consume it and then decide to invest it instead. Most of that which is invested is destined to that purpose in the first place and would otherwise never be produced at all.

open to wealth, the rich man will be in a position to make his favor solicited, his ill-will feared, and may, of course, turn his situation to material profit if so disposed. Accumulations are necessary to lavish displays or magnificence of any kind. On the other hand, we must suppose that where accumulation is limited to consumption goods, it will be subject to considerable costs, for storage, preservation, protection, and doubtless inevitable deterioration.[145]

It will be evident that differences among the individual members of society in economic position and taste with reference to the time of use of goods create a situation in which exchange will be mutually advantageous. To one, a present or early allotment of goods in advance of his own production and against an obligation to repay later will be or seem a benefit, while to another, with an accumulated and growing idle stock, a dependable obligation[146] for the future delivery of a certain amount of value, may be highly preferable to the possession of the goods themselves.

If the balance of the time preference in the population as a whole is in favor of the present, no appreciable net accumulation of goods will take place. Those disposed to accumulate will transfer their surplus production as fast as made to others disposed to draw on the future. The conditions of supply and demand will establish a market ratio of exchange between present and future goods which in this case will show a premium on the present, the magnitude of the premium depending on the strength of the excess desire to anticipate the future. Obviously the premium on the present goods will constitute an additional motive for surplus production and a deterrent to surplus present consumption. The rate established will be that at which the amount of surplus present production will equal the amount of surplus present consumptions The repayment of loans does not affect the principles involved, as it is a repetition of the original transaction with the roles of the parties interchanged. In the aggregate an excess of present consumption over current production is, of course, impossible.

If, on the other hand, the balance of time preference is on the side of a disposition to postpone, the result will be an excess for

[145]We pass over here the effects of divergence in suitability for accumulation of different classes of goods, due to differences in bulk, perishability, universality of appeal, elasticity of demand, etc.

[146]We must here assume it to be made absolutely dependable by insurance or otherwise.

the time being of production over consumption with net accumulation in the society as a whole. The exchanges between present and future goods will establish a premium on the latter. The ratio at which exchanges take place must constantly be such as to equate the amounts of each sort of service offered in the market to the amount that will be taken at the price. With a premium on future goods, accumulation will continue at a rate depending in part on the amount of the premium, until the premium disappears or becomes equal to the cost of keeping the accumulated stocks. Any greater premium on the future is impossible as a permanent thing. But the conditions of accumulation might well be such that an indefinitely long time would be required to reach the equilibrium result. In that case the actual condition at any time is a premium on the future with progressive accumulation taking place.

The "premium" or time preference rate under the conditions described, though similar to (positive or negative) interest, must be distinguished from that phenomenon as it is met with in modern industrial life; it is, indeed, an element, but a relatively insignificant one, affecting the interest rate on loans of productive capital.[147]

Time value, presentness or futureness, is perhaps best regarded as a special sort of utility in a good, like nutritive value or beauty or any other quality conferring or enhancing desirability. The rate of payment for it, where separated from other considerations, is evidently determined by "psychological" considerations on both the demand and supply sides, and the current interest theory of the psy-

[147]Wicksteed has an excellent discussion of this point. (See Common Sense of Political Economy, chap, vn.) It is noteworthy that the "usury" against which moralists have universally thundered in pre-industrial society corresponds to the phenomenon just described rather than to modern interest. The productive investment of accumulated wealth was nearly unknown in earlier times and even the purchase of existing productive property was rare. Practically the only productive agencies known were land and slaves. Land was not private property in the modern sense and was hardly ever bought and sold commercially, while slaves were used almost exclusively in connection with land and by its owner even when not legally attached to the land itself. If there had been a free market for consumption loans the correspondence with the phenomenon we have described would have been complete except for the element of risk. The absence of a competitive market was the source of much of the evil of usury, and the payments made doubtless did represent extortion largely. Be it observed, also, that historically speaking modern interest developed out of the consumption loan through the intermediary of passive partnerships in trade ventures and not out of dealings in canoes, fish nets, etc., in which the fancies of a certain school of interest theorists are prone to revel.

chological school is based on a confusion of this phenomenon with interest proper as a distributive share. The subject of interest proper will claim attention at a later stage of the discussion. We shall find that interest in the correct sense may not be met with at all in a society where uncertainty is absent, even if accumulated wealth is productively used and even if the society is progressive with respect to the accumulation of capital, if knowledge and foreknowledge are complete.

We may now return, and in view of the knowledge obtained of the role of time in economic conduct take up the relations of property in the simple sense of productive agencies separable from the persons of their owners and subject to lease and sale. It must be borne in mind that for the present we exclude any possibility of either increase or decrease in the property or any physical change of such a character as to modify its functioning. Such changes and their effects belong to our third division of economics, which deals with changes in the conditions of the production and consumption of wealth. To realize static conditions they must be abstracted. It will be convenient to refer to property of the sort we have in view as "land,"[148] since land has been conventionally treated as if qualitatively and quantitatively given once for all by nature. This is not at all the view of land which will be presented in this study when the time comes to discuss the subject. But it is a convenient name at this point for a productive agency of a certain described character. We assume, as a matter of course, that such property is limited in amount (i.e., subject to "diminishing returns") and that there is no other sort of property present in the society. On the production side, then, the side of demand, and in relation to functional distribution it will be exactly like other agencies (human services), but its presence may affect the personal distribution of income very considerably.

Supposing the final adjustment to have been reached in the organization of production, any piece of property such as described may be regarded as a right or title to a commodity or money income in perpetuity. As such, its bearings on conduct are closely related to the time distribution of consumption. A piece of land

[148]With the actual history of property we are, of course, not concerned. Doubtless, the first approximation to private productive property was in human beings, slaves, or, perhaps, women or children, while the last thing to become really privately owned was land. But the proper order for our purpose is not chronological, but rather that of increasing complexity.

represents future goods in the very special form of a value income distributed uniformly throughout all future time. We may assume without argument that such a piece of property will be desirable and that under conditions of free contract a definite market rate of exchange between land and consumption goods will be established. More accurately this price will be a ratio between the income from the land (of which there is no significant measure other than its income) and a quantity of present goods also measured in value terms. The price could, therefore, be stated as a certain number of years' purchase or a rate per cent per annum, and represents the familiar phenomenon of capitalization. Our present problem is to formulate the conditions determining this capitalization rate.

Land will be in demand especially by persons disposed to store up wealth for future use; i.e., to discount the present. It is in effect future goods, but the manner of their distribution in the future imposes a new special limitation on the conditions of their demand. We have seen that it is reasonable and common for human beings to prefer future goods to present, within limits, as compared with a uniform distribution in time. Most civilized persons, in fact, plan for a rising standard of living through life rather than a constant, much less a falling one. But when infinite time comes under consideration the case is different.

Any finite amount of consumption or enjoyment distributed uniformly through infinite time becomes a zero rate of real income. Hence there must be an apparent discount on the future in the demand for perpetual income goods. Indeed, it is self-evident that future incomes must be discounted at some rate greater than zero or they would have infinite present worth. The discount of the present in favor of the future can hold good only for finite periods of time in a society where present goods are limited at all; i.e., under economic conditions. We must note also, however, that when a capitalization rate and a market price for land have been established, the land will be convertible at will into a fund of present consumption goods. The existence of a free market for permanent income goods makes the apparent rate of time preference uniform for all real (finite) intervals. The individual who may not wish to keep on postponing to the end of a long period knows that he does not need to do so unless he wishes; for at any time he can realize upon his accumulation in present consumption form as rapidly as he may wish. There must be a premium on present over future goods in the market for perpetual income property; but such a premium, even if high, is not incompatible with a premium on the future over the present for any finite interval, and might perfectly well exist in a society where every individual and the group as a whole distributed its consumption in time in a curve ascending at any finite slope.

Under these conditions a person could arrange, by the purchase and sale of income property, for any desired distribution of consumption over any specified period, or, through an appropriate life insurance organization, over the uncertain period of his life. Those wishing to postpone consumption, to secure a rising distribution of real income, would buy such property in the earlier years and gradually sell it off in the later ones. Those wishing to anticipate future production and secure a descending curve of consumption would progressively sell off their land. (Persons possessing no land could make the anticipation arrangement only in the manner described above in discussing a situation where such goods were absent.) The society as a whole cannot anticipate future production unless there is some other society from which it can borrow. It can postpone in the aggregate only as in the situation above described, through an actual accumulation of consumption goods. The process of net accumulation would again tend toward an equilibrium with current production and consumption equal, though the goal might be an indefinite distance in the future. There must at any time be an equilibration of the two sorts of motives through the discount rate established, together with, in the case just mentioned, a certain rate of net accumulation.

The rate at which perpetual income goods are capitalized in the market is not yet a rate of interest in the sense of a distributive share. Nor would there be any necessity under the conditions we have described for lending money in connection with the transfer or use of income-bearing property (though consumption loans might be effected in much the familiar form). The capital loan for productive purposes is, as we shall presently see, a device for separating the ownership of value equities in production goods from the direct ownership of the goods themselves. It is mainly the presence of the risk or uncertainty factor which makes such a separation desirable. In a progressive society some motives for specializing to individuals other than the savers the function of making the investment might exist even in the absence of uncertainty. In the society which we have described with both uncertainty and progress absent, there would be no motive for lending or borrowing value funds for the purchase of productive agencies.

Chapter 5. Change and Progress with Uncertainty Absent

We turn now to the third grand division of theoretical economics, the study of the use of resources in the increase of resources for the making of goods and in the refinement of wants alongside of and alternative to their direct use in making goods for consumption. The relations of these three theoretical problems are somewhat complex and confusions in regard to them have been a prolific source of error in economic thinking. The first problem is the use of given goods in the satisfaction of given wants (with a given distribution of the goods to begin with, and free exchange) and its analysis and solution constitute the theory of market price. Market prices, besides determining the apportionment of given stocks of goods, the product of past industry, at the same time show the social estimate of the relative importance of different goods according to which the apportionment of resources under the second problem is worked out. In this first division, production goods do not enter at all, since costs already incurred have no bearing on price; as Jevons puts it, "bygones are forever bygones."

The second problem deals with the use of given productive resources in the production of goods to be used, (always in accordance with market price principles) in the satisfaction of given wants; it has become known as the problem of the static society or "static state," and has two aspects. The first phase relates to the value of productive services separately; the second, to the values of particular consumption goods, in relation to the values of the productive services which go into them, or their costs; this is the problem of the long-time or normal prices of consumption goods. In a sense it is, as Marshall suggests, a case of two classifications crossing each other. The first problem classifies on the basis of consumption goods, showing the equation of the value of a commodity to that of the bundle of productive services entering into it. The second takes the productive service as a basis and shows the equation of the value of each unit of productive service to the value of the portion of each kind of consumption goods in whose creation it is used, for which it is responsible. The first is the long-time "value" problem, the second is the short-time "distribution" problem. The changes in supply (and value) of consumption goods are studied in relation to fixed conditions of production, including especially fixed supplies and methods of organization of productive resources.

The third general problem also relates to both value and distribution phenomena. Changes in the "fundamental conditions of demand and supply" of goods give rise to what Marshall calls "secular changes in normal price." But the principal "fundamental conditions" subject to change are the supplies of the different productive services which evidently affect still more directly the prices of these services, the distributive shares. Our discussion, like Marshall's, will be practically limited to this more simple and direct effect, the modification of the distribution situation, and its tendency toward an equilibrium.[149]

---

[149]Marshall's organization of economic theory about the fundamental problems is not very clear. We have already seen that he does not bring out the relations between market and normal price in the case of consumption goods. He refers to the problem of secular changes in normal price, but relegates discussion of the subject to later volumes not yet published. In his treatment of distribution he fails to make clear that the short-time distribution problem is a phase of the same fundamental analysis as normal prices of consumption goods. Moreover, he has very little interest in this short-time distribution problem. Book vi of the Principles is almost entirely devoted to the long-time equilibrium tendencies of the distributive shares, hardly more than passing notice being given to the conditions of equilibrium from the standpoint of distribution at any given time or for short periods when the supply is to be taken as fixed. Nor does he identify or even explicitly connect the question of the long-time tendencies in distribution with that of secular changes in normal price, which are phases or points of view in the analysis of the same fundamental problem of social economic organization. In the writer's view the problem of intelligible exposition and of fundamental comprehension of the price organization can be greatly lightened by the recognition and emphasis of these lines of relation. In addition, it is helpful to stress the close analogy in methodology of treatment between the short-time price theory of value and that of distribution, and similarly with respect to the two long-time or normal price theories.

First, let us try to formulate clearly and accurately what is involved in the problem of progress. What new variables come in for study? What is the exact content of the "general conditions of demand and supply," or the "given resources used in the satisfaction of given wants," which our previous analysis has assumed? And finally, what are the changes in these factors which call for consideration in order to bring our society into the closest possible approximation to reality? Marshall, whom the present study more closely follows

---

In this connection it is interesting to compare Marshall with Professor J. B. Clark, who is especially known in connection with the use of the static hypothesis in this country. Clark's organization is even more inadequate, and it is especially striking that he does not acknowledge the connection between his method and that of Marshall. The "static state" of Clark is the same problem as Marshall's long-time normal price, while his economic dynamics corresponds with the secular changes in the field of value and the long-time tendencies in distribution. But Clark, under Austrian and German historical influence as Marshall was under. English classical, gives us as the theory of distribution the short-time analysis, and hardly goes beyond recognizing the existence of the problem of progressive change, the long-run results or conditions of equilibrium of which are Marshall's almost exclusive concern. He is, indeed, much less satisfactory in this field than is Marshall in the short-time theory, for the latter does give, in passing, a very fair statement of the productivity analysis. It would, of course, be a serious error to confuse Clark's "static state" with the "stationary state" of the classical economists. The stationary state of these writers was the naturally static or equilibrium condition, which is the goal of progress or the subject matter of the third division of the study, not a state made static by arbitrary abstraction as a methodological device. It seems, however, that virtually all discussion of static conditions is vitiated by the failure to distinguish adequately between these two concepts. And we still lack a complete discussion of distribution which will give due weight to both the short-time and long-time problems; i.e., separate the assumption of fixed supplies of productive agencies from the assumption that supply is a function of price. A rough tabulation of the natural divisions of the theory may help to clarify their relations:

	Value (consumption goods)	*Distribution (productive services)*
Problem I *Given supplies of goods and given wants to be satisfied.* *(The situation at a moment.)*	*Market price.*	*No problem of distribution.*
Problem II. *Given productive resources given wants to be satisfied.*	*Normal price (Marshall's long-time normal price)* *Supply a function of price.*	*Short-time or market price distribution theory.* *(Fixed supply.)*
Problem III. *Use of resources to increase resources, change wants & satisfy existing wants.*	*Secular changes normal price.*	*Long-time or normal-price distribution theory* *Supply a function of price.*

than it does any other writer, seems to avoid, not to say evade, answering this question explicitly. He does at one point begin an enumeration of elements, but cuts it short at once with the blanket expression quoted above.[150] A well-known explicit list of static state or dynamic factors to be excluded is that of Professor J. B. Clark, whose name is especially associated with the contrast between static and dynamic problems in this country. He gives these five elements of progress:[151] (1) growth of population; (2) accumulation of new capital; (3) progress in technology; (4) improvement in methods of business organization; (5) development of new wants. Professor Seager modifies this list, and in the writer's view greatly improves it, by combining the third and fourth factors and adding a new one, the impairment of natural resources or discovery of new natural wealth.

It will aid in clarifying the issues if we first consider separately the conditions of demand and of the supply of goods. Conditions of demand seem to include the following fundamental facts :

1. The population considered as consuming units; its numbers and physical composition as to age, sex, race, etc.

2. The psychic attributes of the population, its behavior attitudes toward the consumption of all sorts of goods, both inherited "instincts" (in whatever sense such things exist), and the "social inheritance" of habit, custom, tastes, standards, mores, and what-not, including, of course, actual knowledge or beliefs as to the real characteristics of commodities. We must also include here any institutional facts as to the control of the consumption of some persons by other persons, such as authority of parents, sumptuary laws, etc.

3. Immediately, the money income of the population both as to aggregate amount and distribution. Ultimately, in the equilibrium adjustment, the income and its distribution depend on the whole set of conditions of the supply of goods, especially the amount and distribution of productive resources in the society. It is imperative to remember that the end result of the competitive adjustment depends on the initial facts in all these respects.

4. For completeness it is important, also, to consider the given facts as to the geographic distribution of the population as consuming units; this is determined, of course, by the distribution of productive resources and of environmental conditions affecting desirability of sites for habitation. Differences here would also produce

[150]Cf. Principles of Economics, 6th ed., p. 379.

[151]The Distribution of Wealth, chap. v.

effects ramifying throughout the whole organization.

Given conditions of supply include especially the supply of the factors of production, but there are other vital considerations. We may classify as follows:

1. The population considered as labor force, numbers, and composition.

2. The psychic or behavior attitudes, tastes, prejudices, etc., toward productive activities, inherited or acquired.

3. Immediately, money income and its distribution; ultimately, the distribution of ownership of productive resources of every kind. There is no difference between personal ability and productive property in this respect. It is obvious that income affects disposition to engage in productive activities and enters as a variable, independent of taste.

4. Although it belongs logically under number 3, or is at most a corollary from it, we specify separately the institutional situation as to the meaning and extent of private property. This includes all facts as to (a) control of the use of productive services and (b) of valid and enforceable rights to income. There is again no distinction to be made between personal powers and other productive facts.

5. The amount and form of material agents of production in existence. Under the static conditions hitherto discussed these can include only natural agents in the narrowest sense, or, what would amount to the same thing, implements inherited from past generations, and in either case subject to neither deterioration nor improvement.

6. The geographical distribution of productive agencies.

7. The state of the arts; the development of technology, business organization, etc.

Combining the two groups and removing duplication we find the following factors in regard to which change or the possibility of change must be studied:

1. The population, numbers and composition.

2. The tastes and dispositions of the people.

3. The amounts and kinds of productive capacities in existence, including

a. Personal powers.

b. Material agents.

i. Given by nature.[152]

[152]This distinction follows conventional usage; it will be examined presently

ii. Artificially produced.[153]

4. The distribution of ownership of these, including all rights of control by persons over persons or things. (Impersonal control, by laws or mores, is indistinguishable from number 2, tastes and dispositions.)

5. Geographic distribution of people and things. This stands in close relation to the facts of technology.

6. The state of the arts; the whole situation as to science, education, technology, social organization, etc.

Systematic completeness would call for a survey of possible changes in each of these elements and the relation of such changes to both value and distribution phenomena, the prices of consumption goods and of productive services (and in addition their relations to the capitalization rate, the sale prices of productive agencies). No such ambitious program can be entered upon, however. We shall merely point out some of the more important price bearings of changes and make such comments as seem especially significant in illuminating dark places in theory. The point for especial emphasis is that the really far-reaching effects of change are not the results of the fact of change itself, but of the uncertainty which is involved in a changing world. If any or all of these changes take place regularly, whether progressively or periodically or according to whatever known law, their consequences in the price system and the economic organization can be briefly disposed of. Through the machinery of the exchange of present and future values all of them will be fully "discounted" an indefinite time before they occur. They will not upset human calculations or destroy universal perfect equalization of alternatives. Hence, in particular, changes, if foreseeable, do not disturb the prerequisites of perfect competition for productive services, bringing about exact equivalence between costs and values, with absence of profit.

As a matter of fact the effects of changes in the general conditions of the production and consumption of goods upon the prices of consumption goods are either so obvious or so complicated and hopeless of practical prediction that it does not seem worth while to attempt systematic treatment of them. Our discussion will be confined almost entirely to the theory of distribution. In this field,

---

and shown to be untenable. (See below, pp. 159 ff.)

[153]This distinction follows conventional usage; it will be examined presently and shown to be untenable. (See below, pp. 159 ff.)

also, let us note that progressive changes can usually be fairly well foreseen and discounted and their effects are not generally important over short periods of time. They produce relatively little real disturbance in the competitive adjustment and are not a significant cause of profit. The significant disturbances and sources of profit are rather the short-period and erratic fluctuations, and the irregularities of progressive change, not the change itself. The increase in population and accumulation of new capital are not disturbing facts to any appreciable extent, and the disturbances arising from invention and improvement are due to the local and spasmodic way in which they originate, not to the general tendency.

In discussing the short-time theory of distribution (distribution under conditions of fixed supplies of productive agencies) we have repeatedly emphasized the absence of any valid ground for a general classification of productive agencies, either along the lines of the traditional three factors or along any other lines. That is, on the demand side they are alike or differ by innumerable imperceptible gradations, and for short-time problems the conditions of supply — given quantities in existence — are also obviously identical for all. The long-time point of view, however, brings in the new question of changes in supply, in regard to which there are real differences. These differences in the conditions of supply afford a basis for legitimate classification, somewhat along the lines of the tripartite division. It is superficially reasonable to recognize three categorically different conditions of supply. First we should have agencies whose supply is given once for all even over long periods, things not subject to increase or decrease, improvement or deterioration. The traditional definition of land fits this description. (We do not here raise the question whether anything exists to which the definition applies.) In the second place, some productive goods may be, and obviously are, freely reproducible in the same manner as consumption goods, under conditions in which supply becomes a definite function of the price of their services. The traditional view of capital gives it this character. (Again we make no assertions as to the correctness of the view.) And finally, the supply of still other agencies may be variable, but not a function of price, or not connected with price in an immediate or direct way. The traditional treatment of the long-time supply of labor (the merits of which are also reserved for later examination) differentiate it in this respect from other productive powers. This traditional classification is not accepted as valid, even from the long-time point of view, and will be criticized at length as we proceed. But the superficial basis for it and the fact that it is well established in the thought and terminology of the science may justify taking it as a starting-point.

The ramifications and interconnections of effects of any particular change are ultimately rather complicated, and may be followed out until nearly every aspect of the adjustment is modified in some way. This is obviously true of the first of the static characteristics named. Historically the population question has been considered with distribution in connection with wage theory through its relation to the supply of labor. Of course, an increase of population is an increase in the demand for goods and hence in the demand for all the productive services including labor itself. But the demand for any productive service depends finally upon two elements, the total output of industry and the relative importance of that service in increasing the output. In accordance with the law of diminishing returns and the specific productivity theory based upon that law, a relative increase in the supply of labor will increase the product of industry less than proportionally and decrease the relative productivity of labor. Both effects tend to lower wages per man. The same reasoning applies to any other productive service as well as to labor.

Much confusion has arisen in economic discussion through different meanings given to a distributive share. We may speak of wages, for example, as above, as wages per man, and similarly of other incomes in relation to the concrete agency which produces them. The problem of distribution from this point of view Cannan calls "pseudo-distribution,"[154] seemingly an unfortunate term, for this is surely the phase of the subject in which we have the greatest and most direct interest. The classical economists themselves, led by Ricardo, usually centered their discussion around the fraction of the total social produce received by the "factor" under discussion. Another clearly possible meaning is the aggregate share of a "factor" measured in absolute terms.

The effect of an increase in a factor (meaning a large group of physically interchangeable productive units) on the fraction of the social income it will receive, depends on the rate of diminishing returns realized from the application of that agency to others in the vicinity of the proportions already in existence. If the increase in total production is nearly proportional to the increase in the fac-

[154]Theories of Production and Distribution, chap. VII.

tor (remembering that it cannot be equal or greater), its fractional share will rise; if much less, it will fall. The aggregate absolute share of income falling to the agency will increase unless the falling-off in product is in equal or greater ratio with the increase in the agency. Both points, however, are rather remote from the problem of immediate interest. If the income per unit is known, the relative and absolute shares of the factor can more naturally be determined indirectly.

Obviously a shift in the amount of any productive agency will, through its effect on incomes, react on the demands for goods, and ultimately affect nearly every feature of the organization of industry and of the price system. The resulting changes in the prices of consumption goods are what Marshall calls secular changes in normal price. It does not seem profitable, if indeed it is possible, to discuss these in the abstract. About the only general observation which seems worth making is that those goods in whose production any particular agency predominates will tend to fall in value as the supply of that agency increases, other things being equal.

The really difficult problem in the theory of progress relates not so much to the effects of particular changes. These effects, though complicated, can be traced out by the application of the principles of the market, the "laws" of supply and demand. The difficulty comes in the prediction of the changes themselves. What are the conditions of supply of the productive services? What changes in the supplies of the different services may be reasonably anticipated, and to what goals or equilibria do they tend? The question is of especial interest because it was in terms of these ultimate equilibrium levels that the classical theory of distribution was almost exclusively worked out. In our opinion the meaning of these equilibrium conditions was misconceived in classical economics and their significance perhaps somewhat overestimated. The early writers regarded the equilibrium condition as constantly at hand in a sense analogous to the normal price equilibrium between the production and consumption, cost and value, of consumption goods. Their "static state" was, if not the actual condition of society, a condition on which it constantly verged.[155] It makes a great deal of difference in the theory when we recognize, as the facts require, that the equilibrium is an indefinite and usually a very great distance in the future. The condition must then be viewed as the theoretical result of a particular tendency

[155]Mills, Principles of Political Economy, book iv, chap, iv, sec. 4.

only, which may be modified to any extent or reversed by the effect of other tendencies, or the conditions may be entirely changed by unforeseen developments long before any considerable approach to the equilibrium has been made. The equilibrium, then, in a particular case, is not a result actually to be anticipated; a concrete prediction of the future course of events must take into account all the tendencies at work and estimate their relative importance, and in addition must always be made subject to wide reservations for unpredictable influences. In fact, as we shall see, the interrelations of the various factors of progress are so complicated, and the functions themselves are so inaccurately known and are affected by so many unknown variables, that definite predictions extending any considerable distance into the future seem to be quite out of the question.

Turning now to the question of the conditions influencing the progress variables and of the changes to be expected in regard to each, we may begin with the factor of population once more and go through the list. The plan, of course, is not to investigate hypotheses at random, but to inquire seriously about the facts of the world we live in. The only arbitrary or unreal element in the procedure is the selection of the outstanding dominant features and their isolation with a view to ascertaining if possible their own inherent tendencies. The products of such an inquiry are, like all theoretical deductions, — all general principles, — partial truths which cannot be applied uncritically, but must be combined according to circumstances and supplemented with empirical data. Historic population theory, or Malthusianism, pictured laborers as analogous to a good supplied under conditions of constant cost. Wages were accordingly held to tend toward an equilibrium level equal to this cost, the (real or commodity, not money) cost of maintaining a static population. The premise was not, of course, that the production of laborers takes place from motives of pecuniary profit,[156] but that in consequence of

[156]It is a neglected fact that in the "lower" strata of society the production of children is by no means so unrelated to the ordinary economic calculation as generally assumed. The age of marriage and the size of families probably depend much more in fact on the amount of economic gain or loss between the prospective earning of children and the cost of their keep while under their parents' control than they do upon calculations as to the possibility of maintaining standards of living from one generation to another. (Of course, the two sets of considerations are interrelated.) A comparison of birth-rates with living conditions in the city and country and in different social environments, also a study of the effects of child labor and compulsory education laws on birth-rates, are very suggestive in this connection.

the physiological-psychological law of population, the supply varied in a strictly analogous way. The tendency of wages to the minimum of subsistence is indeed a natural and correct deduction from the tendency of population to press constantly upon the supply of the necessaries of life.[157]

This early version of the theory of the cost of labor was manifest themselves in the market, and assume perfect intercommunication and freedom of movement, the migration factors would quickly come to an equilibrium.

The second of our progress variables is the psychological element, the dispositions and tastes of the people. Like the number and composition of the population, it affects conditions on both the consumption and production sides of the problem. Changes and great changes do, of course, take place in wants for consumption goods and in attitudes toward different lines of productive activity.[158] Most of these changes cannot profitably be treated as functions of price and no conditions of equilibrium can be formulated for them. They remain in the class of external disturbing causes little subject to prediction, especially on the production side. Tendencies can often be noted, such as the "lure of the city" which now operates to increase industrial production at the expense of agriculture. In America the irrational preference for white-collar jobs has raised the wages of mechanics above those of clerical tasks calling for much more ability and education. Other preferences and vogues for particular kinds of work must be passed over with the mere pointing-out that they are part of the given conditions of the economic process and that changes in them have widely ramified effects. These considerations apply to uses of property as well as to personal powers, though in a

[157]It is hardly necessary to point out that the famous "iron law" of wages of Lassalle and the Marxian socialists is this classical theory of the equilibrium wage taken over bodily, but with the logical foundation on which it rested repudiated indignantly. If the tendency of wages to a minimum is based on a principle of population, all schemes of social reorganization (except in so far as they affect that principle) are helpless to produce any result save possibly a temporary amelioration, with a later increase in misery. This, it will be recalled, is the very thesis which the essay on population was originally written to prove in answer to the millennial hopes held out by Godwin's Political Justice.

[158]Strong social disapproval of any line of business or occupation undoubtedly tends to aggravate any real evil connected with it, by throwing it into the hands of persons (of whom there is never any dearth) to whom social approval and disapproval are a matter of indifference. Conspicuous examples are money-lending in the Middle Ages (and the same type of money-lending now) and the liquor business in modern times.

much less degree.

On the consumption side there is a very important problem more amenable to scientific treatment, though still very treacherous to deal with. We refer to the familiar fact of the use of economic resources by private business to develop, create, or direct consumptive wants; i.e., the phenomenon of advertising.[159] The increase of value through advertising, whether informative or merely persuasive, is quite parallel to any other form of production, or "creation of utilities." Such values are largely transferred from other goods, but except in so far as they result from a positive disparagement of competing commodities they are to be regarded as merely an additional utility in the advertised commodity.[160]

The business of want creation is, of course, very uncertain and aleatory or "risky"; but it is evident that, as with other changes, in so far as the results of action can be foreseen, competition will equalize gains with those in other fields. Costs will then be equal to values throughout the system, the conditions of profitless adjustment being present. Whether the creation of wants is subject to diminishing returns, the process consequently tending toward an equilibrium, where it would no longer take place, or whether it is inherently a perpetual cause making for continued change, is a matter we cannot discuss on its merits. The writer's guess would favor the latter alternative.

In regard to the third progress factor, the amount of productive

---

[159]Efforts on the part of society, the public, organized and unorganized, to direct consumption along approved lines, fall outside the scope of a study of private competitive organization.

[160]Disparagement of competing commodities must be eliminated from consideration for the same reasons as burglary and such crude fraud as the dispensing of gold bricks, liquozone, etc. It will be recalled that we have expressly eliminated effects of interests not represented in market transactions.

The suggestion may seem fanciful, but I find it impossible to differentiate between elements in the physical form and appearance of a commodity which make no difference in its efficiency for the purpose intended (an agreeable color, decorative ornament often actually interfering with its uses, fancy containers, etc.), on the one hand, and on the other an element of appeal due to a high-sounding name or any other form of "puffing." These things do make a difference in the commodity to the consumer and in an exchange system the consumer is the last court of appeal. If they are different to him, they are different; if he is willing to buy one sort in preference to the other, then the first is superior to the second; it contains "utilities" which the other does not have. I do not see that it makes any real difference whether these utilities are in the thing itself or in some associated fact.

resources in existence, the first question relates to the classification of these resources from the standpoint of changes in supply. We have shown above that differences must be recognized somewhat along the lines of the conventional tripartite division, but we must emphasize that the differences have been much exaggerated and that definite classification along the traditional lines cannot be maintained.[161]

The long-time conditions of the supply of labor consist of two elements: The first, the population, has already been discussed. The second is the factor of education, taken in the broad sense. Now training, which results in increased productive efficiency, is evidently similar to a material productive agency or capital good created by the diversion of resources from present consumptive uses. Even the population itself, as observed above, depends to a large extent upon considerations of pecuniary profit in the case of the social classes which subsist mainly by labor. The distinction between labor and capital thus shows a tendency to fade away. A degree of distinction, indeed, persists. Technical training cannot be sold or leased for use separate from its owner, and cannot in any direct sense be perpetuated beyond the owner's working life. Capital is at least less attached to its owner's personality (it is important to note that it is never absolutely detached) and may function in perpetuity. In addition the investment in education is more affected by other than profit seeking motives, and in consequence is not so closely adjusted by effective competition to equality of return with other forms of investment.[162] Investment in the improvement of human powers is rather a long-time proposition, yet does not look so far ahead as many other forms of investment; in other ways, however, it is subject to a very high degree of uncertainty. After all there seems to be as much difference between different cases or types of labor production and between different varieties of material productive goods creation as there is between the two classes of investment of resources as types. In so far as uncertainty is absent and competition

---

[161]It will be kept in mind that from the standpoint of short-time problems, where changes in supply are not at issue, and demand alone determines distributive relations, no classification at all is valid.

[162]The fact that so many opportunities for the profitable investment of resources in the development of human potentialities are neglected, and so many wasteful investments of the same kind made, is perhaps one of the most serious criticisms of existing society. The fault, however, is in the family system rather than in the private enterprise organization of industry in any sense in which the two may be dissociated.

obtains, it is clear that investment will distribute itself between the two fields and over all parts of each in such a way as constantly to equalize their net advantages. Which is to say (remembering that costs merely register competing attractions) that with uncertainty absent costs and values would be equal throughout the system; that is, there would be a perfect, profitless organization of production and exchange.

There is a fundamental similarity in the conditions of supply of all the productive services involving the investment of resources. In every case there is a diversion of productive power from use in making present consumption goods to the creation of sources of new consumption goods income. A discussion of the conditions of equilibrium for any of them will therefore be postponed until all can be dealt with together. The general theory of equilibrium in this case is in fact the long-run theory of interest.

The classical economist treated land, or natural agents, as given in supply. This assumption was the basis for propounding a theory of rent different from the reasoning by which the other distributive shares were explained,[163] and for positing a special relation between rent and cost. The definition given for land to make it fit the description of a fixed supply — the original and inexhaustible powers of the soil — is indeed drastic in its limitation. Later, this dogma of unconditional fixity of supply was made the basis for the single-tax propaganda. We cannot discuss this position at length, but must take space to remark quite briefly that it is utterly fallacious. It should be self-evident that when the discovery, appropriation, and development of new natural resources is an open, competitive game, there is unlikely to be any difference between the returns from resources put to this use and those put to any other. Moreover, any disparity which exists is either a result of chance and as likely to be in the favor of one field as the other, or else is due to some differ-

[163]The differential theory of rent has long since been recognized as applying equally well to the other shares. See J. B. Clark, "Distribution as Determined by a Law of Rent," and J. A. Hobson, "The Law of the Three Rents," Quarterly Journal of Economics, vol. v. It is not so generally recognized that in consequence it explains none of them. It is especially remarkable that the theory of distribution propounded by General Francis A. Walker, whose book was long a standard text in American colleges, amounted to nothing more than an elaboration of the proposition that each factor gets what is left after the others are paid. It is easy to show that the differential theory when stated in its significant form is identical with the specific productivity theory. Cf. A. A. Young, Ely's Outlines of Economics, 3d ed., pp. 415-16.

ence in psychological appeal between the fields; i.e., goes to offset some other difference in their net advantages. Viewing as a whole the historic process by which land is made available for productive employment, it must be said to be "produced"; i.e., to have its utility conferred upon it in a way quite on a par with that which holds for any other exchangeable good. This, of course, again abstracts from the factor of uncertainty. In real life a large speculative element is introduced; but this cannot be said to differentiate land generically from any other class of goods, though the results are met with on an especially large scale in the case of land.

A new form of productive resource has become of very great importance in modern society, consisting of special methods of production or exclusive technical processes, whether patented or kept secret, or merely not "yet" extended in use over the whole field of production. Such a process is a source of income like any other agent, and is produced in the first place in the same way, by the investment of present resources (in research and experiment). They are different from most capital goods, however, in that their cost of maintenance and multiple reproduction is so low[164] that it is profitable to multiply them to the point of becoming free goods, except in so far as they inhere in the persons of their possessors. They thus tend to revert to the category of enhanced individual capacities, unless in some way "monopolized." New productive processes are like natural resources in being produced under conditions in which the gambling element is large, but in so far as the results of operations can be foreseen they also tend to equality of return on investment in comparison with other fields.

We turn, therefore, to the ordinary and simple case of the investment of resources in the creation of new productive capacities; i.e., to the case of capital goods. In this connection we can conveniently discuss the general case, subsequently returning briefly to the problems of human powers, natural agents, and productive methods just mentioned. The argument will be closely related to, in fact may

[164]Ideas are not, however, free from these costs, as sometimes assumed. Thus A. S. Johnson (Rent in Modern Economic Theory, p. 120) contends that an idea cannot be regarded as productive, because it is "its nature" to multiply itself indefinitely. It would simplify the problem of education if it were so! But perhaps we should wish some discrimination to be exercised in the extension of the quality to ideas generally! Even so, if the "natural" tendency is obstructed, the idea limited in application seems to be productive in the sense in which anything else is productive. (See below, chapter vi.)

be said to take up and continue, the discussion in the last chapter on the subject of time preference and the purchase and sale of productive goods. We now have the further complication that our productive goods are no longer fixed in supply, but that opportunity exists for the indefinite creation of such goods through the diversion of resources from the production of present consumption goods. For it will be seen that to the individual the investment of present goods (their use to pay productive agencies while the latter, being liberated by the "advance,"[165] devote themselves to the making of the new equipment) is equivalent to their exchange for productive services already in existence in the possession of others; it is an alternative method for securing the same result. The previous discussion of the motivation involved, therefore, applies to the present case; i.e., it fits the assumptions usually made as to the motives for capital formation. We would emphasize the importance of a new motive not present in the former hypothetical case, the opportunity to create, which we hold to be a motive on its own account very distinct from, or at least very much more than, the mere desire to possess the thing created. However, in this brief survey, it seems necessary to abstract from the complicating factors in the motive for saving and to treat new productive equipment as a perpetual value-income merely (with the possibility of cashing in by sale at any time, as in the previous case). [166]

[165]The classical writers' view of capital as "advances to laborers" was correct except for the failure — natural from their labor theory point of view — to include the other productive factors as well as labor.

[166]Beyond the dogma that the desire to secure the income from capital is the sole motive for saving, it is a still further and questionable assumption that the strength of the motive varies in proportion to the size of the income expected or is connected with it by some simple law. Again we make, for convenience, the conventional simple supposition, merely taking this opportunity to record grave doubts as to the validity of any of this procedure. The saving of capital seems to us to be in fact the result mainly of two or three motives of which the desire for increased consumption of goods in the future is only one and probably one of the less important. Like other acts of man in society, it is largely a mere matter of established social custom, good form, the thing to do, the mores. Then«we must emphasize the impulse to create. Probably the greatest single source of saving is the putting of income back into a business, because of sheer interest in the business and the desire to make it grow. That the desire for the increased income is not the dominant motive in much of this is proved by the fact that men invest as desperately in an enterprise never likely to be profitable as they do in the most prosperous concern, and by the further fact that much of the reinvestment in society is made by directors of corporations who will not get the fruits of the work for themselves at all.The truth is, we believe, that the real

The demand for capital goods is, therefore, merely the demand for future income, already discussed. Assuming a static and universally known technology, all forms of such goods will necessarily be kept at a uniform level of productivity in relation to the investment necessary to create them, and they can be treated as a homogeneous class. The demand for capital goods in industry, like that for any other productive agency, is subject to the twofold law of diminishing productivity already familiar, and the more of such goods created the lower the value income they will yield, in terms of the goods themselves measured physically. But the base on which the investor figures is not the physical productive goods created. These are as non-existent to his calculation. He is interested exclusively in the relation between (a) the amount (i.e., value) of present goods he gives up and (b) the size of the value income which he receives. Hence, we have in this case a really fourfold law of diminishing effective demand: (1) The creation of producers' goods involves a diversion of resources from the making of consumption goods, and this transfer takes place subject to diminishing physical returns. The sacrifice of a given amount and kind of consumption goods makes possible the creation of a smaller amount of any given kind of capital goods the further the process is carried.[167] (2) Those productive goods which are more readily multiplied by the investment of resources must increase relatively to the other agents with which they are combined in production, and become subject to diminishing physical returns in their use. (3) To the extent that the relatively increased agencies enter into the production of certain commodities more than of others these commodities will have their supply relatively increased and will fall in price relatively to other commodities. (4) Finally, as present goods are progressively sacrificed to the creation of future income, the relative preference of the latter to the former must fall

---

motives of human life, at least of those people who do big things, are idealistic in character. The business man has the same fundamental psychology as the artist, inventor, or statesman. He has set himself at a certain work and the work absorbs and becomes himself. It is the expression of his personality; he lives in its growth and perfection according to his plans.

[167]The statement is applicable to the other methods of investing resources — the development of new natural agents, training of labor and improvement of technology — as well as to the creation of capital goods in the narrow sense. The use of resources to increase population in numbers appears to be exceptional as population subsists upon consumption goods themselves, and no change in the forms of production is involved. This action, however, is only to a very limited extent a matter of the calculated exchange of present for future goods.

off as more of it becomes available.

Other things being equal, the investment of resources should ultimately be carried to a point of equilibrium at which the amount of value income and the amount of present value which must be sacrificed to create it become equal to every person in the system. As long as the income which can be produced by sacrificing a given amount of present goods has a sufficient appeal to induce new savings, the new savings must continue to be made and to reduce the amount of value income obtainable from a given amount of investment. A point must ultimately be reached at which the product of investment is just attractive enough to hold in existence capital already saved, without calling forth new savings. Of course some individuals may at any time be consuming capital previously saved, while others are saving and investing, provided the two offset each other.[168]

The above is a brief statement of the "eclectic" theory of interest. The equilibrium ratio of the annual value income yielded by the capital goods created to the present value sacrificed in creating them — that ratio at which no further net conversion (saving and investment) takes place — is the theoretical long-time rate of interest. It is the magnitude toward which, as Marshall says,[169] the interest rate constantly "tends." Of course, "other things" must be assumed to be "equal." But in the nature of the case other things are not and cannot be equal. As investment takes place, the new income derived from it makes the saving of any given amount constantly easier, thus progressively changing the conditions of supply of new capital. In addition it is inconceivable that wants and tastes, or even the state of the arts, should remain static while such an adjustment worked

[168] A caution is in place against taking this equilibrium as strictly analogous to the normal price of a consumption good. A consumption good is destroyed in use. The equilibrium condition in regard to it is equality in the rates of its consumption and production with a negligible amount of the good actually in existence. (Durable consumers' goods are, of course, capital in fact.) Capital, on the other hand, accumulates, new production being constantly added to the whole net product of the past. The equilibrium in its case is a constant amount in existence, current production and consumption amounting in the equilibrium condition only to replacement of wear and tear. In this respect capital is like gold in the theory of its valuation. It is like gold, again, in the respect which we proceed to discuss, that the equilibrium condition is actually an indefinite distance in the future, that new production is constant and sure, but still small in amount in comparison with the existing supply, and that, therefore, conditions of production have a negligible effect on value over moderate periods of time.

[169] Principles, 6th ed., p. 536.

itself out. The theory is logically sound if correctly understood. It describes conditions under which the interest rate would not tend to change, and is of service in predicting the future movements of the rate. But it gives a very incomplete view of the facts which must be taken into account in an actual prediction. Changes in the other things — especially the psychology of spending and saving (partly a matter of the size of income) — in the given amounts of agencies not freely reproducible through investment, and the development of technology, not to mention wars and other catastrophes — do in fact commonly exert quite as much influence on the interest rate as does the tendency to equilibrium due to progressive saving and investment.[170]

But the most serious criticism to be made of the eclectic theory as it is currently presented (e.g., in Marshall) is its failure to recognize the true meaning of the equilibrium, and its assumption that actual

[170]Mention should also be made of banking, speculation, and the vicissitudes of foreign trade, which may completely dominate the rate for very short periods. Passing over such phenomena as the call-loan rate and the relation of international transactions to the interest rate, a word should be said on the subject of the bank rate. An issue of new currency by banks through an expansion of loans creates a momentary new supply of capital and, other things equal, tends to lower the interest rate. The effect is chiefly limited to those short-time loans in which banks mainly deal, but perhaps not entirely so. It is imperative to recognize, however, that inflation produces its effect through an actual saving, a diversion of income from present consumption to capital goods creation. The new currency which the bank lends to the investor is not new purchasing power from the standpoint of society as a whole. It is axiomatic in theory that the aggregate real value of the circulating medium is independent of the number of units of which it is composed. When inflation occurs, therefore, purchasing power is not created, but merely transferred from the previous owners of circulating medium to the persons into whose hands the new currency is placed for its first expenditure. The enormous r6le played in history by inflationism and the persistence of the heresy rest upon the fact that the effects of the expenditure of the new money are more conspicuous than the diminished effects of that which already existed. It is another case of the familiar type, "ce qu'on voit et ce qu'on ne voit pas."

However, it is to be emphasized also, that the psychology of business is fundamental in the economic process and that it is a very complex, sensitive, even treacherous thing. It will not do to draw conclusions as to policy from mere cause-and-effect reasoning based on any simple or reasonable assumptions about human behavior. Bank loans may, after all, create more demand for capital than they supply. But it is outside our plan to enter into the intricate problem of changes in business conditions or the business cycle. Some interesting suggestions in this field may be found in a series of articles on " Commercial Banking and Capital Formation," by H. G. Moulton and Myron W. Watkins, Journal of Political Economy, 1918 and 1919.

conditions at a given time approach that state. The contrary is true; the case is similar to that of population already discussed, but more striking and important. At a given moment in a society where new investment is taking place the rate of capitalization is the technical ratio of conversion of present goods into future income. It is the "productivity" ratio of new investment, the ratio between the annual value yield of the capital goods to be created[171] and the value of the present goods sacrificed to create them. Where the possibility of conversion — of saving and investment or of consuming capital already in existence through inadequate maintenance — exists, it cannot be otherwise. The psychology of saving and spending can have no appreciable influence on the interest rate at a moment. The supply of capital is not for short periods a function of the interest rate, but a fixed physical fact. Changes in psychical attitudes may cause people to save (or consume) a little more or a little less, but the effect will be insignificant in comparison with the total supply and demand of capital in the society. The rate of time preference fixes the rate at which new capital accumulates, and influences the rate of interest at future times, but not at the moment. The possibility of conversion impels every individual to equate his time preference rate to the existing productivity rate, which is causal, by saving more or less of his income or consuming more or less capital already saved.

There are no limits to the time which may be requisite at any moment to bring about the equilibrium adjustment, even assuming all other things static. Throughout the modern industrial period the rate of interest has been above the equilibrium level, social conditions being as they are (including human psychology, the mores, and especially the concentration of income in a few hands), as is proved by the fact that capital has constantly and rapidly accumulated.

---

[171]In real life, where uncertainty is present, it is the product generally anticipated in the market, which may not be the same as that subsequently realized in any particular case.

The correct statement of the productivity theory as given in the text manifestly sidetracks the objection of Professor Fetter and the time discount school that the product of capital is not homogeneous with the capital, and that consequently no such ratio can exist until the capitalization process has been applied to the capital itself. Before the investment is made the capital and its anticipated product are quite homogeneous, and it is in the market for capital not yet invested that the interest rate is determined. Capital goods once created are, of course, valued by capitalization; this operation presupposes an interest rate, which is therefore in no wise affected by the relation between capital goods and their income.

How long it would take to reach the equilibrium, if the demand for capital and other things remained constant, depends on the rate at which people save corresponding to any divergence between the actual interest rate and the equilibrium rate (allowance being made for the increase in income and reduction in the psychic cost of saving) and the rapidity of operation of the law of diminishing returns in the application of new capital to other productive agencies existing in society. Historically, of course, the other things have been so far from equal — especially the demand for capital has increased so rapidly through the increase of population and opening-up of new natural resources — that the interest rate shows an astonishing constancy. We should note, also, that improvements in technology generally tend to economize labor and land and relatively increase the demand for capital. The conditions of equilibrium we can formulate; the actual course of the events which are to bring about those conditions or the length of time they will occupy are probably matters of pure and unfruitful speculation. It is quite unnecessary to believe that there will really be any progress toward equilibrium, and it goes without saying that the failure of such progress to occur militates against neither the logical soundness nor the practical utility of the theory itself.

The above analysis does not refer to an interest rate in the ordinary sense of the term, but merely to a capitalization rate or ratio of exchange between present consumption goods and income property which is also the ratio of productivity of investment to the investment where the opportunity for investment is open. It is not clear whether the phenomenon of lending free capital at interest would be met with in a society where uncertainty was absent. The capital loan is an institution or device for separating the ownership of the value of a productive agent from the ownership of the concrete thing itself. The principal, if not the only significant motive for this separation, is the uncertainty as to future changes in the value of the agents. Where this value is not subject to change, or where it is variable, but the variations are predictable, the sale price of the agency will inevitably be such as to make it a matter of complete indifference to a prospective user whether he leases the agency or buys it with borrowed funds. The loan contract is an alternative to a rental contract. Producers borrow capital and invest it, converting it into productive goods by "advancing" it to laborers, landlords, and capitalists, who furnish the resources to make the new equipment.

It is apparent that the original owner of the capital could just as well invest it himself and lease the agencies thus created as to lend the money. Investment would be a practically costless operation in a world where the future was perfectly foreknown. However, it may be reasonable to suppose that the inevitable minimum of care and trouble would be sufficient to specialize the investment function and separate it from the furnishing of the capital. If so, the capital loan and interest proper would appear, the rate of interest being, of course, the capitalization and productivity ratio just discussed (less pay for investment costs if these were appreciable).

After investment is once made we have already observed that the income is simply a matter of the value yield of the goods, and the value of the agency is determined by capitalization of this yield at the interest rate determined in the market for free capital. But with freely reproducible productive goods this value can never diverge appreciably from the cost of production. Capital goods in fact differ widely in the length of time required to adjust supply to changes in demand. If there are any agencies not subject to reproduction through investment at all, they conform to the classical description of land. It is the writer's view that such agents are practically negligible and that in the long run land is like any other capital good. Investment in exploration and development work competes with investment in other fields and is similar in all essential respects to other production costs. The distinction between goods relatively flexible and those relatively inflexible in supply and the recognition of a special category of income (Marshall's "quasi-rent ") for the latter is possibly expedient. With uncertainty absent such a distinction is, of course, irrelevant.

We must deal briefly with the remaining items in the list of factors assumed invariable in discussing the static state. The fourth was the distribution of ownership of productive services. The only points to be noted here are that the condition affects personal powers (labor) in precisely the same way as property, and that the facts depend entirely on social institutions. It is only because we have been accustomed to it that we think in terms of rights to income from either inherited property or inherited ability. Nor is it any more inevitable that out-and-out ownership (nearly unlimited right of control plus right to entire income) should be conferred even for his own lifetime upon an individual who by the investment of present income has developed productive powers, whether in his own person, or in produced capital goods, or by the discovery and development of natural resources.[172] That we should separate the two categories in our thinking, taking property rights for granted in the case of inherited personal powers and stigmatizing the yield of inherited material goods as "unearned income" seems to be quite inexplicable. Society will always have to find some way to encourage the development and serious, interested use of productive capacities of all sorts (as it may always have to recognize family relationships in securing continuity of control from one generation to another). But many other ways are conceivable for doing these things, though their practical availability is not a subject for discussion here. It is to be noted that society is now progressing rapidly in the limitation of ownership, on both the control and income sides; more and more restrictions are being thrown around the use of property and the conditions under which an individual may agree to work, and more and more income is being taken through taxation for "social" purposes.

In regard to geographical distributions — much might be said on this neglected topic, but space and the plan of this work do not permit. The question of mere concentration of population, irrespective of where it is concentrated, i.e., of city versus country, is far-reaching and fascinating. Immigration and emigration and internal migration are obviously important and intricate problems. In this field also we can recognize the condition of an ultimate equilibrium wherein the advantages of all locations would be equalized; and here also progress toward the theoretical goal is slow in comparison with the interval which separates us from it at any particular time. Changes in wants, and activities directed to change wants from motives of private gain, are especially important in this connection. It is hardly too much to say that the political as well as economic history of America has been dominated by real estate speculation and by the cheap money controversy, largely an offshoot from the former. The

[172]It is noteworthy that in the fourth great field for the investment of resources, the improvement of productive methods through research and experiment (we are not including the numerical increase of population) perpetual rights to the earnings of the improvement are not conferred upon the person who makes the advance. The individual may retain a monopoly on his idea as long as he can keep it secret or otherwise prevent its being copied, but this is usually quite impracticable for any length of time. In the case of specified sorts of technical inventions, society confers and protects a temporary monopoly in the form of a patent. (In the United States we find a growing tendency to limit the method of exploitation of even this temporary monopoly. Witness the prohibition of tying contracts.)

actual distribution of population is, of course, largely determined by the distribution of natural productive resources and by the topography of the country in relation to transportation; partly also by mere desirability of locations for residential purposes. But it is interesting to observe that considerations of consumption and social motives alone would probably bring people together in groups of all sizes and degrees of compactness even in a world whose physical conditions were absolutely uniform.

Static conditions include finally static technology and knowledge in general, and this is one of the most treacherous concepts of all as a subject for scientific discourse. Activities directed to the increase of knowledge may be very productive, but it is too great a strain on the imagination to try to think of their results as being predictable in a particular case. We have, however, an approach to predictability in large groups; in many fields research can even now be carried on more or less "intelligently" where the scale of operations is sufficiently large. It seems almost fanciful also to speak seriously of a condition of equilibrium where the rewards or chances of reward from further effort would no longer be adequate to entice productive energy into this field. But it is clear that even here, in so far as results can be foreseen, resources will be distributed so as to secure equality of return over the whole field of investment and under competition every value realized will be just equal to the cost incurred in creating it. In this field uncertainty is indeed an inevitable concomitant of progress. Yet there is an approach to predictability, a variation in the amount of unpredictability independent of variation in the amount of progress and the two factors must be separated in the causal analysis, for their effects are very different.

This completes the list of progressive changes. In every case the necessary and sufficient condition of a perfect, remainderless distribution of the product of industry among the agencies causally concerned in creating it, in addition to perfect competition itself, is that the change can be anticipated over the period of time to which producers' calculations relate. Where the results of the employment of resources can be foreseen, competition will force every user of any productive resource to pay all that he can afford to pay, which is its net specific contribution to the total product of industry. No sort of change interferes with the no-profit adjustment if the law of the change is known.

Chapter 6. Minor Prerequisites for Perfect Competition

In Part Two we have attempted an analytical construction of a perfectly competitive society, with a view to determining the precise meaning of the theoretical tendencies of a private property, free exchange organization of society, and especially the conditions necessary to the realization of those tendencies. The abstract conditions first enumerated in chapter III represented in part divergencies in degree only from real life, and were in part arbitrary abstractions from fundamental characteristics of the pecuniary organization made for the purpose of a separate study of the constituent elements. Those of the latter type have been dealt with in chapters IV and V, and the result, up to the present point, is an outline picture of the essentials of a perfect competitive system.[173] The first, rather preliminary, objective of the study has thus been achieved, as far as the author is prepared or feels it advisable to go. The second and more fundamental purpose is to contrast this ideal, perfect competition with the facts of ordinary life, to examine the limitations

[173]There is one important exception to this statement. As observed in chapters i and ii, the presence of uncertainty in regard to individual events does not necessarily obstruct the workings of competition or prevent the realization of its theoretical result in a remainderless distribution of the product of industry among the productive agents. If the uncertainty in a particular case is measurable, it may in effect be eliminated by the grouping or clubbing of a sufficient number of cases to secure certainty in regard to the group. This point cannot be dealt with until after the general theory of risk and uncertainty has been presented. (See chapter vm.)

of the general principles developed, and to inquire as to the directions in which they must be supplemented by detailed, empirical data before completely applicable conclusions can be drawn.

But it is not the intention to cover this field with any great degree of exhaustiveness. Only one of the theoretical simplifications is to be studied in detail, the assumption of perfect knowledge. Part Three of the essay will be devoted to a discussion of the meaning and consequences of uncertainty, the incompleteness and inaccuracy of the beliefs and opinions upon which economic conduct is based. But it is desirable to have as a background some brief notice of the other abstracted factors.[174]

It will readily be seen that many of the objections to the pure theory of distribution commented upon in chapter IV relate to these necessary scientific idealizations, and have real significance as limitations on the completeness and accuracy of the generalizations of theory. They are not, therefore, valid objections to the theory and have been advanced as such only because of the common failure to comprehend the nature of scientific reasoning, the meaning and use of general principles. This is especially applicable to the first point to be noticed, the assumption of continuous variability in the magnitude of all factors dealt with. The question of the size of the "marginal unit" is clearly relative to that of the flexibility of industrial organization, and the two must be considered together. When we give up the illicit procedure of funding productive agents into "factors" and deal with the actual competing units on their own account, this problem becomes of practical significance and constitutes

[174]Specifications numbered (2) and (5) in chapter in — that people are perfectly rational and that there is perfect intercommunication among them — are clearly phases of the problem of perfect knowledge to be taken up in Part Three. In the present chapter we are concerned especially with numbers (3) and (4) — formal freedom of action and perfect mobility, implying perfect divisibility; (6) and (7) the absence of monopoly and predation. Numbers (8), (9), (10), and (11) have already been considered, but some further remarks will be in place in regard to the first point mentioned under number (8), the relations of social as contrasted with individual wants. We may note here that the timelessness of the production process necessary to secure perfect mobility has been dealt with in one aspect in chapter iv. In addition it retards the speed of readjustments by holding productive forces committed to certain uses for an interval after it would otherwise be profitable for them to change. But it does not affect the final results, the character of adjustment when achieved. Some discussion of the intermediate effects is necessary in connection with the study of profits, and the whole subject of "friction" will be gone into after the treatment of uncertainty has cleared the way for a discussion of profit.

an effective limitation on the application of the theory. In the case of labor especially, with which we are here particularly concerned, the human individual is a very effective unit; not only does he bargain as a unit, but he cannot practically be divided up between different establishments, and the range of occupations in which he can engage in any short interval of time is also very narrowly restricted. He may also be in a high and surprising degree unique; he does not always shade off by imperceptible gradations from one variety to another to the extent that perfect competitive imputation demands. His numbers (in proportion to the number of variants) are not nearly always so large as to make an individual a negligible fraction of a group of similars.[175]

As a consequence of the appreciable dimensions of the natural agent, the flexibility of the economic organization as a whole is restricted, and the criticism made by Mr. J. A. Hobson and Professor Wieser against the productivity theory is true to a considerable extent in many individual cases. There are many productive organizations consisting of small numbers of rather unique agents which very effectively supplement each other and are not so effectively demanded elsewhere. In such a case competition does not afford means of distributing the entire yield of the group among its members; an appreciable part of it resists automatic division and remains a joint product, dependent on the peculiar effectiveness of the particular organization. Many partnerships illustrate this point. Imputation goes as far as the group, giving that its proper income, but fails to distribute accurately within it. In case of a partnership this division between the members is usually made on ethical grounds or on the basis of "bargaining power," sheer personal force. In industry at large the special product of the organization above that competitively assigned to its components is likely to go, largely at least, to the entrepreneur, though bargaining power or the strategic situation always plays a large part in the proceedings.

The same factors give rise to a peculiar difficulty in dealing with the law of diminishing returns. When any agent is by its physical nature or any particular circumstances available only in relatively

[175]It is not necessary that he be an infinitesimal fraction of the productive power of a particular establishment. The imputation process works itself out through the competition of establishments for the different agents. If a number of establishments exist in which a certain type of agencies is on an indifference margin, the income of all similar agencies will be accurately determined.

large blocks, so that only a few, perhaps only one, is used in a single competitive organization, the technological features of particular combinations may cause apparent exceptions to the "law" at some points; these may be apparent for certain sections of the curve for the simple reason that one element is not subject to decrease and the best proportions can be secured only by increasing the other elements. A conspicuous example is the case of railways, the principal crucial "agent" being the right of way. If the demand for transportation were large enough to require an indefinite number of tracks the curve would be smoothed out and would ultimately show increasing costs from the other elements in the equipment. So with gas or water mains, until a certain size has been reached, and many similar cases. The fact of limited divisibility is responsible for all differences in the economy of operation of establishments of different sizes. The amounts of certain agencies or elements in the operations not being continuously variable, other things have to be proportioned to them to get the best ratio, thus imposing restrictions on the size of the plant as a whole. Many, if not most, of these questions of size ultimately come back to the human being as a relatively indivisible unit.

Preliminary to a discussion of predatory activity, or acquisition which is not production, we must again refer to the question of the ethical implications of the productivity analysis. The purely causal meaning of productivity in a scientific explanation of economic phenomena is apt to be confused with social or moral issues which belong in an entirely different sphere. We have insisted that the word "produce" in the sense of the specific productivity theory of distribution, is used in precisely the same way as the word "cause" in scientific discourse in general. But the word "cause" itself is vague in ordinary speech, and it is natural that confusion should arise in regard to the economic synonym. For example, the socialists, with no lack of suggestion and justification from the loose usage of words by economists of non-socialistic schools, have insisted that all wealth is "produced" by labor. We need do no more than mention the names of Smith and Ricardo in this connection, while among contemporary writers Professor Taussig exemplifies the same practice, expressly stating that labor produces all wealth, but may not be entitled to all.[176]

[176]Paper entitled "Outlines of a Theory of Wages," read at the twenty-second annual meeting of the American Economic Association. See Proceedings, pp. 143-44, note.

We should say that the reverse is more correct, that labor does not "produce" all wealth, but may be entitled to all, on ideal grounds.

Inasmuch as any assertion of a cause and effect relation between particular events is always (as already pointed out) made on the ground of some special human interest or "bias," there is much justification for such usage, but this only makes the more imperative, a clear separation from the "scientific," use of causal terminology. Thus it is quite proper to say, in ordinary speech, that the cook "prepares " the meal, that the opening of the throttle of the locomotive by the engineer is the "cause" of the starting of the train, and that his failure to see the signal is the "cause" of the wreck and the deaths of the passengers. In an analogous way a small group of agents might for some purposes be credited with nearly the whole output of a large establishment; "other things equal," the product depends on their cooperation.

But it must be evident that scientific economics cannot use the word "produce" in this sense. The product of any productive service can for scientific purposes be only what we have defined it to be, that which is really dependent upon the service in question, that which can be produced by its aid and which cannot be produced without it, in the social situation as it is, allowing for the change in organization which would accompany its withdrawal from use. It follows that we cannot properly speak of the "product" of an economic "factor," even if we use the word "factor" in the possibly legitimate sense of a group of physically interchangeable things. The product of "labor," "land," or "capital," as aggregates, involves a still more illicit and meaningless use of terms. The only specific product which can be recognized is that of a single agent as such, an individual human being or machine, or such a parcel of land (or of liquid capital) as is actually bargained for and used in the production process (and for perfect competition to take place it must be negligible in size).

More important, however, is the error of attributing any sort of moral significance to economic productivity. It is a physical, mechanical attribute, attaching to inanimate objects quite as properly as to persons, and to non-moral or even immoral as well as virtuous activities of the latter. The confusion of causality with desert is an inexcusable blunder for which the bourgeois psychology of modern society is perhaps ultimately to blame, though productivity theorists are not guiltless.[177] We must guard against thinking of the

[177]Notably Professor J. B. Clark. Cf . above, p. 109. The concessions of

"natural" adjustment of the competitive system as having any moral import, though it is of course "ideal" in the scientific sense of being a condition of stability. To call it the "best possible" arrangement is merely to beg the question or to misuse words. The natural arrangement is only that under which, with the given conditions as to the demand and supply of goods, especially the existing distribution of productive power, no one is under any inducement to make any change. If we pass over the question of how far individual wants for specific things really dominate conduct, and neglect equally the whole category of wants for certain social relationships and interests in other individuals (not absolutely dependent), and assume in addition (we shall investigate the point presently) that no interests are involved in any exchange except those of the direct parties to it — then the result is a mere mechanical equilibrium of the pull and haul of interacting individual self-interests.

It is imperative that we bear in mind that the serpent's tail is always in the serpent's mouth, that what the competitive system tends to give back is just what is put into it in the way of human motives and human powers, natural, acquired, or conferred, and has in itself no moral attribute whatever. In real life the possession of property (or superior training) is supposed to represent saving or invention or some contribution to social progress. But it is clear that there is no technical (much less moral) equivalence between these services and the right to their entire fruits in perpetuity, and to confer it on one's heirs and assigns forever — particularly when we consider the enormous element of pure luck in all operations of this sort. The only sense and the only degree in which rewards for service are ethical is that of the necessity of paying the reward in order to get the service performed. From this point of view the only defense of most of the existing system is the difficulty of suggesting a workable alternative.

We must now turn again briefly to the point mentioned above, the extent to which outside interests not represented in agreements between individuals are affected by them (otherwise than through

---

Professor J. M. Clark {he. cit.) seem to me to cover only a portion of the ground. I see nothing morally ideal in a distribution according to innate personal ability — certainly not ability measured by pecuniary demand suggest that such a distribution would yield vastly more inequality, misery, and despair than does the present order. Nor, in the abstract, can I see any connection between innate ability and moral desert. Is inherited ability on any better footing morally than inherited property?

direct competition in the market). The mere mechanical effectiveness of competitive free contract in producing a reconciliation of individual interests under given conditions depends largely on the answer to this question. Obviously, outsiders may be affected either advantageously or disadvantageously. In the former case voluntary agreements will not be carried far enough to secure maximum social (total individual) advantage, while in the latter case they will be carried too far. These facts form the most important source of the need for social interference. Many services, such as communication and education, not to mention the administration of justice, confer a general benefit on the community in addition to the special benefit to the individual, and must be encouraged by bounties or actually taken over and performed by public agencies or they will not be developed to the point of maximum benefit. The most familiar illustrations of the opposite case in our society relate to the use of land for purposes which damage the neighborhood, or are thought to do so. It is perhaps of nearly equal importance that improvements on land and industrial developments generally may benefit neighboring property, and might be made much more readily and in ways involving less injustice if there were some practicable way of assessing these benefits. This is notably true of public and quasi-public works, which effect enormous uncompensated transfers of values. It may be doubted whether in fact any agreement between individuals is ever made which does not affect for good or ill many persons other than the immediate parties, and a large proportion have wide ramifications over "society.'

In this brief sketch we can only mention and insist on the fundamental importance of the fact that a large part of what men want relates directly to other members of society. Man is, after all, *zoon politikon* and quite on a par with his personal needs are all sorts of interests in furthering the plans of people whom he likes and, always relatively and generally absolutely, obstructing those of others, in a wide scale of gradations down to Thackeray's "'e's a furriner; 'eave a 'arf a brick at 'im!" or, "kill the nigger!" The relative importance of other-regarding motives and desires, directed not to material things, but to forms of social relationships, is sure to be underestimated by any one treating economic phenomena in a "scientific" way.

The extreme phase of the problem of the moral character of the economic system relates to positively predatory activity. Davenport, following Veblen, has stressed the contrast between (private) acquisition and (social) production, making much of the hiring of sluggers, assassins, and incendiaries as part of the demand for labor, the productivity of burglars and their implements, and the like. It is not really very difficult in most cases for one who is disposed to do so to distinguish between theft or brigandage and free contract, and perhaps all that is needful to say of them in treating the theory of contractual organization is that they are obviously outside of it. A large part of the critics' strictures on the existing system come down to protests against the individual wanting what he wants instead of what is good for him, of which the critic is to be the judge; and the critic does not feel himself called upon even to outline any standards other than his own preferences upon a basis of which judgment is to be passed. It would be well for the progress of science if we had less of this sort of thing and more serious effort to formulate standards and to determine the conditions under which free contract does or does not promote individual interests harmoniously and realize social ideals, in addition it is most desirable that some attempt be made to separate the evils for which the form of organization is more or less reasonably blamable from those which are inherent in nature and human nature, or in organization as such, irrespective of its form and to keep the question in view, in criticizing the exchange system, of whether any other conceivable system would offer any possible chance for change or improvement.[178]

[178]See Davenport, Economics of Enterprise, chap, ix, especially p. 127; and cf. L. H. Haney, "The Social Point of View," Quarterly Journal of Economics, vol. xxviii, pp. 319-21.

Though the case of the pickpocket offers no real difficulty and is not likely to be taken seriously, there are many cases where standards of productivity are very hard to define. Gambling, for example, is definitely ambiguous. If the men who gamble know what they are about, play for fun, at a game which is "fair," and do not risk more than they can afford to pay for the excitement, I should say that the gains of the banker represent product. If all are interested in winning only, and play because they expect to win, I suppose the operation is unproductive and produces a transfer, not a production of wealth. It will doubtless be conceded that there is such a thing as a transfer of wealth, distinguishable from production, or else receiving gifts must also be classed as productive work!

Other cases are more difficult still, since no clear line can be drawn between being tricked and gratifying a perverted taste. The difficulty is the ultimate impossibility of saying what one "really" wants. In cases where each knows what he is getting and what he is giving — no "compulsion" (artificial manipulation of alternatives) being present — and actually gets the means of satisfying his actual want, we must hold that the operation is a production of utility in the economic sense. But what we may call "crude" fraud must be classed outside of exchange relations along with forced transfers. The man who sells whiskey,

There is a close connection between the moral aspect of the economic order and the problem of monopoly. This subject is of especial importance in the theory of profit, since profit has often been ascribed wholly or in part to monopoly gain, as already noticed in the case of Macvane and the Clark School. "Monopoly" is a word used to cover things which for present purposes must be kept distinct, and its meaning must first be made clear. Monopoly is usually defined as the control of the supply of a commodity. A common but disastrous error is the confusion of control with natural limitation of supply. We need not pause longer than to characterize as a serious misuse of words the denomination of land rent, for example, as a monopoly income. Even J. S. Mill fell into the error of defining monopoly as limitation, and it is exemplified in its extreme form by Mr. F. B. Hawley, who virtually calls all income due to the "scarcity" of any productive resource a monopoly return. Now, as all income, from the distributive standpoint, is dependent on the scarcity of the agents which produce it, and all in exactly the same way, the meaninglessness of such a description is apparent. And of course the same applies to "scarcity income" in general, whether called monopoly gain or not. There is under free competition no other sort of income, qualitatively or quantitatively, and the designation neither distinguishes or in any significant way describes anything.

It is no part of our present purpose to go into an exhaustive discussion of monopoly, and we may pass over the ordinary type of the

---

patent medicine, corrupt literature or art, etc., to people who want them and are willing to pay for them is productive; but one who sells gilded chunks of lead to unsuspecting rustics for gold bricks clearly is not. If the buyer be in a position where it never can make any difference whether the metal is lead or gold and never could find out which it is, the action is hard to classify, but we must consider that he could have had what he got for vastly less money, if he had known. Is the buyer of an imitation jewel or antique for a genuine, and who never knows the difference, really cheated? And suppose the purchaser of Liquozone or Peruna is really cured of his (real or imaginary) ailment! And suppose he is not! Was it the medicine, or a cure, that he really bought?

We are carried back to the already oft-reiterated observation that any scientific thinking about conduct presupposes that wants are given entities, and that exchange organization of the satisfaction of wants presupposes that their character is known. Capricious and experimental conduct are not amenable to scientific treatment (unless subject to prediction in large groups, a case which we have postponed for later consideration). In the language of abstract logic, a must remain a throughout the discussion. This it can do either by remaining sensibly unchanged or by changing in accordance with a known law. The last alternative reverts to the first, since such a change can be thought of only as an expression of an inner, unchanging attribute of the thing changing.

phenomenon very briefly. In its original meaning the word signified an exclusive right to produce or sell a certain commodity, and was essentially a legal concept. The "legitimate" representative of the type in modern industry is the patented article for consumption — not patented production process (including machines, etc.), which will be considered later. Monopoly may also be based on mere financial power, on the threat of local underselling, boycott, and other forms of "unfair competition"; this amounts in effect to a voice in the control of property owned by others or their persons as well; that is, to part ownership. Free competition, of course, involves the complete, separate ownership of every productive agent or natural unit, and the exploitation of every one in a way to secure its maximum value yield. Any sort of violent interference with competition manifestly contradicts this assumption and may be roughly designated monopoly.

In the same category of monopoly (control of a consumption good) we may place two other varieties significant in the modern economic world. The first is the "corner," in which only a temporary control is secured, amounting in reality to control over the time of marketing of an existing stock not subject to rapid increase at the moment by further production. The other is the use of trademarks, trade names, advertising slogans, etc., and we may include the services of professional men with established reputations (whatever their real foundation). The buyer being the judge of his own wants, if the name makes a difference to him it constitutes a peculiarity in the commodity, however similar it may be in physical properties to competing wares. And the difference from physically equivalent goods may be very real, in the way of confidence in what one is getting. Such goods are then commodities whose supply is controlled by the producer, and competition with other makes or brands is a case of substitution of more or less similar goods, such as a monopolist always has to take into account.

A monopoly, of the category described, is evidently "productive" in the economic or mechanical causality sense. It may be viewed either as a separate productive element, in which case it is property in perfectly good business standing, and may be exchanged for other property on an income basis. Allowance will be made for the security of the income, but this allowance is perhaps as likely to be in favor of the monopoly as against it. Or we may take the view that the monopoly of a consumption good confers superior productivity on the agencies producing it, above physically identical agencies in other uses. As long as these are debarred in any way from producing the monopolized good the effect is the same as that of a physical incapacity to do so, and they are, like the branded article, economically differentiated, however similar physically. If the monopoly is of the character of a patent, and freely salable separately from the plant producing the goods, it is better to treat it as a productive agency on its own account.

Again, monopoly may consist in the exclusive control of the supply of some productive agency, physically defined as a group of interchangeable units. The only incentive to obtain such a monopoly is the desire to secure one of the former type, the power to restrict the supply of some consumption good. The control of any type of productive agent, of course, gives control of the supply of commodities whose production is dependent on the use of that agent, through the power to withhold the agent from use altogether or restrict its use in the making of any particular commodity while leaving its employment in other uses free. Whether the monopolist produces these goods himself or leases his monopolized agency to others, he can secure the entire increase in the net revenue from the final commodity as a rent on the restricted and restricting agency. It is evident in this case also that the restriction on the use of the agency, whatever its basis, is equivalent in effect to a physical peculiarity, and that the causal productivity of the agency is increased by its limitation in the same way as if part of it had gone out of existence or undergone some incapacitating change. Nor should it be necessary to insist again on the separation of the causality aspect of the case from the question of social policy.

A somewhat different case is the exclusive control of a peculiarly effective method or system of organization of production. The question of the productivity of a special process protected by patent or kept secret is a difficult one. Treatment of it in economic literature varies from that of Lavergne,[179] who insists that the *idee productrice* is an independent factor, always present along with land, labor, and capital, to that of A. S. Johnson, who contends that an idea or method cannot be regarded as productive because it is the nature of an idea to multiply itself indefinitely.[180] Here, again, the crucial test can only be the facts in the case. Does the method or idea get prod-

[179] Bertrand Lavergne, Theorie des marches Economiques. Paris, 1910.
[180] Rent in Modern Economic Theory, p. 120, note.

uct imputed to it? This is largely a question of whether it is salable and so takes on capital value. If so, it is productive in the sense of economic causality. If it is not salable it will represent an element in the productivity of its possessor and its yield will accrue to him in the form of a wage. The moral question, whether it "ought" to be a source of income, is of course another matter. It seems evident[181] on the one hand that the highest social advantage would require the most rapid and general extension of the use of the best methods, and it is of significance that this can theoretically be done nearly without cost. On the other hand, it is equally evident that both justice and expediency demand a fair reward for the origination of better ways of doing things. It would seem to be a matter of political development to provide a better way of rewarding these services than even a temporary monopoly of their use; but this inquiry belongs in the theory of progress, and as a question of social policy is outside the scope of the present study.

We must again insist, however, that the method must be recognized as being productive, or as conferring superior productivity on the agencies employed in connection with it.[182] An arbitrary restriction is again causally equivalent to physical limitation. The method or idea is merely less productive of goods (and more productive of exchange value) than it would be if its use were unrestricted. The same paradox holds for any productive good; if multiplied indefinitely it would yield more goods in physical units, but have no value at all. The only difference in the case of a method of production is that it can be multiplied indefinitely without much cost (after once worked out), an important distinction from the standpoint of social policy (perhaps), but not significant from the standpoint of a cause and effect explanation of things. And we must again insist that the danger of reasoning about social totals of exchange value, and still more the extreme treachery of all reasoning about human welfare in terms of any such concept as economic utility, be borne in mind in attempting to reach conclusions as to social policy.[183]

[181]Supposing the desideratum to be the greatest possible consumption of commodities. Supposing it to be maximum happiness, the case is not so clear, while the question of maximum "welfare" involves us in still greater uncertainty.

[182]There is a danger in over-emphasizing the difference between these two views of productivity. Remembering that all production is joint, it is clear that any separate productivity of a particular agency means ultimately superior productivity conferred upon others used in connection with it.

[183]It seems in place to remark that a confusion is involved in laying down "ap-

The position taken above, that monopoly is productive, is in opposition to the doctrine of Professor J. B. Clark and his followers that the monopolist merely appropriates product created by other agents. But when monopoly income is said to be "diverted from its real producers,"[184] or is called "exploitative," in the sense that it "is not secured by the agent that creates it,"[185] the words "create" and "produce" are not used in their correct (causal) meaning. Monopoly is impossible except on the basis of some control over an element essential in the production of a commodity, and the extra product is rightly imputed to this essential element, or to the condition which makes control possible, if separable from the rest of the situation.

Monopoly of productive agencies has hitherto been of restricted importance in actual affairs, for several reasons. Most productive resources are specialized only to a limited extent, and are subject to effective competition from a wide range of substitutes. And in the hitherto undeveloped and rapidly changing condition of the world, most agencies, even of the most specialized types, have been rapidly and irregularly increasing in supply through new discoveries, and open to deliberate increase through moderate expenditures in exploration and development work. Finally, the technique of the large-scale organization requisite to secure unified control has been crude and imperfect, while the opposition of public opinion has been increasing in force. It is of some interest to inquire into the implica-

propriability" or what might be called competitive self-assertion, as a condition of economic productivity. Productivity is a matter of limitation. If an agency is limited relatively to the need for its use, it must be appropriated by some one, to be administered, to decide who is to have the use of it and who is to do without. And any productivity conferred on an object by appropriation must come through and in connection with restriction on its use. Thus Professor Young (Outlines of Economics, by R. T. Ely and others, ed. of 1908, pp. 555-56) contends that the Strait of Gibraltar would be productive wealth if the British Government were to charge for its use. But they could not charge for its use without reducing its volume; it would be a case of monopoly merely. This and several other confusions are involved in Veblen's contention (on the "Nature of Capital," Quarterly Journal of Economics, vol. xxii, pp. 917 ff., and vol. xxiii, pp. 104 ff.) that the world's stock of knowledge is its most important "capital," which is without value merely because not privately exploited. It could be exploited only by having its use restricted; i.e., by monopoly. The notion that capital is significant as limiting access to the world fund of technical knowledge is absurd, for the reason, already noted, that production is joint, and the productivity of anything may be viewed as a productivity conferred on other things.

[184] Willett.

[185] Johnson, pp. 106. 107.

tions of absolutely free competition in this regard.

With perfect intercommunication it would seem that the assumed absence of collusion is very improbable, as organization costs would naturally tend to a low level. Under static conditions (with the existing stocks of all agencies fixed and known), a great development of monopoly would apparently be inevitable. It is not unreasonable to suppose even that in the absence of organized social interference conditions would approach the result contended for by the Marxian socialists, monopoly universal, or at least prevalent to an extent involving the complete breakdown of the competitive system of organization.

A further consideration, which goes back to the requirement of negligible size in the marginal unit as a condition of effective competition, tends to reinforce this view. In the ordinary sense of monopoly, concentration of control is not profitable unless it is nearly complete. But with organization costs absent or small, there might be a continuous incentive to increase the size of the bargaining unit. It is true, as some objectors to the productivity theory of distribution contend, that as the bargaining unit is larger the product theoretically dependent upon it is larger in greater ratio, and this fact affords a small incentive to combine even on a very small scale, and to increase the size of the unit without limit. The extra remuneration of the block over what it could obtain if its constituent units bargained separately would come out of the shares of the other agents used in connection with the one affected, not out of increased payments extorted from consumers as in case of monopoly.

The argument may be shown graphically by recourse to the "dosing method" of explaining specific productivity, made familiar by Professor J. B. Clark. There is no fallacy in this analysis if by a "factor" of production we mean merely a group of physically interchangeable things, and not a sort of labor or capital pulp obtained by putting things of all degrees of heterogeneity through the mill of the competitive process itself and reducing them to value productivity units. We must also remember that the method is a logical device purely, and in no sense represents the process by which productive services actually get evaluated. If, then, we imagine a static society, and fix our attention upon such a group of competing agents, it will be seen that the different units or members composing it may be regarded as placed along the descending curve of diminishing productivity of the familiar diagram. The curve, like that of diminishing utility and diminishing demand price,[186] is purely hypothetical ; the ordinate of each point merely shows what would be the productivity of each unit in the series if the total number were reduced to that indicated by the corresponding abscissa and production reorganized along "natural" lines. It does not indicate differences in productivity, or anything else, at the moment. We also pass over the fact that it is impossible to construct such a curve except for a very limited range in the region of known conditions and that any considerable extension of it (for an important productive service) soon carries us into the realm of pure fantasy.

But ignoring the difficulties and imagining the curve drawn, it is obvious that under theoretical imputation each member of any such group of competing agents will get what is directly dependent upon that which occupies the least important position, which is all that is ultimately "dependent" upon any one. But if two or more such agents combine so as to compete as a unit instead of separately, they can get the total product of that number of units at the lower end of the series, which is more than their separate "marginal" products. Therefore, under perfect competition, they will combine and bargain as a unit; and the same incentive will urge them to keep on combining until a monopoly results.

The situation is easily understood from the conventional diagram. If the curve CD represents the relative importance of successive agents of a series, or units of some really fundable agent, then under perfect competition every unit will get the product DE, and a certain group E'E will get FDE'E. If now these EE' units combine so as to become marginal as a group, they can get instead D'DE'E, gaining D'DF over the former arrangement. The owner of the group can prevent the substitution of a (marginal) unit outside the group for any unit in it, and so cause a larger product to be dependent on the employment of the group than the aggregate marginal products of its members.

Figure 7:

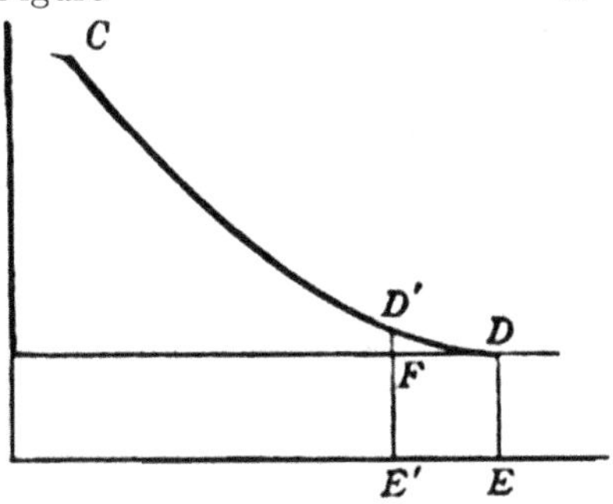

[186]Cf. chapter in.

Similar agencies outside the combination will only get the wage DE, and the surplus income received by our consolidated block will come out of the shares of the agencies with which it is combined, not out of an increase in the price of the product to consumers. The employers of the "block" use no more nor less of the agency than before and make no more nor less product; hence they must sell the same supply at the same price. But the other agencies are forced to take less for their services because the block cannot be replaced a unit at a time from the margin, but only by an equal number of marginal units at once, a transfer which will raise their price all along the line. Only "friction" (human limitations) prevents this in actual society, the "diminishing returns of entrepreneurship."

It need not be remarked that this process would not go far in fact until something would have to be done to stop it. There does seem to be a certain Hegelian self-contradiction in the idea of theoretically perfect competition after all. As to what the end would be, it is fruitless to speculate, but it would have to be some arbitrary system of distribution under some sort of social control, doubtless based on ethics or political power or brute force, according to the circumstances — providing that society or somebody in it had sufficient intelligence and power to prevent a reversion to the *helium omnium contra omnes.* Competitive industry is or hitherto has been saved by the fact that the human individual has been found normally incapable of wielding to his own advantage much more industrial power than, aided by legal and moral restraints, society as a whole can safely permit him to possess. How long this beneficent limitation can be counted upon to play its saving role may in the light of current business development occasion some doubt. With this subject we are not here particularly concerned, but it has seemed worth while to point out, in connection with the discussion of an ideal system of perfect competition, that such a system is inherently self-defeating and could not exist in the real world. Perfect competition implies conditions, especially as to the presence of human limitations, which would at the same time facilitate monopoly, make organization through free contract impossible, and force an authoritarian system upon society.[187]

[187]In addition to the incentives to combination afforded by the gains through increase in the size of the bargaining unit, another tendency might work in the same direction. In many cases it might be profitable for the owner of a considerable block, though not the whole supply of an important productive

In connection with the meaning of productivity it is of interest to raise the question of the economic value of the State. What would be the effect upon our economic life if society as such, acting through the political organization, should assert itself as an economic individual and charge "what the traffic will bear" for its own service? Obviously the Government has a monopoly on an absolutely indispensable commodity. Business could not be carried on at all without the protection of property and enforcement of contract. Into this interesting, but intricate, question it is impossible to enter at length here, but it appears that what the Government could take, its economic product, is hardly limited.[188] The writer is much more optimistic as to the possibilities of a drastic program of taxation for securing a greater degree of economic equality than over most proposals for social interference in contractual relations.

---

service, to restrict its use and so increase the value of the product. Whether the owner of a part of a supply can gain by withholding some of that part from use will depend upon the fraction of the supply which he holds and on the flexibility of the supply obtainable from competing sources and the elasticity of the demand for the product. In view of the fact that practically every business is a partial monopoly, it is remarkable that the theoretical treatment of economics has related so exclusively to complete monopoly and perfect competition.

Attention may be directed to another tendency fatal to free competition under theoretical conditions. This is the matter of the inflation of credit. With all forms of friction eliminated there would seem to be hardly a limit to the substitution of credit for any sort of commodity as a medium of exchange and a stable value-standard would apparently be impossible to establish.

[188]Concerning the "economic surplus" of which much has been made by some writers, notably Hobson, the remark made above (page 188 n.) is applicable. The payment necessary to secure the performance of any service depends on how much of that service is desired. The question is much complicated by human mortality and the fact of inheritance, but in general there are no surpluses available without reducing the volume of the service. This will not be true of monopolized or highly specialized agencies, and there are, no doubt, many remunerations which are too high absolutely and which if reduced would positively increase the volume of the services for which they are paid.

Part III. Imperfect Competition Through Risk And Uncertainty

Chapter 7. The Meaning of Risk and Uncertainty

STARTING with the individual psychology of valuation and adding new factors step by step, we have now built up a competitive industrial society involving valuation and distribution under the highly simplified conditions necessary to perfect competition. The drastic assumptions made were necessary to show the operation of the forces at work free from all disturbing influences; and impossible as the presuppositions have been, the principles involved have not been falsified or changed, but merely exhibited in purity and isolation. Chief among the simplifications of reality prerequisite to the achievement of perfect competition is, as has been emphasized all along, the assumption of practical omniscience on the part of every member of the competitive system. The task of the present chapter is to inquire more fully into the meaning of this assumption. We must take a brief excursion into the field of the theory of knowledge and clarify our ideas as to its nature and limitations, and the relation between knowledge and behavior. On the basis of the insight thus gained, it will be possible to illuminate that large group of economic phenomena which are connected with the imperfection of knowledge.

The problem may be set in view and its significance made clear by recalling certain points already brought out in the previous discussion. In chapter II it was pointed out that the failure of competition and the emergence of profit are connected with changes in economic conditions, but that the connection is indirect. For profit arises from the fact that entrepreneurs contract for productive services in advance at fixed rates, and realize upon their use by the sale of the product in the market after it is made. Thus the competition for productive services is based upon anticipations. The prices of the productive services being the costs of production, changes in conditions give rise to profit by upsetting anticipations and producing a divergence between costs and selling price, which would otherwise be equalized by competition. If all changes were to take place in accordance with invariable and universally known laws, they could be foreseen for an indefinite period in advance of their occurrence, and would not upset the perfect apportionment of product values among the contributing agencies, and profit (or loss) would not arise. Hence it is our imperfect knowledge of the future, a consequence of change, not change as such, which is crucial for the understanding of our problem.

Again, in chapters III and IV, it was found necessary to assume static conditions in order to realize perfect competition. But, as expressly stated, this assumption was made because it follows from it as a corollary that the future will be foreknown, and not for the sake of the proposition itself. It is conceivable that all changes might take place in accordance with known laws, and in fact very many changes do occur with sufficient regularity to be practically predictable in large measure. Hence the justification and the necessity for separating in our study the effects of change from the effects of ignorance of the future. And chapter V was devoted to a study of the effects of change as such with uncertainty absent. Here it was found that under such conditions distribution or the imputation of product values to production services will always be perfect and exhaustive and profit absent.

Furthermore, it is unnecessary to perfect, profitless imputation that particular occurrences be foreseeable, if only all the alternative possibilities are known and the probability of the occurrence of each can be accurately ascertained . Even though the business man could not know in advance the results of individual ventures, lie could operate and base his competitive offers upon accurate foreknowledge of the future if quantitative knowledge of the probability of every possible outcome can be had. For by figuring on the basis of a large number of ventures (whether in his own business alone or in that of business in general) the losses could be converted into fixed costs. Such special costs would, of course, have to be given full weight, but they would be costs merely, like any other necessary outlays, and would not give rise to profit, which is a difference between cost and selling price. Such situations in more or less pure form are also common in everyday life, and various devices for dealing with them form an important phase of contemporary business organization. Some of the more important of these devices will come up for brief discussion later. At present we are concerned only to emphasize the fact that knowledge is in a sense variable in degree and that the practical problem may relate to the degree of knowledge rather than to its presence or absence *in toto*.

The facts of life in this regard are in a superficial sense obtrusively obvious and are a matter of common observation. It is a world of change in which we live, and a world of uncertainty. We live only by knowing *something* about the future; while the problems of life, or of conduct at least, arise from the fact that we know so little. This is as true of business as of other spheres of activity. The essence of the situation is action according to *opinion*, of greater or less foundation and value, neither entire ignorance nor complete and perfect information, but partial knowledge. If we are to understand the workings of the economic system we must examine the meaning and significance of uncertainty; and to this end some inquiry into the nature and function of knowledge itself is necessary.[189]

[189]The problem of uncertainty and risk in economics is, of course, not new. Some reference has already been made to the literature. It has been recognized and discussed in three connections: (1) insurance; (2) speculation; and (3) entrepreneurship. For a full treatment of the last named it is necessary to go to the German works cited in the historical portion of this study. English economics has been too exclusively occupied with long-time tendencies or with "static" economics to give adequate attention to this problem. For a very general discussion of uncertainty see, in addition to works already cited, Ross, Uncertainty as a Factor in Production, Annals, American Academy, vol. viii, pp. 304 ff. See also Leslie, T. E. Cliffe, "The Known and the Unknown in the Economic World," Essays in Political Economy, pp. 221-42; Lavington, F., "Uncertainty in its Relation to the Rate of Interest," in Economic Journal, vol. xxn, pp. 398-409; and "The Social Interest in Speculation," ibid., vol. xxiii, pp. 36-52; Pigou, A. C, Wealth and Welfare, part v; Haynes, John, "Risk as an Economic Factor," Quarterly Journal of Economics, July, 1895.

In this superficial sketch of the theory of knowledge it has not seemed important to give extended reference to philosophic literature. It will be evident that the doctrine expounded is a functional or pragmatic view, with some reservations. By way of further "reservation" we should point out that the tone of the discussion merely results from the fact that it is the function of consciousness and knowledge in relation to conduct that we are interested in, for present purposes, and the text must not be taken as expressing any view whatever as to

The first datum for the study of knowledge and behavior is the fact of consciousness itself. Apparently the higher mental operations of reason are different only in degree, only elaborations of what is inherent in the first spark of "awareness." The essence of mentality from a functional standpoint seems to be its forward-looking character. Life has been described as internal adaptations to external coexistences and sequences. On the vegetable or unconscious plane, the internal changes are simultaneous with the external. The fundamental difference in the case of animal or conscious life is that it can re Act to a situation before that situation materializes; it can "see things coming." This is what the whole complicated mechanism of the nervous system is "for," in the biological sense. The readjustments by which the organism adapts itself to the environment require time, and the farther ahead the organism can "see," the more adequately it can adapt itself, the more fully and competently it can live.

Just what consciousness as such has to do with it is a mystery which will doubtless remain inscrutable.[190] It is a mere brute fact that wherever we find complicated adaptations we find consciousness, or at least are compelled to infer it. Science can find no place for it, and no role for it to perform in the causal sequence. It is epiphenomenal. An explanation of the readjustment necessarily runs in terms of stimulus and reaction, in this temporal order. Yet in our own experience we know that we do not react to the past stimulus, but to the "image" of a future state of affairs; and for common sense, consciousness, the "image," is both present and operative wherever adaptations are dissociated from any immediate stimulus; i.e., are "spontaneous" and forward-looking. It is evident that all organic reactions relate to future situations, farther in the future as the type of life and activity is "higher." However successful mechanistic science may be in explaining the reaction in terms of a past cause, it will still be irresistibly convenient for common sense to think of it as prompted by a future situation present to consciousness. The role of consciousness is to give the organism this "knowledge" of the future. For all we can see or for all that science can ever tell us, we might

---

the ultimate nature of reality or any other philosophic position. The writer is in fact a radical empiricist in logic, which is to say, as far as theoretical reasoning is concerned, an agnostic on all questions beyond the fairly immediate facts of experience.

[190]See the brilliant lectures of E. DuBois-Raymond, " Uber die Grenzen des Naturerkennens" and "Die sieben Weltratsel."

just as well have been unconscious automata, but we are not. At least the person speaking is not, and he cannot help attributing to other creatures similarly constituted and behaving in the same way with himself "insides," to use Descartes' picturesque term, like his own. We *perceive* the world before we react to it, and we react not to what we perceive, but always to what we *infer.*

The universal form of conscious behavior is thus action designed to change a future situation inferred from a present one. It involves perception and, in addition, twofold inference. We must infer what the future situation would have been without our interference, and what change will be wrought in it by our action. Fortunately or unfortunately, none of these processes is infallible, or indeed ever accurate and complete. We do not perceive the present as it is and in its totality, nor do we infer the future from the present with any high degree of dependability, nor yet do we accurately know the consequences of our own actions. In addition, there is a fourth source of error to be taken into account, for we do not execute actions in the precise form in which they are imaged and willed. The presence of error in these processes is perhaps a phase of the fundamental mystery of the processes themselves. It seems to be an earnest of their non-mechanical character, for machines, generally speaking, do not make mistakes. (Though it may not be legitimate to draw inferences from the crude machines of our own construction to the infinitely more sensitive and intricate physico-chemical complexes which make up organic systems.) In any case the fact of liability to err is painfully familiar and is all that concerns us here. It is interesting to note that the perceptive faculties seem often to be less acute and dependable in the higher forms of life than in some of the lower. At least civilized man is often weak in this respect in comparison with primitive man and the higher animals. Higher powers of inference may take the place of perceptive faculties to a large extent, and we have undoubtedly developed reasoning power and lost ground with respect to keenness of sense.

It must be recognized further that no sharp distinction can be drawn between perception and reason. Our perceptive faculties are highly educated and sophisticated, and what is present to consciousness in the simplest situation is more the product of inference, more an imaginative construct than a direct communication from the nerve terminal organs. A rational animal differs from a mere conscious one in degree only; it is *more* conscious. It is immaterial whether we say that it infers more or perceives more. Scientifically we can analyze the mental content into sense data and imagination data, but the difference hardly exists for consciousness itself, at least in its practical aspects. Even in "thought" in the narrow sense, when the object of reflection is not present to sense at all, the experience itself is substantially the same. The function of consciousness is to infer, and all consciousness is largely inferential, rational. By which, again, we mean that things not present to sense are operative in directing behavior, that reason, and all consciousness, is forward-looking; and an essential element in the phenomena is its lack of automatic mechanical accuracy, its liability to error.

The statement that a situation not in physical relations with an organism, not even in existence, influences that organism, is of course in a sense figurative; the influence is indirect, operating through a situation with which the organism is in contact at the moment. Hence, as already pointed out, it is always theoretically possible to ignore the form of the conscious relation, and interpret the reaction as a mechanical effect of the cause actually present. But it remains true that practically we must regard the situation present to consciousness, not the one physically present, as the controlling cause. In spite of rash statements by over-ardent devotees of the new science of "behavior," it is preposterous to suppose that it will ever supersede psychology (which is something very different) or the theory of knowledge, in something like their historic forms.

It is evident that the possibility of a situation not present, operating through one which is present, is conditioned upon some sort of dependable relation between the two. This postulate of all knowledge and thought has been variously formulated as the "law" or "principle" of "causality," and "uniformity" or "regularity" of nature, etc. Remembering that we are speaking of the surface facts, not metaphysical interpretations, we may say that all reasoning rests on the principle of analogy. We know the absent from the present, the future from the now, by assuming that connections or associations among phenomena which have been valid will be so; we judge the future by the past. Experience has taught us that certain time and space relations subsist among phenomena in a degree to be depended upon. This dogma of uniformity of coexistence and sequence among phenomena is a fairly satisfactory statement of the postulate of thought and forward-looking action from the standpoint of the philosopher. But from the more superficial standpoint of common sense (and hence of an inquiry such as the present) the term "phenomenon" is rather vague and elusive, and a more serviceable formulation seems possible. Common sense works in terms of a world of objects or merely "things." Consequently the idea of things manifesting *constant modes of behavior* seems to be a better "category" than that of uniformity of relation among phenomena. This may be unsatisfactory to the philosopher, who will protest at once that the thing is merely a sum of its modes of behavior, that no such separation is really possible. It is the ancient riddle which so puzzled Locke, of the attribute and substratum, the substratum, of course, tending to evaporate under critical scrutiny. But this weakness may prove rather a source of strength for the use which we intend to make of the notion, as will be argued.

We have, then, our dogma which is the presupposition of knowledge, in this form; that the world is made up of things, which, *under the same circumstances*, always *behave in the same way.* The practical problem of inference or prediction in any particular situation centers around the first two of these three factors: what things are we dealing with, and what are the circumstances which condition their action? From knowledge of these two sets of facts it must be possible to say what behavior is to be expected. The chief logical problem, as already noticed, lies in the conception of a "thing." For it is obvious that the "circumstances" which condition the behavior of any particular thing are composed of other things and their behavior. The assumption that under the same circumstances the same things behave in the same ways thus raises the single question of how far and in what sense the universe is really made up of such "things" which preserve an unvarying identity (mode of behavior). It is manifest that the ordinary objects of experience do not fit this description closely, certainly not such "things" as men and animals and probably not even rocks and planets in the strict sense. Science has rested upon the further assumption that this superficial divergence of fact from theory arises because the "things" of everyday experience are not the "ultimate" things, but are complexes of things which really are unchanging. And the progress of science has consisted mostly in *analyzing* variable complexes into unvarying constituents, until now we have with us the electron.

But *workable* knowledge of the world requires much more than the assumption that the world is made up of units which maintain an unvarying identity in time. There are far too many objects to be dealt with by a finite intelligence, however unvarying they might be, if they were all different. We require the further dogma of identical similarity between large numbers of things. It must be possible not merely to assume that the same thing will always behave in the same way, but that the same kind of thing will do the same, and that there is in fact a finite, practically manageable number of kinds of things. Hence the fundamental role which *classification* has always played in thought and the theory of thought. For our limited intelligence to deal with the world, it must be possible to infer from a perceived similarity in the behavior of objects to a similarity in respects not open to immediate observation. That is, we must assume that the properties of things are not shuffled and combined at random in nature, but that the number of groupings is limited or that there is constancy of association. This is the dogma of the "reality of classes," familiar to students of logic.

But even this is not enough. If the classification of objects be restricted to the grouping of things in all respects similar or substantially identical, there would still be a quite impossible number of *kinds* of things for intelligence to grasp. Even in the sense of practical degrees of completeness of similarity, identity to ordinary observation, our groups would be far too small and too numerous. It is questionable whether classification would be carried far enough on this basis to be of substantial assistance in simplifying our problems to the point of manageability. It is not that kind of a world. And even abstracting from mere differences in degree such as size and the like, for which intelligence readily makes allowance, the same would still hold true. It is clear that to live intelligently in our world, — that is, to adapt our conduct to future facts, — we must use the principle that things similar in some respects will behave similarly in certain other respects even when they are very different in still other respects. We cannot make an exhaustive classification of things, but must take various and shifting groupings according to the purpose or problem in view, assimilating things now on the basis of one common property (mode of behavior) and now on the basis of another. The working assumption of practical inference about the environment is thus a working number of properties or *modes of resemblance* between things, not a workable number of kinds of things; this latter we do not have. That is, the properties of things which influence our reactions toward them must be sufficiently limited in number and in modes of association for intelligence to grasp.

We may sum up these facts about the environment of our lives which are fundamental for conduct in the following propositions :

1. The world is made up of objects which are practically infinite in variety as aggregates of sensible qualities and modes of behavior not immediately sensible. And when we consider the number of objects which function in any particular conduct situation, and their possible variety, it is evident that only an infinite intelligence could grasp all the possible combinations.

2. Finite intelligence is able to deal with the world because

a. The number of distinguishable properties and modes of behavior is limited, the infinite variety in nature being due to different combinations of the attributes in objects.

b. Because the properties of things remain fairly constant and

c. Such changes in them as take place occur in fairly constant and ascertainable ways.

d. The non-sensible properties and modes of behavior of things are associated with sensible properties in at least fairly uniform ways.

It is to be noted under (a) that differences in kind are referred to rather than differences in degree, and we should add that

3. The quantitative aspect of things and the power of intelligence to deal with quantity is a fundamental element in the situation.

4. It is also fundamental that in regard to certain properties objects differ only in degree, that mass and spacial magnitude are *universal* qualities of things, which do not exhibit differences in kind.

5. Following out the same principle of (4) many of the most significant properties are common to very large groups; in respect to the qualities most important for conduct, there are a very few kinds. The intelligibility of the world is enormously increased if not actually made possible by the simplicity of the great divisions into solid, liquid, and gas, into living and not-living things, and the like. And there is a hierarchy of attributes[191] in order of generality down to the slight peculiarities which probably distinguish in some mariner "and degree (other than mere situation) every nameable thing in the universe from every other, giving it individuality.

6. The postulates of intelligent behavior would be very incomplete without formal insistence on the role played by the fact of consciousness in "objects" outside ourselves, human beings and animals. The behaviorist notwithstanding, the inferences as to the behavior to be anticipated which we draw from the configuration of

[191] Cf. Comte's Classification of the Sciences.

the lines about the mouth, the gleam or "twinkle" of an eye or a shrill or "soft" vocal sound, are not made from these physical features as such or alone, but through "sympathetic introspection"[192] into what is going on in the "mind" of the "object" contemplated, and would be impossible without this mysterious capacity of interpretation. It is always possible for the scientist to argue the contrary, as it is for him to demonstrate that we are not really conscious ourselves, but common sense properly revolts against the one conclusion as against the other.

7. It goes without saying that we must know ourselves as well as the world. Hence we must list our sense of our own powers of movement, etc.

It is perhaps superfluous to speak here of the syllogism and its place in logical theory. Empirical logicians such as Mill and Venn have ventilated the subject sufficiently and shown that no real inference is involved in the syllogism itself, that the inference takes place in the formulation of the premises and consists in the recognition of a constant factual connection between the predicates denoted by the different terms.

We are rather concerned here with pointing out that the theory of knowledge as it is worked out by logicians is primarily a theory of exact knowledge, of rigorous demonstration. It has become somewhat the fashion, especially since Bergson came into vogue, to be irrationalistic, and question the validity of logical processes. It seems to the writer that there is much ground for this position, but that its implications are very liable to be misunderstood. There is to my mind no question of understanding the world by any other method. There is, however, much question as to how far the world is intelligible at all. This will be seen to be a question of the facts as to the uniformity of behavior of natural objects and the similarities subsisting between them, on the ground of which inference is made from one to another. In so far as there is "real change" in the Bergsonian (i.e., Heracleitean) sense it seems clear that reasoning is impossible. In addition we have to make the still more questionable assumption that the situation elements or fundamental kinds of object properties upon which we fall back for simplicity (practically finitude) in view of the unmanageable number of kinds of objects as wholes, are unvarying from one "combination" (i.e., one object) to another. This assumption is doubtless valid in some connections.

[192]Professor Cooley's descriptive phrase. See Social Organization, chap. i.

Thus weight, inertia, etc., are undoubtedly the same in a living as in a non-living object. But that the quality "living" is really the same in any two kinds of living things is more open to doubt. In so far as these general attributes are not uniform and cannot be given a definite meaning which is the same for all the objects in the class which they designate, reasoning from one member of the class to another is clearly invalid. That is, valid classification assumes identity in some respect. It is not absolutely certain that the ground on which we ascribe similarity to things and class them together and reason from the behavior of one to that of the other is always of this character. The power of one thing to suggest another is often quite mysterious, and may possibly not rest upon the possession of any common real qualities which will support a valid inference.[193]

The practical limitation of knowledge, however, rests upon very different grounds. The universe may not be ultimately knowable (we speak, of course, only of objective phenomena, of behavior, not of problems which transcend ordinary experience of fact); but it is certainly know able to a degree so far beyond our actual powers of dealing with it through knowledge that any limitations of knowledge due to lack of real consistency in the cosmos may be ignored. It probably occasions surprise to most persons the first time they consider seriously what a small portion of our conduct makes any pretense to a foundation in accurate and exhaustive knowledge of the things we are dealing with.

It is only when our interest is restricted to a very narrow aspect of the behavior of an object, dependent upon its physical attributes of size, mass, strength, elasticity, or the like, that exact determination is theoretically possible; and only by refined laboratory technique that the determination can be actually made. The ordinary decisions of life are made on the basis of "estimates" of a crude and superficial character. In general the future situation in relation to which we act depends upon the behavior of an indefinitely large number of objects, and is influenced by so many factors that no real effort is made to take account of them all, much less estimate and summate their separate significances. It is only in very special and crucial cases that anything like a mathematical (exhaustive and quantitative) study can be made.

The mental operations by which ordinary practical decisions are made are very obscure, and it is a matter for surprise that neither lo-

[193]See James, Psychology, chap, xxii, on "Association by Similarity."

gicians nor psychologists have shown much interest in them. Perhaps (the writer is inclined to this view) it is because there is really very little to say about the subject. Prophecy seems to be a good deal like memory itself, on which it is based. When we wish to think of some man's name, or recall a quotation which has slipped our memory, we go to work to do it, and the desired idea comes to mind, often when we are thinking about something else — or else it does not come, but in either case there is very little that we can tell about the operation, very little "technique." So when we try to decide what to expect in a certain situation, and how to behave ourselves accordingly, we are likely to do a lot of irrelevant mental rambling, and the first thing we know we find that we have made up our minds, that our course of action is settled. There seems to be very little meaning in what has gone on in our minds, and certainly little kinship with the formal processes of logic which the scientist uses in an investigation. We contrast the two processes by recognizing that the former is not reasoned knowledge, but "judgment," "common sense," or "intuition." There is doubtless some analysis of a crude type involved, but in the main it seems that we "infer" largely from our experience of the past as a whole, somewhat in the same way that we deal with intrinsically simple (unanalyzable) problems like estimating distances, weights, or other physical magnitudes, when measuring instruments are not at hand.[194]

The foregoing discussion of reasoning relates to ideal or complete inference based on uniformity of association of predicates and which can be formulated in universal propositions. The theory of formal deductive logic has, of course, always recognized also reasoning from what are undescriptively called "particular" propositions — "occasional " would be a better term — asserting that two predicates *sometimes* belong to the same subject, or that two classes of objects overlap. The goal of science is always to get rid of this form of assertion, to "explain" the occurrence and non-occurrence of the quality by finding some other general fact in the past history of the object with which the association is universal. But there are large classes of cases in which this cannot be done even scientifically, and the rough operations of everyday unscientific thinking employ the form quite commonly. In the crude form of "*some* X is Y," such generalizations are very unsatisfactory to the scientific mind and practically useless

[194]Marshall remarks that the business manager's decisions are guided by "trained instinct" rather than knowledge. (Principles, 6th ed., p. 406.)

except as a challenge and starting-point for further inquiry. But when, as is so commonly the case, it is impossible or impracticable to do better, the data can often be put in a form of a great deal of scientific utility. This is done by ascertaining the numerical proportion of the cases in which X is associated with F, which yields the familiar probability judgment. If, say, ninety per cent of X is Y, — i.e., if that fraction of objects characterized by property X shows also property Y, — the fact may obviously have much the same significance for conduct as if the association were universal.[195]

Furthermore, even if the proportion is not approximately one hundred per cent, even if it is only half or less, the same fact may hold good. If, in a certain class of cases a given outcome is not certain, nor even extremely probable, but only contingent, but if the numerical probability of its occurrence is known, conduct in relation to the situation in question may be ordered intelligently. Business operations, as already observed, illustrate the point perfectly. Thus, in the example given by von Mangoldt, the bursting of bottles does not introduce an uncertainty or hazard into the business of producing champagne; since in the operations of any producer a practically constant and known proportion of the bottles burst, it does not especially matter even whether the proportion is large or small. The loss becomes a fixed cost in the industry and is passed on to the consumer, like the outlays for labor or materials or any other. And even if a single producer does not deal with a sufficiently large number of cases of the contingency in question (in a sufficiently short period of time) to secure constancy in its effects, the same result may easily be realized, through an organization taking in a large number of producers. This, of course, is the principle of insurance, as familiarly illustrated by the chance of fire loss. No one can say whether a particular building will burn, and most building owners do not operate on a sufficient scale to reduce the loss to constancy (though some do). But as is well known, the effect of insurance is to extend this base to cover the operations of a large number of persons

[195]When variations in degree in the attributes X and Y are taken into account, the problem must be dealt with by applying the statistical theory of correlation, which is a further development of probability theory. See especially the works of K. Pearson and F. Y. Edgeworth. An elementary discussion will be found in any treatise on statistics. A. L. Bowley's Measurement of Groups and Series is particularly serviceable for the general reader. A rough idea may be obtained from Elderton's Primer of Statistics. Pearson's Grammar of Science, chaps, IV and V, may be consulted on the whole ground of the present chapter.

and convert, the contingency into a fixed cost. It makes no difference in the principles whether the grouping of eases is effected through a mutual organization of the persons directly affected or through an outside commercial agency.

It will be evident that the practical difficulties of ordering conduct intelligently are enormously increased where the inference is contingent instead of being positive. The difficulties of establishing an association between predicates are great enough where the association is universal; so great, as we have already seen, that it is never done with any approach to accuracy except for critical cases of very special importance justifying extensive study in laboratory or "field." Where the connection is occasional, demonstration of a dependable connection is vastly more difficult, and there is the added problem of ascertaining the precise proportion of cases in which the connection occurs. In relation to everyday problems, where rigorous scientific procedure is excluded, the difficulty and chance of error are, of course, multiplied in still greater degree. We have to "estimate" not merely factors whose associates, implications, or effects are known, but in addition the degree of dependability of the association between the (estimated) factors (the immediately perceptible attributes or modes of behavior) and the inferred factors with relation to which our action in the case is to be controlled. Most of the real decisions of life are based on "reasoning" (if such it may be called) of this still more tenuous and uncertain character, and not even that which has already been described. We have to estimate the given factors in a situation and also estimate the probability that any particular consequence will follow from any of them if present in the degree assumed.

For logical accuracy and in order to understand the different kinds of situations and modes of dealing with them in practice, a further distinction must be drawn, a distinction of far-reaching consequences and much neglected in the discussion of economic problems. There are two fundamentally different ways of arriving at the probability judgment of the form that a given numerical proportion of X's are also Ys. The first method is by a priori calculation, and is applicable to and used in games of chance. This is also the type of case usually assumed in logical and mathematical treatments of probability. It must be strongly contrasted with the very different type of problem in which calculation is impossible and the result is reached by the empirical method of applying statistics to actual instances. As an illustration of the first type of probability we may take throwing a perfect die. If the die is really perfect and known to be so, it would be merely ridiculous to undertake to throw it a few hundred thousand times to ascertain the probability of its resting on one face or another. And even if the experiment were performed, the result of it would not be accepted as throwing any light on the actual probability. The mathematician can easily calculate the probability that any proposed distribution of results will come out of any given number of throws, and no finite number would give certainty as to the probable distribution. On the other hand, consider the case already mentioned, the chance that a building will burn. It would be as ridiculous to suggest calculating from a priori principles the proportion of buildings to be accidentally destroyed by fire in a given region and time as it would to take statistics of the throws of dice.

The import of this distinction for present purposes is that the first, ma thematical or a priori, type of probability is practically never met with in business, while the second is extremely common. It is difficult to think of a business "hazard" with regard to which it is in any degree possible to calculate in advance the proportion of distribution among the different possible outcomes.[196] This must be dealt with, if at all, by tabulating the results of experience. The "if at all" is an important reservation, which will be discussed presently. It is evident that a great many hazards can be reduced to a fair degree of certainty by statistical grouping — also that an equally important category cannnot. We should note, however, two other facts. First, the statistical treatment never gives closely accurate quantitative results. Even in such simple cases as mechanical games of chance it would never be final, short of an infinite number of instances, as already observed. Furthermore, the fact that a *priori* methods are inapplicable is connected with a much greater complication in the data, which again carries with it a difficulty, in fact impossibility, of securing the same degree of homogeneity in the instances classed together. This point will have to be gone into more fully. The second fact mentioned in regard to the two methods is that the hazards or probabilities met with in business do admit of a certain small degree of theoretical treatment, supplementing the application of experience data. Thus in the case of fire risk on buildings, the fact that the cases are not really homogeneous may be offset in part

---

[196]The calling of bonds by lot is an illustration. In Germany bondholders often insure against this chance.

by the use of judgment, if not calculation. It is possible to tell with some accuracy whether the "real risk" in a particular case is higher or lower than that of a group as a whole, and by how much. This procedure, however, must be treated with caution. It is not clear that there is an ultimate separation between the calculation of departures from a standard type and more minute classification of types. There is, however, a difference in form, and insurance companies constantly follow both practices, that of defining groups as accurately as possible and also that of modifying or adjusting the coefficient applied within a class according to special circumstances which are practically always present.

We thus find that there are two logically different types of inference included in the probability judgment. We shall refer to these for brevity under the names of the "a priori " and the "statistical" respectively. The relations between the two concepts as employed in the crude usage of common sense are much confused and the ideas themselves blurred, so that it is important to emphasize the contrast. The precise meaning of "real probability" will have to be examined more in detail presently, but we can see that there is a difference in this respect in our feelings toward the two classes of cases. It seems clear that the probability of getting a six in throwing a die is "really" one in six, no matter what actually happens in any particular number of throws; but no one would assert confidently that the chance of a particular building burning on a particular day is "really" of any definite assigned value. The first statement has intuitive certainty with reference to a particular instance; in case of the second it is merely an empirical generalization with reference to a group. Possibly the difference is partly a matter of habit in our thinking and to some extent illusory, but it is none the less real and functional in our thinking. There is, indeed, a sort of logical paradox in the problem. If the probability in a game of chance is questioned, there is no test except that of experimental trial of a large number of cases, and under some circumstances we should conclude that the die was probably "loaded." This would itself be a probability judgment, to be sure, and would depend on the fact of our ignorance of the composition and manufacture of the die. Given this ignorance, a mathematician could tell the probability that the die is false, indicated by any given number and distribution of throws.

The practical difference between a priori and statistical probability seems to depend upon the accuracy of classification of the instances grouped together. In the case of the die, the successive throws are held to be "alike" in a degree and a sense which cannot be predicated of the different buildings exposed to fire hazard. There is, of course, a constant effort on the part of the actuary to make his classifications more exact, dividing groups into subgroups to secure the greatest possible homogeneity. Yet we can hardly conceive this process being carried so far as to make applicable the idea of real probability in a particular instance.

There is a further difficulty, amounting to paradox, in the idea of homogeneous grouping. Much is made of this point in treatises on statistics, the student being warned against drawing conclusions from distributions in nonhomogeneous groups. Perhaps the most familiar example is the age and sex distribution of population aggregates. An illustration (used by Secrist) is the death rate of the American soldiers in the Philippines, which was lower than that of the general population in the United States. The fallacy in the inference as to healthfulness of environment is, of course, that the "general population" is not a homogeneous group, but is made up of numerous age, sex, race, and occupation classes, "naturally" subject to widely different death rates. The paradox, which carries us at once into the heart of the logical problem of probability, is that if we had *absolutely* homogeneous groups we should have uniformity and not probability in the result, or else we must repudiate the dogma of the ultimate uniformity of nature, the persistence of identity in things . If the idea of natural law is valid at all, it would seem that men exactly alike and identically circumstanced would all die at once; in any particular interval either all or none would succumb, and the idea of probability becomes meaningless. So even in the case of the dice; if we believe in the postulates which make knowledge possible, then dice made alike and thrown alike will fall alike, and that is the end of it.

Yet practically there is no danger, figuratively speaking, that any of these phenomena will ever be amenable to prediction in the individual instance. The fundamental fact underlying probability reasoning is generally assumed to be our ignorance. If it were possible to measure with absolute accuracy all the determining circumstances in the case it would seem that we should be able to predict the result in the individual instance, but it is obtrusively manifest that in many cases we cannot do this. It will certainly not be proposed in the typical insurance situations, the chance of death and of fire loss, probably not even in the case of gambling devices. The question arises whether we should draw a distinction between necessary and only factual ignorance of the data in a given case. Take the case of balls in an urn. One man knows that there are red and black balls, but is ignorant of the numbers of each; another knows that the numbers are three of the former to one of the latter. It may be argued that "to the first man" the probability of drawing a red ball is fifty-fifty, while to the second it is seventy-five to twenty-five. Or it may be contended that the probability is "really" in the latter ratio, but that the first man simply does not know it. It must be admitted that practically, if any decision as to conduct is involved, such as a wager, the first man would have to act on the supposition that the chances are equal. And if the real probability reasoning is followed out to its conclusion, it seems that there is "really" no probability at all, but certainty, if knowledge is complete. The doctrine of real probability, if it is to be valid, must, it seems, rest upon inherent unknowability in the factors, not merely the fact of ignorance. And even then we must always consult the empirical facts, for it will not do to assume out of hand that the unknown causes in a case will distribute themselves according to the law of indifference among the different instances. We seem to be driven back to a logical impasse. The postulates of knowledge generally involve the conclusion that it is really determined in the nature of things which house will burn, which man die, and which face of the thrown die will come uppermost. The logic which we actually use, however, assumes that the result is really indeterminate, that the unknowable causes actually follow a law of indifference. The phenomenal constancy of distribution to which we are forced to appeal justifies this reasoning on the whole, but clearly is not its actual basis in our thinking. Wherever we find that there is not indifference, that the results show "bias," we assume some determinable cause at work; and the results of experience on the whole justify this assumption also.

There is a further point of some interest in regard to our probability reasoning. Examination of the mathematical theory of probability will show that the argument always proceeds on the assumption that there is no middle ground between complete determination and complete indifference. That is, the *elementary* probabilities in any form of problem must always be equal. If the chance of any particular result is more or less than one half, it is held to be axiomatic that there is a greater number of possible alternatives which yield this result (or do not yield it) than of the other kind; the alternatives themselves must be equally probable. The whole mathematical theory of probability is obviously a simple application of the principles of permutations and combinations for finding out the number of alternatives. Absolute indifference between the alternatives is taken for granted. Wherever the results do not show complete indifference between alternatives it is assumed that these are not simple, and further analysis is applied to reduce them to combinations of equally possible ones. And experience confirms these assumptions also.

Are we, then, to assume real indeterminateness, in the cosmos itself? This was the view of Cournot, and the mere ignorance theory common among writers on probability seems inadequate and untenable. There are, to be sure, cases which it seems to fit, like that referred to, where the probability of drawing a red or black ball is even to one who knows only that there are balls of the two colors in the urn, but is ignorant of the numbers of each.[197] But the case of the man who does know the numbers of each seems to be different. The dogmatic determinist can always maintain that there are causes at work which decide the result, but common sense is not satisfied. How does it "happen" that experience justifies the calculation of probabilities unless these unknown causes are really indifferent? Whenever we find "bias" in the results, a divergence from the anticipations on the basis of probability theory, we assume the presence of some cause which is not indifferent, and this procedure is also justified of its fruits. When we can be sure that we have eliminated every circumstance which can be measured or which might act consistently, we feel confident in assuming that in a large number of trials the results will come out in accordance with the assumption that the factors not subject to measurement or elimination are in fact indifferent. And not merely do we feel this way, but "it works."

It is interesting to observe that the common applications of probability in games of chance relate to some action of the human organism itself, the drawing of a card from a deck or ball from an urn after random manipulations, the impulse given to a wheel or coin or die, etc. The facts suggest a connection with that other age-old

---

[197]Professor Irving Fisher is particularly insistent upon the interpretation of probability as due to ignorance alone. See The Nature of Capital and Income, chap, xvi, sec. 1.

bone of contention, the freedom of the will.[198] If there is real indeterminateness, and if the ultimate seat of it is in the activities of the human (or perhaps organic) machine, there is in a sense an opening of the door to a conception of freedom in conduct. And when we consider the mystery of the role of consciousness in behavior and the repugnance which is felt by common sense to the epiphenomenal theory, we feel justified in further contending for at least the possibility that "mind" may in some inscrutable way originate action. Just how much or what sort of significance the admission may have for practical ethics is another question, which must be passed over here. Of course we cannot prove that the exact distribution of all the *coups* of the roulette wheels at Monte Carlo was *not* stowed away somewhere in the primeval nebula; the final appeal must be to "intrinsic reasonableness," the inveterate and necessary preference of intelligence for the simplest formulation which conforms to the facts. And about this, there may indeed be differences of opinion, and from these there is apparently no appeal.[199]

There may be different brands of "common sense" (which some wag has averred is so called because so very uncommon). In the writer's view the doctrine of ignorance or "insufficient reason" is untrue to the feelings of unsophisticated intelligence. We do not merely feel that we know no reason why the coin shall fall heads or tails; we know in a positive sense that there *is no reason*, and only under this condition do we make the probability judgment with any confidence. And furthermore, as already argued, it appears that only on condition that there is no reason would the results of experience confirm the judgment, as they do. The entire science of probability in the mathematical sense is based on the dogmatic assumption that

[198]Cf. E. Borel, Le Hasard, pp. 196-97.

[199]See Karl Pearson's essay on "The Scientific Aspects of Monte Carlo Roulette," in The Chances of Death and Other Studies in Evolution. The necessity of constant appeal to a dogmatic preference of simple to complicated hypotheses is brilliantly treated in Poincare's chapter on "Probabilities," in The Foundations of Science, Science and Hypothesis, chap, XI. See also Poincare's fascinating treatment of the relations between small causes and large effects in the same volume, Science and Method, chap. IV. Poincare bases the doctrine of equal probability on the mathematical principle that for small changes any continuous analytical function changes in the same ratio as the variable. The same unsatisfactory, if not absurd, doctrine of "intrinsic reasonableness" (for how can one thing be "intrinsically" more probable than another?) is developed from a different point of view in Balfour's Theism and Humanism, lecture vii, on "Probability, Calculable and Intuitive."

the ultimate alternatives are really *equally probable*, which seems to the writer to mean real indeterminateness.[200]

Professor Irving Fisher's view of probability as "always an estimate" becomes conditionally valid, however, on two interpretations. In the first place, it may be saved "theoretically" if the term "estimate" is construed broadly enough. If there is no difference between our a *priori* judgment of the absence of any cause which should lead a coin or a die to fall on one face rather than another and an "estimate" of equal probability, then there is no opposition between the two views. This is, however, repugnant to common sense (the present writer's brand). We seem to experience an "apodeictic certainty" about the situation of a game of chance, on a level with our confidence in the axioms of mathematics, and quite different from an "estimate." To illustrate, suppose we are allowed to look into the urn containing a large number of black and red balls before making a wager, but are not allowed to count the balls; this would give rise to an estimate of probability in the correct sense; it is something very different from either the mere consciousness or ignorance on which we act if we know only that there are balls of both colors without any knowledge or opinion as to the numbers or the exact knowledge of real probability attained by an accurate counting of the balls. In the second place, we must admit that the actual basis of action in a large proportion of real cases is an estimate. Neither of these interpretations, however, justifies identifying probability with an estimate.

But the probability in which the student, of business risk is interested is an estimate, though in a sense different from any of the propositions so far considered. To discuss the question from this new point of view we must go back for a moment to the general principles of the logic of conduct. We have emphasized above that the exact science of inference has little place in forming the opinions upon which decisions of conduct are based, and that this is true whether the implicit logic of the case is prediction on the ground of exhaustive analysis or a probability judgment, a priori or statistical. We act upon estimates rather than inferences, upon "judgment"

[200]For an excellent brief discussion of the issue, with references to the literature, the reader is referred to Arne Fisher, The Mathematical Theory of Probability, chap, I: "General Principles and Philosophic Aspects." The writer's position is that taken by Fisher and designated the principle of "cogent reason" in opposition to the older view common among mathematicians, of "insufficient reason." Compare also La Place, Essay on the Philosophical Theory of Probability.

or "intuition," not reasoning, for the most part. Now an estimate or intuitive judgment is somewhat like a probability judgment, but very different from either of the types of probability judgment already described. The relations between the two sorts" are in fact amazingly complex and as fraught with logical paradox as the probability judgment itself. If the term "probability" is to be applied to an estimate — and the usage is so well established that there is no hope of getting away from it — a third species under that genus must be recognized. Such a third type of probability fits very nicely in a scheme of classification with the two already discussed. We have insisted that there is a fundamental difference between "a priori" probability, on the one hand, and "statistical," on the other. In the former the "chances" can be computed on general principles, while in the latter they can only be determined empirically. This distinction is in opposition to the views of writers such as Venn and Edgeworth,[201] who reduce the former type to the latter on the basis of an empirical law of large numbers and accept practically the assumption of real indeterminateness. We have already raised the question of accuracy of classification in this connection, suggesting that the "*instances*," "*throws*," or "*coups*" in a game of chance form a homogeneous group in a higher sense than can be predicated on life or fire hazards. This view and our entire theory tend to be confirmed by the attempt to secure complete homogeneity through more minute classification. The end result of this endeavor would be groupings in which only really indeterminate factors should differ from one instance to another.

Taking, then, the classification point of view, we shall find the following simple scheme for separating three different types of probability situation:

1. A priory probability. Absolutely homogeneous classification of instances completely identical except for really indeterminate factors. This judgment of probability is on the same logical plane as the propositions of mathematics (which also may be viewed, and are viewed by the writer, as "ultimately" inductions from experience).

2. Statistical probability. Empirical evaluation of the frequency of association between predicates, not analyzable into varying combinations of equally probable alternatives. It must be emphasized that any high degree of confidence that the proportions found in the past will hold in the future is still based on an a priori judgment of

[201] "The Philosophy of Chance," Mind, vol. 9, 1884.

indeterminateness. Two complications are to be kept separate: firsts the impossibility of eliminating all factors not really indeterminate; and, second, the impossibility of enumerating the equally probable alternatives involved and determining their mode of combination so as to evaluate the probability by a priori calculation. The main distinguishing characteristic of this type is that it rests on an empirical classification of instances.

3. Estimates. The distinction here is that there is no valid basis of any kind for classifying instance s. This form of probability is involved in the greatest logical difficulties of all, and no very satisfactory discussion of it can be given, but its distinction from the other types must be emphasized and some of its complicated relations indicated.

We know that estimates or judgments are "liable" to err. Sometimes a rough determination of the magnitude of this "liability" is possible, but more generally it is not. In general, any determination of the value of an estimate must be merely empirical, secured by the tabulation of instances, thus reducing it to a probability of the second or statistical type. Indeed, since, as we have noticed, entirely homogeneous classification of instances is practically never possible in dealing with statistical probability, it is clear that the divergence from it of this third type where all classification is excluded is a matter of degree only. There are all gradations from a perfectly homogeneous group of life or fire hazards at one extreme to an absolutely unique exercise of judgment at the other. All gradations, we should say, except the ideal extremes themselves; for as we can never in practice secure completely homogeneous classes in the one case, so in the other it probably never happens that there is *no* basis of comparison for determining the probability of error in a judgment.

The theoretical difference between the probability connected with an estimate and that involved in such phenomena as are dealt with by insurance is, however, of the greatest importance, and is clearly discernible in nearly any instance of the exercise of judgment. Take as an illustration any typical business decision. A manufacturer is considering the advisability of making a large commitment in increasing the capacity of his works. He "figures" more or less on the proposition, taking account as well as possible of the various factors more or less susceptible of measurement, but the final result is an "estimate" of the probable outcome of any proposed course of action.

What is the "probability" of error (strictly, of any assigned degree of error) in the judgment? It is manifestly meaningless to speak of either calculating such a probability a *priori* or of determining it empirically by studying a large number of instances. The essential and outstanding fact is that the "instance" in question is so entirely unique that there are no others or not a sufficient number to make it possible to tabulate enough like it to form a basis for any inference of value about any real probability in the case we are interested in. The same obviously applies to the most of conduct and not to business decisions alone.

Yet it is true, and the fact can hardly be overemphasized, that a judgment of probability is actually made in such cases. The business man himself not merely forms the best estimate he can of the outcome of his actions, but he is likely also to estimate the probability that his estimate is correct. The "degree" of certainty or of confidence felt in the conclusion after it is reached cannot be ignored, for it is of the greatest practical significance. The action which follows upon an opinion depends as much upon the amount of confidence in that opinion as it does upon the favorableness of the opinion itself. The ultimate logic, or psychology, of these deliberations is obscure, a part of the scientifically unfathomable mystery of life and mind. We must simply fall back upon a "capacity" in the intelligent animal to form more or less correct judgments about things, an intuitive sense of values. We are so built that what seems to us reasonable is likely to be confirmed by experience, or we could not live in the world at all.

Fidelity to the actual psychology of the situation requires, we must insist, recognition of these two separate exercises of judgment, the formation of an estimate and the estimation of its value. We must, therefore, disagree with Professor Irving Fisher's contention[202] that there is only one estimate, the subjective feeling of probability itself. Moreover, it appears that the original estimate maybe a probability judgment. A man may act upon an estimate of the chance that his estimate of the chance of an event is a correct estimate. To be sure, after the decision is made he will be likely to sum all up in a certain degree of confidence that a certain outcome will be realized, and in practice may go farther and assume that the outcome itself is a certainty.

Two sorts of difficulty tend to obscure the relation between our

[202]See The Nature of Capital and Income, p. 266.

second and third types of probability, that which rests upon an empirical classification of instances and that which rests upon no classification, but is an estimate of an estimate. In the first place, nothing in the universe of experience is absolutely unique any more than any two things are absolutely alike. Consequently it is always possible to form classes if the bars are let down and a loose enough interpretation of similarity is accepted. Thus, in the case above mentioned, it might or might not be entirely meaningless to inquire as to the proportion of successful factory extensions and the proportion of those which are not. In this particular case it is hard to imagine that any one would base conduct upon a judgment of the probability of success arrived at in this way, but in other situations the method could conceivably have more or less validity. We must keep in mind that for conduct a probability judgment based on mere ignorance may be determining if it is the best that can be had. It would be a question, however, whether the person placed in the position of our business manager should regard the probability for him of success as that indicated by statistics of "similar" instances or simply even chances each way based on the fact of pure ignorance. What does appear certain is that his own estimate of the value of his own judgment would be given far greater weight than either sort of computation.

A still more interesting complication, and one of much greater practical significance, is the possibility of forming a class of similar instances on entirely different grounds. That is, instead of taking the decisions of other men in situations more or less similar objectively, we may take decisions of the same man in all sorts of situations. It is indisputable that this procedure is followed in fact to a very large extent and that an astounding number of decisions actually rest upon such a probability judgment, though it cannot be placed in the form of a definite statistical determination. That is, men do form, on the basis of experience, more or less valid opinions as to their own capacity to form correct judgments, and even of the capacities of other men in this regard. To be sure, both bases of classification are more or less taken into account; the estimate (by A or any one else) of the probability that the outcome of a situation will be that which A has predicted is not based on a perfectly general estimate of A's capacity to form judgments, but of his powers in a more or less defined field of prediction. It will at once occur to the reader that this capacity for forming correct judgments (in a more or less extended or restricted field) is the principal fact which makes a man serviceable in business; it is the characteristic human activity, the most important endowment for which wages are received. The stability and success of business enterprise in general is largely dependent upon the possibility of estimating the powers of men in this regard, both for assigning men to their positions and for fixing the remunerations which they are to receive for filling positions. The judgment or estimate as to the value of a man is a probability judgment of a complex nature, indeed. More or less based on experience and observation of the outcome of his predictions, it is doubtless principally after all simply an intuitive judgment or "unconscious induction," as one prefers.

It seems likely that a still further distinction may be drawn, leading to the recognition of another basis of classification of instances in order to reach a probability judgment. We mean the subjective feeling of confidence of the person making a prediction. I may have an intuitive feeling or "hunch" that a situation will eventuate in a certain way, and this feeling may inspire a more or less deliberative confidence by its very strength and persistence. The confidence in a prediction which is based on the strength of an intuition may appear to be compounded to the point of nonsense, but in so far as there exist such feelings reached unconsciously or without deliberation and in so far as they may become the objects of deliberative contemplation, the situation is none the less real. However, we cannot extend our inquiry to cover all the grounds on which men, even educated men, actually make decisions, or it will degenerate into a catalogue of superstitions. Let us try, then, to sum up the conclusions, significant for present purposes, to which the argument of the chapter leads.

The importance of uncertainty as a factor interfering with the perfect workings of competition in accordance with the laws of pure theory necessitated an examination of foundations of knowledge and conduct. The most important result of this survey is the emphatic contrast between knowledge as the scientist and the logician of science uses the term and the convictions or opinions upon which conduct is based outside of laboratory experiments. The opinions upon which we act in everyday affairs and those which govern the decisions of responsible business managers for the most part have little similarity with conclusions reached by exhaustive analysis and accurate measurement. The mental processes are entirely different in the two cases. In everyday life they are mostly subconscious. We know as little why we expect certain things to happen as we do the mechanism by which we recall a forgotten name. There is doubtless some analogy between the subconscious processes of "intuition" and the structure of logical deliberation, for the function of both is to anticipate the future and the possibility of prediction seems to rest upon the uniformity of nature. Hence there must be, in the one case as in the other, some sort and amount of analysis and synthesis; but the striking feature of the judging faculty is its liability to error.

The real logic or psychology of ordinary conduct is rather a neglected branch of inquiry, logicians having devoted their attention more to the structure of demonstrative reasoning. This is in a way inevitable, since the processes of intuition or judgment, being unconscious, are inaccessible to study. Such attention as has been given to the problem of intuitive estimation has been connected with and largely vitiated by confusion with the logic of probability. A brief examination of the probability judgment shows it to fall into two types, which we called the a priori and the statistical. In the latter type of situation, we cannot, as we can in the former, calculate the true probability from external data, but must derive it from an inductive study of a large group of cases. This limitation involves a serious logical weakness, since at best statistics give but a probability as to what the true probability is. In practice we are still further handicapped by the impossibility of attaining complete homogeneity in our groups of instances, in the sense in which the "coups" in a priori probability are homogeneous; that is, that the divergences are practically indeterminate as well as undetermined.

The liability of opinion or estimate to error must be radically distinguished from probability or chance of either type, for there is no possibility of forming in any way groups of instances of sufficient homogeneity to make possible a quantitative determination of true probability. Business decisions, for example, deal with situations which are far too unique, generally speaking, for any sort of statistical tabulation to have any value for guidance. The conception of an objectively measurable probability or chance is simply inapplicable. The confusion arises from the fact that we do estimate the value or validity or dependability of our opinions and estimates, and such an estimate has the same form as a probability judgment; it is a ratio, expressed by a proper fraction. But in fact it appears to be meaningless and fatally misleading to speak of the probability, in an objective sense, that a judgment is correct. As there is little hope of breaking away from well-established linguistic usage, even when vicious, we propose to call the value of estimates a third type of probability judgment, insisting on its differences from the other types rather than its similarity to them.

It is this third type of probability or uncertainty which has been neglected in economic theory, and which we propose to put in its rightful place. As we have repeatedly pointed out, an uncertainty which can by any method be reduced to an objective, quantitatively determinate probability, can be reduced to complete certainty by grouping cases. The business world has evolved several organization devices for effectuating this consolidation, with the result that when the technique of business organization is fairly developed, measurable uncertainties do not introduce into business any uncertainty whatever. Later in our study we shall glance hurriedly at some of these organization expedients, which are the only economic effect of uncertainty in the probability sense; but the present and more important task is to follow out the consequences of that higher form of uncertainty not susceptible to measurement and hence to elimination. It is this *true uncertainty* which by preventing the theoretically perfect outworking of the tendencies of competition gives the characteristic form of "enterprise" to economic organization as a whole and accounts for the peculiar income of the entrepreneur.

Chapter 8. Structures and Methods for Meeting Uncertainty

TO PRESERVE the distinction which has been draw in in the last chapter between the measurable uncertainty and an unmeasurable one we may use the term "risk" to designate the former and the term "uncertainty" for the latter. The word "risk" is ordinarily used in a loose way to refer to any sort of uncertainty viewed from the standpoint of the unfavorable contingency, and the term "uncertainty" similarly with reference to the favorable outcome; we speak of the "risk" of a loss, the "uncertainty" of a gain. But if our reasoning so far is at all correct, there is a fatal ambiguity in these terms, which must be gotten rid of, and the use of the term "risk" in connection with the measurable uncertainties or probabilities of insurance gives some justification for specializing the terms as just indicated. We can also employ the terms "objective" and "subjective" probability to designate the risk and uncertainty respectively, as these expressions are already in general use with a signification akin to that proposed.

The practical difference between the two categories, risk and uncertainty, is that in the former the distribution of the outcome in a group of instances is known (either through calculation a priori or from statistics of past experience), while in the case of uncertainty this is not true, the reason being in general that it is impossible to for m a group of instances, because the situation dealt with is in a high degree unique. The best example of uncertainty is in connection with the exercise of judgment or the formation of those opinions as to the future course of events, which opinions (and not scientific knowledge) actually guide most of our conduct. Now if the distribution of the different possible outcomes in a group of instances is known, it is possible to get rid of any real uncertainty by the expedient of grouping or "consolidating" instances. But that it is possible does not necessarily mean that it will be done, and we must observe at the outset that when an individual instance only is at issue, there is no difference for conduct between a measurable risk and an unmeasurable uncertainty. The individual, as already observed, throws his estimate of the value of an opinion into the probability form of "a successes in b trials" (a/b being a proper fraction) and "feels" toward it as toward any other probability situation.

As so commonly in this subject fraught with logical difficulty and paradox, reservations must be made to the above statement. In the first place, it does not matter how unique the instance, if a real probability can be calculated, if we can know with certainty how many successes there *would* be in (say) one hundred trials if the one hundred trials could be made. If we know the odds against us it does not matter in the least whether we place all our wagers in one kind of game or in as many different games as there are wagers; the laws of probability hold in the second case just as well as in the first. But in business situations it so rarely happens that a probability can be computed for a single unique instance that this qualification has less weight than might be supposed. However, in so far as objective probability enters into a calculation, it is hard to imagine an intelligent individual considering any single case as absolutely isolated. The only exception would be a decision in which one's whole fortune (or his life) were at stake. The importance of the contingency and probable frequency of recurrence in the individual lifetime of situations similar in the magnitude of the issues involved should make a difference in the attitude assumed toward any one case as well as the mathematical probability of success or failure.

A second reservation of more importance is connected with the possibility referred to in the preceding chapter, of forming classes of cases by grouping the decisions of a given person. That is, even though we do not get a quantitative probability by the process of grouping, still there is some tendency for fluctuations to cancel out and for the result to approach constancy in some degree. There appear to be in the making of judgments the same two kinds of elements that we find in probability situations proper; i.e., (a) determinate factors (the quality of the judging faculty, which is more or less stable) and (b) truly accidental factors varying from one decision to another according to a principle of indifference. The difference between the uncertainty of an opinion and a true probability is that we have no means of separating the two and evaluating them, either by calculation a *priori* or by empirical sorting. But in the second case the difference is not absolute; the sorting method does apply to some extent, though within narrow limits. Life is mostly made up of uncertainties, and the conditions under which an error or loss in one case may be compensated by other cases are bafflingly complex. We can only say that "in so far as" one confronts a situation involving uncertainty and deals with it on its merits as an isolated case, it is a matter of practical indifference whether the uncertainty is measurable or not.

The problem of the human attitude toward uncertainty (not for the present purpose distinguishing kinds) is as beset with difficulties as that of uncertainty itself. Not merely is the human reaction to situations of this character apt to be erratic and extremely various from one individual to another, but the "normal" reaction is subject to well-recognized deviations from the conduct which sound logic would dictate. Thus it is a familiar fact, well discussed by Adam Smith, that men will readily risk a small amount in the hope of winning a large when the adverse probability (known or estimated) against winning is much in excess of the ratio of the two amounts, while they commonly will refuse to incur a small chance of losing a larger amount for a virtual certainty of winning a smaller, even though the actuarial value of the chance is in their favor. To this bias must be added an inveterate belief on the part of the typical individual in his own "luck," especially strong when the basis of the uncertainty is the quality of his own judgment. The man in the street has little more sense of the real value of his opinions than he has knowledge of the "logic" (if such it may be called) on which they rest. In addition, we must consider the almost universal prevalence of superstitions. Any coincidence that strikes attention is likely to be elevated into a law of nature, giving rise to a belief in an unerring "sign." Even a mere "hunch" or "something tells me," with no real or imaginary basis in the mind of the person himself, may readily be accepted as valid ground for action and treated as an unquestionable verity.

Doubtless in the long run of history there is a tendency toward rationality even in men's whims and impulses. And if for no other reason than the impossibility of intelligently dealing with conduct on any other hypothesis, we seem justified in limiting our discussion to rational grounds of action. We shall assume, then, that if a man is undergoing a sacrifice for the sake of a future benefit, the expected reward must be larger in order to evoke the sacrifice if it is viewed as contingent than if it is considered certain, and that it will have to be larger in at least some general proportion to the degree of felt uncertainty in the anticipation.[203] It is clearly the subjective uncertainty which is decisive in such a case, what the man believes the chances to be, whether his degree of confidence is based upon an objective probability in the situation itself or in an estimate of his own powers of prediction. We hold also that both the objective and subjective types may be involved at the same time, though no doubt most men do not carry their deliberations so far; the man's opinion or prediction may be an estimate of an objective probability, and the estimate itself be recognized as having a certain degree of validity, so that the degree of felt uncertainty is a product of two probability ratios. It is to be emphasized again that practically all decisions as to conduct in real life rest upon opinions, and doubtless the greater part rest upon opinions which on scrutiny easily resolve themselves into an opinion of a probability — though as noted this "scrutiny" may not in most cases be given to the judgment by the individual making it.

The normal economic situation is of this character: The adventurer has an opinion as to the outcome, within more or less narrow limits. If he is inclined to make the venture, this opinion is either an expectation of a certain definite gain or a belief in the real probability of a larger one. Outside the limits of the anticipation any other result becomes more and more improbable in his mind as the amount thought of diverges either way. Hence it is correct to treat

[203]The chief limitation in fact relates less to the proposition as stated than to the dogma of "conduct" or activity exclusively in order to a future reward. Means and end seem to be the form in which we think about our behavior rather than the actual form of the behavior itself. The literature of ethics is one long record of failure to find any absolute end; in life every end becomes a means to some new and farther goal. The attempt to rationalize human behavior seems to be a perpetual chase after one's own shadow, and the conclusion forces itself upon us that the "summum bonum" or any other objective "bonum" is an ignis fatuus. We are compelled to believe that in a great proportion of cases we take more interest in action whose fruition is only probable than we would if it were certain.

all instances of economic uncertainty as cases of choice between a smaller reward more confidently and a larger one less confidently anticipated.

At the bottom of the uncertainty problem in economics is the forward-looking character of the economic process itself. Goods are produced to satisfy wants; the production of goods requires time, and two elements of uncertainty are introduced, corresponding to two different kinds of foresight which must be exercised. First, the end of productive operations must be estimated from the beginning. It is notoriously impossible to tell accurately when entering upon productive activity what will be its results in physical terms, what (a) quantities and (b) qualities of goods will result from the expenditure of given resources. Second, the wants which the goods are to satisfy are also, of course, in the future to the same extent, and their prediction involves uncertainty in the same way. The producer, then, must estimate (1) the future demand which he is striving to satisfy and (2) the future results of his operations in attempting to satisfy that demand.

It goes without saying that rational conduct strives to reduce to a minimum the uncertainties involved in adapting means to ends. This does not mean, be it emphasized, that uncertainty as such is abhorrent to the human species, which probably is not true. We should not really prefer to live in a world where everything was "cut and dried," which is merely to say that we should not want our activity to be all perfectly rational. But in attempting to act "intelligently" we are attempting to secure adaptation, which means foresight, as perfect as possible. There is, as already noted, an element of paradox in conduct which is not to be ignored. We find ourselves compelled to strive after things which in a "calm, cool hour" we admit we do not want, at least not in fullness and perfection. Perhaps it is the manifest impossibility of reaching the end which makes it interesting to strive after it. In any case we do strive to reduce uncertainty, even though we should not want it eliminated from our lives.

The possibility of reducing uncertainty depends again on two fundamental sets of conditions: First, uncertainties are less in groups of cases than in single instances. In the case of a priori probability the uncertainty tends to disappear altogether, as the group increases in inclusiveness; with statistical probabilities the same tendency is manifest in a less degree, being limited by defectiveness of classification. And even the third type, true uncertainties, show some tendency toward regularity when grouped on the basis of nearly any similarity or common element. The second fact or set of facts making for a reduction of uncertainty is the differences among human individuals in regard to it. These differences are of many kinds and an enumeration of them will be undertaken presently. We may note here that they may be differences in the men themselves or differences in their position in relation to the problem. We may call the two fundamental methods of dealing with uncertainty based respectively upon reduction by grouping and upon selection of men to "bear" it, "consolidation"[204] and "specialization," respectively. To these two methods we must add two others which are so obvious as hardly to call for discussion: (3) control of the future, and (4) increased power of prediction. These are closely interrelated, since the chief practical significance of knowledge is control, and both are closely identified with the general progress of civilization, the improvement of technology and the increase of knowledge. Possibly a fifth method should be named, the "diffusion" of the consequences of untoward contingencies. Other things equal, it is a gain to have an event cause a loss of a thousand dollars each to a hundred persons rather than a hundred thousand to one person; it is better for two men to lose one eye than for one to lose two, and a system of production which wounds a larger number of workers and kills a smaller number is to be regarded as an improvement. In practice this diffusion is perhaps always associated with consolidation, but there is a logical distinction between the two and they may be practically separable in some cases. We must observe also that consolidation and specialization are intimately connected, a fact which will call for repeated emphasis as we proceed. In addition to these methods of dealing with uncertainty there is (6) the possibility of directing industrial activity more or less along lines in which a minimal amount of uncertainty is involved and avoiding those involving a greater degree.

One of the most immediate and most important consequences of uncertainty in economics may be disposed of as a preliminary to a detailed technical discussion. The essence of organized economic activity is the production by certain persons of goods which will be used to satisfy the wants of other persons. The first question which arises then is, which of these groups in any particular case, producers or consumers, shall do the foreseeing as to the future wants to be

---

[204]Professor Irving Fisher's term {The Nature of Capital and Income, p. 288). I should prefer simply "grouping" as both shorter and more descriptive.

satisfied. It is perhaps obvious that the function of prediction in the technological side of production itself inevitably devolves upon the producer. At first sight it would appear that the consumer should be in a better position to anticipate his own wants than the producer to anticipate them for him, but we notice at once that this is not what takes place. The primary phase of economic organization is the production of goods for a general market, not upon direct order of the consumer. With uncertainty absent it would be immaterial whether the exchange of goods preceded or followed actual production. With uncertainty (in the two fields, production and wants) present it is still conceivable that men might exchange productive services instead of products, but the fact of uncertainty operates to bring about a different result. To begin with, modern society is organized on the theory (whatever the facts, about which some doubt may be expressed) that men predict the future and adapt their conduct to it more effectively when the results accrue to themselves than when the results accrue to others. The responsibilities of controlling production thus devolve upon the producer.

But the consumer does not even contract for his goods in advance, generally speaking. A part of the reason might be the consumer's uncertainty as to his ability to pay at the end of the period, but this does not seem to be important in fact. The main reason is that he does not know what he will want, and how much, and how badly; consequently he leaves it to producers to create goods and hold them ready for his decision when the time comes. The clue to the apparent paradox is, of course, in the "law of large numbers," the consolidation of risks (or uncertainties). The consumer is, to himself, only one; to the producer he is a mere multitude in which individuality is lost. It turns out that an outsider can foresee the wants of a multitude with more ease and accuracy than an individual can attain with respect to his own. This phenomenon gives us the most fundamental feature of the economic system, production for a market, and hence also the general character of the environment in relation to which the effects of uncertainty are to be further investigated. Before continuing the inquiry into other phases and methods of the consolidation of risks, we shall turn briefly to consider the differences among individuals in their attitudes and reactions toward measurable or unmeasurable uncertainty.

We assume, as already observed, that although life is no doubt more interesting when conduct involves a certain amount of uncertainty, — the proper amount varying with individuals and circumstances, — yet that men do actually strive to anticipate the future accurately and adapt their conduct to it. In this respect we may distinguish at least five variable elements in individual attributes and capacities. (1) Men differ in their capacity by perception and inference to form correct judgments as to the future course of events in the environment. This capacity, furthermore, is far from homogeneous, some persons excelling in foresight in one kind of problem situations, others in other kinds, in almost endless variety. Of especial importance is the variation in the power of reading human nature, of forecasting the conduct of other men, as contrasted with scientific judgment in regard to natural phenomena. (2) Another, though related, difference is found in men's capacities to judge means and discern and plan the steps and adjustments necessary to meet the anticipated future situation. (3) There is a similar variation in the power to execute the plans and adjustments believed to be requisite and desirable. (4) In addition there is diversity in conduct in situations involving uncertainty due to differences in the amount of confidence which individuals feel in their judgments when formed and in their powers of execution; this degree of confidence is in large measure independent of the "true value" of the judgments and powers themselves. (5) Distinct from confidence felt is the conative attitude to a situation upon which judgment is passed with a given degree of confidence. It is a familiar fact that some individuals want to be sure and will hardly "take chances" at all, while others like to work on original hypotheses and seem to prefer rather than to shun uncertainty. It is common to see people act on assumptions in ways which their own opinions of the value of the assumption do not warrant; there is a disposition to "trust in one's luck."

The amount of uncertainty effective in a conduct situation is the degree of subjective confidence felt in the contemplated act as a correct adaptation to the future — number 4 above. It is clear that we may speak in some sense of the "true value" of judgment and of capacity to act, but it is the person's own opinion of these values which controls his activities. Hence the five variables are, from the standpoint of the person concerned, reduced to two, the (subjective or felt) uncertainty and his conative feeling toward it. For completeness we should perhaps add a sixth uncertainty factor, in the shape of occurrences so revolutionary and unexpected by any one as hardly to be brought under the category of an error in judgment at all.

In addition to the above enumeration of five or six distinct elements in the uncertainty situation we must point out that the first three variables named are themselves not simple. Judgment or foresight and the capacity for planning and the ability to execute action are each the product of at least four distinguishable factors, in regard to which the faculties in question may vary independently. These are (a) accuracy, (b) promptness or speed (c) time range, and (d) space range, of the capacity or action. The first two of these require no explanation; it is evident that accuracy and rapidity of judgment and execution are more or less independent endowments. The third refers to the length of time in the future to which conduct is or may be adjusted, and the fourth to the scope or magnitude of the situation envisaged and the operations planned. Familiar also is the difference between individuals who have a mind for detail and those who confine their attention to the larger outlines of a situation. Even this rather complex outline is extremely simplified as compared with the facts of life in that it compasses only a rigidly "static" view of the problem. Quite as important as differences obtaining at any moment among individuals in regard to the attributes mentioned are their differences in capacity for change or development along the various lines. Knowledge is more a matter of learning than of the exercise of absolute judgment. Learning requires time, and in time the situation dealt with, as well as the learner, undergoes change.

We have classified the possible reactions to uncertainty under some half-dozen heads, each of which gives rise to special problems, though the social structures for dealing with these problems overlap a good deal. The most fundamental facts regarding uncertainty from our point of view are, first, the possibility of reducing it in amount by grouping instances; and, second, the differences in individuals in relation to uncertainty, giving rise to a tendency to specialize the function of meeting it in the hands of certain individuals and classes. The most fundamental effect of uncertainty on the social-economic organization — production for a general market on the producer's responsibility — has already been taken up; it is primarily a case of reduction of uncertainty by consolidation or grouping of cases. In the mere fact of production for a market, there is little specialization of uncertainty-bearing, and what there is is on a basis of the producer's position in relation to the problem, not his peculiar characteristics as a man. To isolate the phenomenon of production for a market from other considerations we must picture a pure "handicraft stage" of social organization. In such a system every individual would be an independent producer of some one finished commodity, and a consumer of a great variety of products. The late Middle Ages afford a picture of an approximation to such a state of affairs in a part of the industrial field.

The approximation is rather remote, however. A handicraft organization shows an irresistible tendency to pass over, even before well established, into a very different system, and this further development is also a consequence of the presence of uncertainty. The second system is that of "free enterprise" which we find dominant to-day. The difference between free enterprise and mere production for a market represents the addition of specialization of uncertainty-bearing to the grouping of uncertainties, and takes place under pressure of the same problem, the anticipation of wants and control of production with reference to the future. Under free enterprise the solution of this problem, already removed from the consumer himself, is further taken out of the hands of the great mass of producers as well and placed in charge of a limited class of "entrepreneurs" or "business men." The bulk of the producing population cease to exercise responsible control over production and take up the subsidiary role of furnishing productive resources (labor, land, and capital) to the entrepreneur, placing them under his sole direction for a fixed contract price.

We shall take up this phenomenon of free enterprise for detailed discussion in the next chapter, though we may note here two further facts regarding it; first, the "specialization" of uncertainty-bearing in the hands of entrepreneurs involves also a further consolidation; and, second, it is closely connected with changes in technological methods which (a) increase the time length of the production process and correspondingly increase the uncertainty involved, and (b) form producers into large groups working together in a single establishment or productive enterprise and hence necessitates concentration of control. The remainder of the present chapter will be devoted to a survey of the social structures evolved for dealing with uncertainty. Some of the phenomena will thus be finally disposed of, so far as the present work is concerned, especially those which already have a literature of their own and whose general bearings and place in a systematic treatment of uncertainty alone call for notice here. Other problems will be merely sketched in outline and reserved for fuller treatment in subsequent chapters, as has just been done with the subject of entrepreneurship.

Following the order of the classification already given of methods of dealing with uncertainty, the first subject for discussion is the institutions or special phenomena arising from the tendency to deal with uncertainty by consolidation. The most obvious and best known of these devices is, of course, insurance, which has already been repeatedly used as an illustration of the principle of eliminating uncertainty by dealing with groups of cases instead of individual cases. In our discussion of the theory of uncertainty in the foregoing chapter and at other points in the study we have emphasized the radical difference between a measurable and an unmeasurable uncertainty. Now measurability depends on the possibility of assimilating a given situation to a group of similars and finding the proportions of the members of the group which may be expected to exhibit the various possible outcomes. This assimilation of cases into classes may be exceedingly accurate, and the proportions of the various outcomes may be computable on a priori grounds by the application of the theory of permutations and combinations to determine the possible groupings of equally probable alternatives; but this rarely if ever happens in a practical business situation. The classification will be of all degrees of precision, but the ascertainment of proportions must be empirical. The application of the insurance principle, converting a larger contingent loss into a smaller fixed charge, depends upon the measurement of probability on the basis of a fairly accurate grouping into classes. It is in general not enough that the insurer who takes the "risk" of a large number of cases be able to predict his aggregate losses with sufficient accuracy to quote premiums which will keep his business solvent while at the same time imposing a burden on the insurer which is not too large a fraction of his contingent loss. In addition he must be able to present a fairly plausible contention that the particular insured is contributing to the total fund out of which losses are paid as they accrue in an amount corresponding reasonably well with his real probability of loss; i.e., that he is bearing his fair share of the burden.

The difficulty of a satisfactory logical discussion of the questions we are dealing with has repeatedly been emphasized, due to the fact that distinctions of the greatest importance tend to run together through intermediate degrees and become blurred. This is conspicuously the case with the measurability of uncertainty through classification of instances. We hardly find in practice really homogeneous classifications (in the sense in which mathematical probability implies, as in the case of successive throws of a perfect die) and at the other extreme it is hard to find cases which do not admit of some possibility of assimilation into groups and hence of measurement. Indeed, the very concept of contingency seems to preclude absolute uniqueness (as for that matter there is doubtless nothing absolutely unique in the universe). For to say that a certain event is contingent or "possible" or "may happen" appears to be equivalent to saying that "such things " have been known to happen before, and the "such things" manifestly constitute a class of cases formed on some ground or other. The principal subject for investigation is thus the degree of assimilability, or the amount of homogeneity of classes securable, or, stated inversely, the degree of uniqueness various kinds of business contingencies. Insurance deals with those which are "fairly" classifiable or show a relatively low degree of uniqueness, but the different branches of insurance show a wide range of variation in the accuracy of measurement of probability which they secure.

Before taking up various types of insurance we may note in passing a point which it is superfluous to elaborate in this connection, namely, that different forms of organization in the insurance field all operate on the same principle. It matters not at all whether the persons liable to a given contingency organize among themselves into a fraternal or mutual society or whether they separately contract with an outside party to bear their losses as they fall in. Under competitive conditions and assuming that the probabilities involved are accurately known, an outside insurer will make no clear profit and the premiums will under either system be equal to the administrative costs of carrying on the business.

The branch of insurance which is most highly developed, meaning that its contingencies are most accurately measured because its classifications are most perfect, and which is thus on the most nearly "mathematical" basis is, of course, what is called "life insurance." (In so far as it is "insurance" at all, and not a mere investment proposition, it is clear that it is insurance against "premature" loss of earning power, and not against death.) It is possible, on the basis of medical examinations, and taking into account age, sex, place of residence, occupation, and habits of life, to select "risks" which closely approximate the ideal of mechanical probability. The chance of death of two healthy individuals similarly circumstanced in the above regards seems to be about as near an objective equality, the life or death of one rather than the other about as nearly really indeterminate, as anything in nature. To be sure, when we pass outside the relatively narrow circle of "normal" individuals, difficulties are encountered, but the extension of life insurance outside this circle has also been restricted. Some development has taken place in the insurance of sub-standard lives at higher rates, but it is limited in amount and could be characterized as exceptional.[205]

The very opposite situation from life insurance is found in insurance against sickness and accident. Here an objective description and classification of cases is impossible, the business is fraught with great difficulties and susceptible of only a limited development. It is notorious that such policies cost vastly more than they should; indeed, the companies find it profitable to adopt a generous attitude in the adjustment of claims, raising the premium rates accordingly, it is needless to say. Accident compensation for workingmen, under social control, is on a somewhat better footing, but only on condition that the payments are restricted to not too large a fraction of the actual economic loss to the individual, with nothing for discomfort, pain, or inconvenience. In the whole field of personal, physical contingencies, however, there is nothing that is strictly of the nature of a "business risk," unless it be the now happily obsolescent phenomenon of commercial employers' liability insurance.

The typical application of insurance to business hazards is in the protection against loss by fire, and the theory of fire insurance rates forms an interesting contrast with the actuarial mathematics of life insurance. The latter, as we have observed, is a fairly close approximation to objective probability; it is in fact so close to this ideal that life insurance problems are worked by the formulae derived from the binomial law, in the same way as problems in mechanical

[205]It would be out of place here to go into the social aspects of life insurance, but one observation may be worth making. From the social point of view it is arguable that all classification of risks is a bad thing, except in so far as the special hazard is purely occupational and the cost of carrying it can be transferred to the consumer of the product. It is hard to discover any good reason why the unfortunate should be especially burdened because of their handicaps. It would, therefore, be better if all were insured at a uniform rate. Indeed, we may go farther and contend that the rate should be graduated inversely with the risk (occupational risks excepted, as noted). It goes without saying that only a state compulsory insurance scheme could operate on any such principles; under private profit incentives, competition will compel any insurance agency to classify its risks as accurately and minutely as practicable.

probability. Fire insurance rating is a very different proposition; only in rather recent years has any approach been made to the formation of fairly homogeneous classes of risks and the measurement of real probability in a particular case. At best there is a large field for the exercise of "judgment" even after literally thousands of classes of risks have been more or less accurately defined.[206] More important is the fact that, in consequence, insurance does not take care of the whole risk against loss by fire. On account of the "moral hazard" and practical difficulties, it is necessary to restrict the amount of insurance to the "direct loss or damage" or even to a part of that, while of course there are usually large indirect losses due to the interruption of business and dislocation of business plans which are entirely unprovided for. Thus there is a large margin of uncertainty both to insurer and insured, in consequence of the impossibility of objectively homogeneous groupings and accurate measurement of the chance of loss. Corresponding to this margin of uncertainty in the calculations there is a chance for a profit or loss to either party, in connection with the fire hazard. The probabilities in the case of fire are, of course, complicated by the fact that risks are not entirely independent. A fire once started is likely to spread and there is a tendency for losses to occur in groups. In so far, however, as fire losses in the aggregate are calculable in advance, they are or may be converted into fixed costs by every individual exposed to the possibility of loss, and in so far no profit, positive or negative, will be realized by any one on account of this uncertainty in his business.

The principle of insurance has also been utilized to provide against a great variety of business hazards other than fire — the loss of ships and cargoes at sea, destruction of crops by storms, theft and burglary, embezzlement by employees (indirectly through bonding, the employee doing the insuring), payment of damages to injured employees, excessive losses through credit extension, etc. The unusual forms of policies issued by some of the Lloyd's underwriters have attained a certain amount of publicity as popular curiosities. These various types of contingencies offer widely divergent possibilities for "scientific" rate-making, from something like the statistical certainty of life insurance at one extreme to almost pure guesswork at the other, as when Lloyd's insures the business interests concerned that a royal coronation will take place as scheduled, or guarantees the weather in some place having no records to base calculations upon.

[206]Cf. Huebner, Property Insurance, chaps, xvr, xvn.

Even in these extreme cases, however, there is a certain vague grouping of cases on the basis of intuition or judgment; only in this way can we imagine any estimate of a probability being arrived at.

It is therefore seen that the insurance principle can be applied even in the almost complete absence of scientific data for the computation of rates. If the estimates are conservative and competent, it turns out that the premiums received for insuring the most unique contingencies cover the losses; that there is an offsetting of losses and gains from one venture to another, even when there is no discoverable kinship among the ventures themselves. The point seems to be, as already noticed, that the mere fact that judgment is being exercised in regard to the situations forms a fairly valid basis for assimilating them into groups. Various instances of the exercise of (fairly competent) judgment even in regard to the most heterogeneous problems, show a tendency to approach a constancy and predictability of result when aggregated into groups.

The fact which limits the application of the insurance principle to business risks generally is not therefore their inherent uniqueness alone, and the subject calls for further examination. This task will be undertaken in detail in the next chapter, which deals with entrepreneurship. At this point we may anticipate to the extent of making two observations: first, the typical uninsurable (because unmeasurable and this because unclassifiable) business risk relates to the exercise of judgment in the making of decisions by the business man; second, although such estimates do tend to fall into groups within which fluctuations cancel out and hence to approach constancy and measurability, this happens only after the fact and, especially in view of the brevity of a man's active life, can only to a limited extent be made the basis of prediction. Furthermore, the classification or grouping can only to a limited extent be carried out by any agency outside the person himself who makes the decisions, because of the peculiarly obstinate connection of a moral hazard with this sort of risks. The decisive factors in the case are so largely on the inside of the person making the decisions that the "instances" are not amenable to objective description and external control.

Manifestly these difficulties, insuperable when the "consolidation" is to be carried out by an external agency such as an insurance company or association, fall away in so far as consolidation can be effected within the scale of operations of a single individual; and the same will be true of an organization if responsibility can be adequately centralized and unity of interest secured. The possibility of thus reducing uncertainty by transforming it into a measurable risk through grouping constitutes a strong incentive to extend the scale of operations of a business establishment. This fact must constitute one of the important causes of the phenomenal growth in the average size of industrial establishments which is a familiar characteristic of modern economic life. In so far as a single business man, by borrowing capital or otherwise, can extend the scope of his exercise of judgment over a greater number of decisions or estimates, there is a greater probability that bad guesses will be offset by good ones and that a degree of constancy and dependability in the total results will be achieved. In so far uncertainty is eliminated and the desideratum of rational activity realized.

Not less important is the incentive to substitute more effective and intimate forms of association for insurance, so as to eliminate or reduce the moral hazard and make possible the application of the insurance principle of consolidation to groups of ventures too broad in scope to be "swung" by a single enterpriser. Since it is capital which is especially at risk in operations based on opinions and estimates, the form of organization centers around the provisions relating to capital. It is undoubtedly true that the reduction of risk to borrowed capital is the principal desideratum leading to the displacement of individual enterprise by the partnership and the same fact with reference to both owned and borrowed capital explains the substitution of corporate organization for the partnership. The superiority of the higher form of organization over the lower from this point of view consists both in the extension of the scope of operations to include a larger number of individual decisions, ventures, or "instances," and in the more effective unification of interest which reduces the moral hazard connected with the assumption by one person of the consequences of another person's decisions.

The close connection between these two considerations is manifest. It is the special "risk" to which large amounts of capital loaned to a single enterpriser are subject which limits the scope of operations of this form of business unit by making it impossible to secure the necessary property resources. On the other hand, it is the inefficiency of organization, the failure to secure effective unity of interest, and the consequent large risk due to moral hazard when a partnership grows to considerable size, which in turn limit its extension to still larger magnitudes and bring about the substitution of the corporate form of organization. With the growth of large fortunes it becomes possible for a limited number of persons to carry on enterprises of greater and greater magnitude, and to-day we find many very large businesses organized as partnerships. Modifications of partnership law giving this form more of the flexibility of the corporation with reference to the distribution of rights of control, of participation in income, and of title to assets in case of dissolution have also contributed to this change.

With reference to the first of our two points above mentioned, the extension of the scope of operations, the corporation may be said to have solved the organization problem. There appears to be hardly any limit to the magnitude of enterprise which it is possible to organize in this form, so far as mere ability to get the public to buy the securities is concerned. On the second score, however, the effective unification of interests, though the corporation has accomplished much in comparison with other forms of organization, there is still much to be desired. Doubtless the task is impossible, in any absolute sense; nothing but a revolutionary transformation in human nature itself can apparently solve this problem finally, and such a change would, of course, obliterate all moral hazards at once, without organization. In the meanwhile the internal problems of the corporation, the protection of its various types of members and adherents against each other's predatory propensities, are quite as vital as the external problem of safeguarding the public interests against exploitation by the corporation as a unit.[207]

Another important aspect of the relations of corporate organization to risk involves what we have called "diffusion" as well as consolidation. The minute divisibility of ownership and ease of transfer of shares enables an investor to distribute his holdings over a large number of enterprises in addition to increasing the size of a single enterprise. The effect of this distribution on risk is evidently twofold. In the first place, there is to the investor a further offsetting through consolidation; the losses and gains in different corporations in which he owns stock must tend to cancel out in large measure and provide a higher degree of regularity and predictability in his total returns.

[207]Haney (Business Organization and Combination, chap, xxm) uses the terms "The Corporation Problem" and "The Trust Problem" to designate what I have called the "internal" and "external" problems respectively. He properly emphasizes the importance of the former in view of the tendency of the evils of monopoly, etc., to overshadow it in the popular mind and in much of the literature of the subject.

And again, the chance of loss of a small fraction of his total resources is of less moment even proportionally than a chance of losing a larger part.

There are other aspects of the question which must be passed over in this summary view. Doubtless a significant fact is the greater publicity attendant upon the organization, resources, and operations of a corporation, due to its being a creature of the State and to legal safeguards. It must be emphasized that this type of organization actually reduces risks, and does not merely transfer them from one party to another, as might seem at first glance to be the case. Superficial discussions of limited liability tend to give the impression, or at least leave the way open to the conclusion, that this is the main advantage over the partnership. But it must be evident that the mere fact of limited liability only serves to transfer losses in excess of invested resources from the owners of the concern to its creditors; and if this were the only effect of incorporation, the loss in credit standing should offset the gain in security to the owners. The vital facts are the twofold consolidation of risks, together with greater publicity, and diffusion in a minor role, not really separable from t he fact of consolidation.

It is particularly noteworthy that large-scale organization has shown a tendency to grow in fields where division of labor is absent and consolidation or grouping of uncertainties is the principal incentive. Occupations in which the work is of an occasional and intermittent character tend to run into partnerships and even corporations where there is no capital investment, or relatively little, and the members work independently at identical tasks. Examples are the syndicating of detectives, stenographers, and even lawyers and doctors.

The second of the two main principles for dealing with uncertainty is Specialization. The most important instrument in modern economic society for the specialization of uncertainty, after the institution of free enterprise itself, is Speculation. This phenomenon also combines different principles, and the mere specialization of uncertainty-bearing in the hands of persons most willing to assume the function is probably among the lesser rather than the greater sources of gain. It seems best to postpone for the present a detailed theoretical analysis of the factors of specialization of uncertainty-bearing in the light of the many ways in which individuals differ in their relations to uncertainty; this discussion will be taken up in the next chapter, in connection with the treatment of enterprise and entrepreneurship. At this point we wish merely to emphasize the association in several ways between specialization and actual reduction of uncertainty.

Most fundamental among these effects in reducing uncertainty is its conversion into a measured risk or elimination by grouping which is implied in the very fact of specialization. The typical illustration to show the advantage of organized speculation to business at large is the use of the hedging contract. By this simple device the industrial producer is enabled to eliminate the chance of loss or gain due to changes in the value of materials used in his operations during the interval between the time he purchases them as raw materials and the time he disposes of them as finished product, "shifting" this risk to the professional speculator. It is manifest at once that even aside from any superior judgment or foresight or better information possessed by such a professional speculator, he gains an enormous advantage from the sheer magnitude or breadth of the scope of his operations. Where a single flour miller or cotton spinner would be in the market once, the speculator enters it hundreds or thousands of times, and his errors in judgment must show a correspondingly stronger tendency to cancel out and leave him a constant and predictable return on his operations.

The same reasoning holds good for any method of specializing uncertainty-bearing. Specialization implies concentration, and concentration involves consolidation; and no matter how heterogeneous the "cases" the gains and losses neutralize each other in the aggregate to an extent increasing as the number of cases thrown together is larger. Specialization itself is primarily an application of the insurance principle; but, like large-scale enterprise, it grows up to meet uncertainty situations where, on account of the impossibility of objective definition and external control of the individual ventures or uncertainties, a "moral hazard" prevents insurance by an external agency or a loose association of venturers for this single purpose.

Besides organized speculation as carried on in connection with produce and security exchanges, the principle of specialization is exemplified m the tendency for the highly uncertain or speculative aspects of industry to become separated from the stable and predictable aspects and be taken over by different establishments. This is, of course, what has really taken place in the ordinary form of speculation already noticed, namely, the separation of the marketing function from the technological side of production, the former being much more speculative than the latter. A separation perhaps equally significant in modern economic life is that which so commonly takes place between the establishment or founding of new enterprises and their operation after they are set going. To be sure, by no means all the business of promotion comes under this head, but still the tendency is manifest. A part of the investors in promoted concerns look to the future earnings from regular operations for their return, but a large part expect to sell out at a profit after the business is established, and to devote their capital to some new venture of the same sort. A considerable and increasing number of individual promoters and corporations give their exclusive attention to the launching of new enterprises, withdrawing entirely as soon as the prospects of the business become fairly determinate. The gain from arrangements of this sort arises largely from the consolidation of uncertainties, their conversion by grouping into measured risks which are for the group of cases not uncertainties at all. Such a promoter takes it as a matter of course that a certain proportion of his ventures will be failures and involve heavy losses, while a larger proportion will be relatively unprofitable, and counts on making his gains from the occasional conspicuous successes. That is — to face frankly that paradoxical element which is really involved in such calculations — he does not "expect" to have his "expectations" verified by the results in every case; the expectations on which he really counts are based on an average, on an "estimate" of the long-run value of his "estimates." The specialization in the speculative phase of the business enables a single man or firm to deal with a larger number of ventures, and is clearly a mode of applying the same principle which underlies ordinary insurance.

Other illustrations of the same phenomenon will come to the reader's mind. Industries which utilize land whose value is largely speculative are more likely to rent rather than own their sites where the nature of the utilization makes such a procedure practicable. Even expensive machines and articles of equipment of other sorts, ownership of which involves heavy risks to a small concern, may be rented instead of bought outright. The owner of leased land or equipment is presumably a specialist in that sort of business and his risks are reduced by the grouping of a larger number of ventures.

Other advantages of specialization of speculative functions in addition to the reduction" of uncertainty through consolidation are manifest, and no intention of belittling or concealing them is implied in the separation of the latter aspect of the case in the foregoing discussion. It is apparent in particular that the specialist in any line of risk-taking naturally knows more about the problem with which he deals than would a venturer who dealt with them only occasionally. Hence, since most of these uncertainties relate chiefly to the exercise of judgment, the uncertainty itself is reduced by this fact also. There is in this respect a fundamental difference between the speculator or promoter and the insurer, which must be kept clearly in view. The insurer knows more about the risk in a particular case — say of a building burning — but the real risk is no less because he assumes it in that particular case. His risk is less only because he assumes a large number. But the transfer of the "risk" of an error in judgment is a very different matter. The "insurer" (entrepreneur, speculator, or promoter) now substitutes his own judgment for the judgment of the man who is getting rid of the uncertainty through transferring it to the specialist. In so far as his knowledge and judgment are better, which they almost certainly will be from the mere fact that he is a specialist, the individual risk is less likely to become a loss, in addition to the gain from grouping. There is better management, greater economy in the use of economic resources, as well as a mere transformation of uncertainty into certainty.

The problem of meeting uncertainty thus passes inevitably into the general problem of management, of economic control. The fundamental uncertainties of economic life are the errors in predicting the future and in making present adjustments to fit future conditions. In so far as ignorance of the future is due to practical indeterminateness in nature itself we can only appeal to the law of large numbers to distribute the losses, and make them calculable, not to reduce them in amount, and this is only possible in so far as the contingencies to be dealt with admit of assimilation into homogeneous groups; i.e., in so far as they repeat themselves. When our ignorance of the future is only partial ignorance, incomplete knowledge and imperfect inference, it becomes impossible to classify instances objectively, and any changes brought about in the conditions surrounding the formation of an opinion are nearly sure to affect the intrinsic value of the opinion itself. This is true even of the method of grouping by extending the scale of operations of a single entrepreneur, for the quality of his estimates will not be independent of the number he has to make and the mass of the data involved.

But it is especially true of grouping by specialization, as we have seen. The inseparability of the uncertainty problem and the managerial problem will be especially important in the discussion (in the next chapter) of entrepreneurship, which is the characteristic phenomenon of modern economic organization and is essentially a device for specializing uncertainty-bearing or the improvement of economic control. The relation between management, which consists of making decisions, and taking the consequences of decisions, which is the most fundamental form of risk-taking in industry, will be found to be a very intricate as well as intimate one. When the sequence of control is followed through to the end, it will be found that from the standpoint of the ultimately responsible manager, the two functions are always inseparable.

We are thus brought naturally around to a discussion of the most thoroughgoing methods of dealing with uncertainty; i.e., by securing better knowledge of and control over the future. As previously observed, however, these methods represent merely the objective of all rational conduct from the outset, and they call for discussion in such a work as the present only in so far as they affect the general outline of the social economic structure. Thus it is fundamental to the entrepreneur system that it tends to promote better management in addition to consolidating risks and throwing them into the hands of those most disposed to assume them. The only further comment here called for is to point out the existence of highly specialized industrial structures performing the functions of furnishing knowledge and guidance.

One of the principal gains through organized speculation is the provision of information on business conditions, making possible more intelligent forecasting of market changes. Not merely do the market associations or exchanges and their members engage in this work on their own account. Its importance to society at large is so well recognized that vast sums of public money are annually expended in securing and disseminating information as to the output of various industries, crop conditions, and the like. Great investments of capital and elaborate organizations are also devoted to the work as a private enterprise, on a profit-seeking basis, and the importance of trade journals and statistical bureaus and services tends to increase, as does that of the activities of the Government in this field. The collection, digestion, and dissemination in usable form of economic information is one of the staggering problems connected with our modern large-scale social organization. It goes without saying that no very satisfactory solution of this problem has been achieved, and it is safe to predict that none will be found in the near future. But all these specialized agencies for the supply of information help to bridge the wide gap between what the individual business manager knows or can find out by the use of his own resources and what he would have to know to conduct his business in a perfectly intelligent fashion. Their output increases the value of the intuitive "judgments" on the basis of which his decisions are finally made after all, and greatly extends the scope of the environment in relation to which he can more or less intelligently react.

The foregoing relates chiefly to the production side of the problem of economic information. In the field of information for consumers, we have the still more staggering development of advertising. This complex phenomenon cannot be discussed in detail here, beyond pointing out its connection with the fact of ignorance and the necessity of knowledge to guide conduct. Only a part of advertising is in any proper sense of the term informative. A larger part is devoted to persuasion, which is a different thing from conviction, and perhaps the stimulation or creation of new wants is a function distinguishable from either. In addition to advertising, most of the social outlay for education is connected with informing the population about the means of satisfying wants, the education of taste. The outstanding fact is that the ubiquitous presence of uncertainty permeating every relation of life has brought it about that information is one of the principal commodities that the economic organization is engaged in supplying. From this point of view it is not material whether the "information" is false or true, or whether it is merely hypnotic suggestion. As in all other spheres of competitive economic activity, the consumer is the final judge. If people are willing to pay for "Sunny Jim" poetry and "It Floats" when they buy cereals and soap, then these wares are economic goods. If a certain name on a fountain pen or safety razor enables it to sell at a fifty per cent higher price than the same article would otherwise fetch, then the name represents one third of the economic utility in the article, and is economically no different from its color or design or the quality of the point or cutting edge, or any other quality which makes it useful or appealing. The morally fastidious (and naive) may protest that there is a distinction between "real" and "nominal" utilities; but they will find it very dangerous to their optimism to attempt to follow the distinction very far. On scrutiny it will be found that most of the things we spend our incomes for and agonize over, and notably practically all the higher "spiritual" values, gravitate swiftly into the second class.

Somewhat different from the production and sale of information is the dealing in actual instructions for the guidance of conduct directly. Modern society is characterized by the rapid growth of this line of industry also. There have always been a few professions whose activities consisted essentially of the sale of guidance, notably medicine and the law, and more or less the preaching and teaching professions. Recent years, however, have witnessed a veritable swarming of experts and consultants in nearly every department of industrial life. The difference from dealing in information is that these people do not stop at diagnosis; in addition they prescribe. They are equally conspicuous in the fields of business organization, accounting, the treatment of labor, the lay-out of plants, and the processing of materials; they are the scientific managers of the managers of business; and though they by no means serve business or its managers for naught, and in spite of a large amount of quackery, they probably pay their way and more on the whole in increasing the efficiency of production. Certainly they do a useful work in forcing the intelligent, critical consideration of business problems instead of a blind following of tradition or the use of guesswork methods.[208]

The last of the alternatives named for meeting uncertainty relates to the problem of a tendency to prefer relatively predictable lines of activity to more speculative operations. It is common to assume[209] that society pays for the assumption of risk in the form of higher prices for commodities whose production involves uncertainty and a deficient supply of these in comparison with goods of an opposite character. This subject will come up again in connection with the closely related question of a tendency of profit to zero, and it seems best to postpone discussion of it for the present.[210] We shall find reasons for being very skeptical as to the reality of any such abhorrence of uncertainty as to decrease productivity in any line below the level that an equivalent fixed cost would bring about.

---

[208]On the production and sale of "guidance" see J. M. Clark, Journal of Political Economy, vol. 26, Nos. 1 and 2.

[209]Cf . Willett, Economic Theory of Risk and Insurance, chap. ni. 8 Cf. chapter XI.

[210]Cf. chapter XII.

Chapter 9. Enterpise and Profit

We MUST now consider more concretely and in detail the effects of uncertainty on the general form of organization of economic life. The best method seems to be to take up a society in which uncertainty is absent, imagine uncertainty introduced, and try to ascertain what changes will take place in its structure. We therefore return to the argument of chapter IV in which the mechanics of exchange and competition were studied with uncertainty (and progress) absent. The same method will be followed, beginning with the problem in as simple a form as possible and studying the effects of different factors separately, analyzing the complexity of real life "synthetically" by building it up in imagination out of its elements.

To secure the minimum degree of uncertainty and at the same time keep the discussion as close to reality as possible, it is necessary to exercise some care in defining the assumptions with which we are working. The most obvious initial requirement is to eliminate the factors of social progress from consideration and consider first a static society. But this postulate calls for discrimination in handling. In an absolutely unchanging social life there would, as we have repeatedly observed, be no uncertainty whatever, and our analysis in chapter IV proceeded on this assumption. Such conditions are thoroughly incompatible with the most fundamental facts of the world in which we live, but their study serves the analytic purpose of isolating the effects of uncertainty. For different kinds of change and different degrees of change are real facts, and it will therefore involve less abstraction to study hypothetical conditions under which change is restricted to the most fundamental and ineradicable kind and amount. Societies may be and have been nearly unprogressive, and the obvious simplification to make is therefore the elimination of progressive change.

After abstracting all the elements of general progressive change enumerated in chapter V a large amount of uncertainty will be left in human life, due to changes of the character of fluctuations which cannot be thought away without violence to material possibility. Strictly accurate formulation of conditions involving a realistic minimum of uncertainty cannot be made, but are not necessary; it is sufficient to indicate in a rough way the situation we propose to discuss. Several factors affect the amount of uncertainty to be recognized, and have to be taken into account. The first to be noted is the time length of the production process, for the longer it is, the more uncertainty will naturally be involved. Of very great importance also is the general level of economic life. The lower wants of man, those having in the greatest degree the nature of necessities, are the most stable and predictable. The higher up the scale we go, the larger the proportion of the aesthetic element and of social suggestion there is involved in motivation, the greater becomes the uncertainty connected with foreseeing wants and satisfying them. On the production side, on the other hand, most manufacturing processes are more controllable and calculable as to outcome than are agricultural operations under usual conditions. We must notice also the development of science and of the technique of social organization. Greater ability to forecast the future and greater power to control the course of events manifestly reduce uncertainty, and of still greater importance is the status of the various devices noted in the last chapter for reducing uncertainty by consolidation.

All these perplexities about which some more or less definite assumption must be made can be disposed of by being as realistic as possible. Let us say simply that we are talking about the United States in the early years of the twentieth century, but with abstraction made of progressive changes. That is, we assume a population static in numbers and composition and without the mania of change and advance which characterizes modern life. Inventions and improvements in technology and organization are to be eliminated, leaving the general situation as we know it to-day to remain stationary. Similarly in regard to the saving of new capital, development of new natural resources, redistribution of population over the soil or redistribution of ownership of goods, education, etc., among the people. But we shall not assume that men are omniscient and immortal or perfectly rational and free from caprice as individuals. We shall neglect natural catastrophes, epidemics, wars, etc., but take for granted the "usual" uncertainties of the weather and the like, along with the "normal" vicissitudes of mortal life,[211] and uncertainties of human choice.

Returning now to the kind of social organization described in chapter IV,[212] let us inquire as to what will be the effects of introducing the minimum degree of uncertainty into the situation. The essential features of the hypothetical society as thus far constructed need to be kept clearly in mind. Acting as individuals under absolute freedom but without collusion, men are supposed to have organized economic life with primary and secondary division of labor, the use of capital, etc., developed to the point familiar in present-day America. The principal fact which calls for exercise of the imagination is the internal organization of the productive groups or establishments. With uncertainty entirely absent, every individual being in possession of perfect knowledge of the situation, there would be no occasion for anything of the nature of responsible management or control of productive activity. Even marketing operations in any

---

[211]The situation which we here endeavor to delineate is what Dr. A. H. Willett appears to have in mind under the designation of the "approximate static state." See The Economic Theory of Risk and Insurance, pp. 15, 16. In this connection, again, we cannot be rigorously logical and definite without getting off into mere subtleties. We do not know whether there is ultimately real uncertainty and caprice in either physical nature or human nature. It may be that all changes are self-compensating some time, and that if progress were eliminated we should finally achieve prophetic powers in regard to phenomena in the aggregate (through application of the principle of consolidation) if not in individual instances. But in view of the tragically limited success of science in predicting the weather, for example, it is clear that there is no strain on credulity in assuming a large amount of real uncertainty. We must not forget that the periodicity of change or the interval required for canceling out of fluctuations is in practice relative to the length of human life. If such a cancellation would occur ultimately (as some writers, notably Nietzsche, have ventured to suppose) the period is so long in relation to human life that no advantage of it could be taken.

[212]Chapter V, the reader will recall, dealt with the effects of progress with uncertainty absent. We here retrace our steps somewhat in order to consider uncertainty with progress absent, thus completing the design of studying the two factors separately. After completing the present task we shall (in chapter XI) study them in combination. A confusion between the effects of uncertainty and those of progress, which are largely, though never quite completely, separable facts, has been seen to underlie the reasoning of the "dynamic" theory of profit.

realistic sense would not be found. The flow of raw materials and productive services through productive processes to the consumer would be entirely automatic.

We do not need to strain the imagination by supposing supernatural powers of prescience on the part of men. We can think of the adjustment as the result of a long process of experimentation, worked out by trial-and-error methods alone. If the conditions of life and the people themselves were entirely unchanging a definite organization would result, perfect in the sense that no one would be under an incentive to change. So in the organization of the productive groups, it is not necessary to imagine every worker doing exactly the right thing at the right time in a sort of "preestablished harmony" with the work of others. There might be managers, superintendents, etc., for the purpose of coordinating the activities of individuals. But under conditions of perfect knowledge and certainty such functionaries would be laborers merely, performing a purely routine function, without responsibility of any sort, on a level with men engaged in mechanical operations.

With the introduction of uncertainty — the fact of ignorance and necessity of acting upon opinion rather than knowledge — into this Eden-like situation, its character is completely changed. With uncertainty absent, man's energies are devoted altogether to doing things; it is doubtful whether intelligence itself would exist in such a situation; in a world so built that perfect knowledge was theoretically possible, it seems likely that all organic readjustments would become mechanical, all organisms automata. With uncertainty present, doing things, the actual execution of activity, becomes in a real sense a secondary part of life; the primary problem or function is deciding what to do and how to do it. The two most important characteristics of social organization brought about by the fact of uncertainty have already been noticed. In the first place, goods are produced for a market, on the basis of an entirely impersonal prediction of wants, not for the satisfaction of the wants of the producers themselves. The producer takes the responsibility of forecasting the consumers' wants. In the second place, the work of forecasting and at the same time a large part of the technological direction and control of production are still further concentrated upon a very narrow class of the producers, and we meet with a new economic functionary, the entrepreneur.

When uncertainty is present and the task of deciding what to do and how to do it takes the ascendancy over that of execution, the internal organization of the productive groups is no longer a matter of indifference or a mechanical detail.[213] Centralization of this deciding and controlling function is imperative, a process of "cephalization," such as has taken place in the evolution of organic life, is inevitable, and for the same reasons as in the case of biological evolution. Let us consider this process and the circumstances which condition it. The order of attack on the problem is suggested by the classification worked out in chapter VII of the elements in uncertainty in regard to which men may in large measure differ independently.

In the first place, occupations differ in respect to the kind and amount of knowledge and judgment required for their successful direction as well as in the kind of abilities and tastes adapted to the routine operations. Productive groups or establishments now compete for managerial capacity as well as skill, and a considerable rearrangement of personnel is the natural result. The final adjustment will place each producer in the place where his particular combination of the two kinds of attributes seems to be most effective.

But a more important change is the tendency of the groups themselves to specialize, finding the individuals with the greatest managerial capacity of the requisite kinds and placing them in charge of the work of the group, submitting the activities of the other members to their direction and control. It need hardly be mentioned explicitly that the organization of industry depends on the fundamental fact that the intelligence of one person can be made to direct in a general way the routine manual and mental operations of others. It will also be taken into account that men differ in their powers of effective control over other men as well as in intellectual capacity to decide what should be done. In addition, there must come into play the diversity among men in degree of confidence in their judgment and powers and in disposition to act on their opinions, to "venture." This fact is responsible for the most fundamental change of all in the form of organization, the system under which the confident and venturesome "assume the risk" or "insure" the doubtful and timid by guaranteeing to the latter a specified income in return for an assignment of the actual results.

Uncertainty thus exerts a fourfold tendency to select men and specialize functions: (1) an adaptation of men to occupations on the basis of kind of knowledge and judgment; (2) a similar selec-

---

[213]See above, chapter IV, p. 106, note.

tion on the basis of degree of foresight, for some lines of activity call for this endowment in a very different degree from others; (3) a specialization within productive groups, the individuals with superior managerial ability (foresight and capacity of ruling others) being placed in control of the group and the others working under their direction; and (4) those with confidence in their judgment and disposition to "back it up" in action specialize in risk-taking. The close relations obtaining among these tendencies will be manifest. We have not separated confidence and vent tiresomeness at all, since they act along parallel lines and are little more than phases of the same faculty — just as courage and the tendency to minimize danger are proverbially commingled in all fields, though they are separable in thought. In addition the tendencies numbered (3) and (4) operate together. With human nature as we know it it would be impracticable or very unusual for one man to guarantee to another a definite result of the latter's actions without being given power to direct his work. And on the other hand the second party would not place himself under the direction of the first without such a guaranty. The result is a "double contract" of the type famous in the history of the evasion of usury laws. It seems evident also that the system would not work at all if good judgment were not in fact generally associated with confidence in one's judgment on the part both of himself and others. That is, men's judgment of their own judgment and of others' judgment as to both kind and grade must in the large be much more right than wrong.[214]

The result of this manifold specialization of function is enterprise and the wage system of industry. Its existence in the world is a direct result of the fact of uncertainty; our task in the remainder of this study is to examine this phenomenon in detail in its various phases and divers relations with the economic activities of man and the structure of society. It is not necessary or inevitable, not the only conceivable form of organization, but under certain conditions has certain advantages, and is capable of development in different degrees. The essence of enterprise is the specialization of the function of responsible direction of economic life, the neglected feature of which is the inseparability of these two elements, responsibility and control. Under the enterprise system, a special social class, the

[214]The statement implies that a man's judgment has in an effective sense a true or objective value. This assumption will be justified by the further course of the argument.

business men, direct economic activity; they are in the strict sense the producers, while the great mass of the population merely furnish them with productive services, placing their persons and their property at the disposal of this class; the entrepreneurs also guarantee to those who furnish productive services a fixed remuneration. Accurately to define these functions and trace them through the social structure will be a long task, for the specialization is never complete; but at the end of it we shall find that in a free society the two are essentially inseparable. Any degree of effective exercise of judgment, or making decisions, is in a free society coupled with a corresponding degree of uncertainty-bearing, of taking the responsibility for those decisions.

With the specialization of function goes also a differentiation of reward. The produce of society is similarly divided into two kinds of income, and two only, contractual income, which is essentially rent, as economic theory has described incomes, and residual income or profit. But the differentiation of contractual income, like that of profit, is never complete; neither variety is ever met with in a pure form, and every real income contains elements of both rent and profit. And with uncertainty present (the condition of the differentiation itself) it is not possible even to determine just how much of any income is of one kind and how much of the other; but a partial separation can be made, and the causal distinction between the two kinds is sharp and clear.

We may imagine a society in which uncertainty is absent transformed on the introduction of uncertainty into an enterprise organization. The readjustments will be carried out by the same trial-and-error methods under the same motives, the effort of each individual to better himself, which we have already described. The ideal or limiting condition constantly in view would still be the equalization of all available alternatives of conduct by each individual through the distribution of efforts and of expenditure of the proceeds of effort among the lines open. Under the new system labor and property services actually come into the market, become commodities and are bought and sold. They are thus brought into the comparative value scale and reduced to homogeneity in price terms with the fund of values made up of the direct means of want satisfaction.

Another feature of the new adjustment is that a condition of perfect equilibrium is no longer possible. Since productive arrangements are made on the basis of anticipations and the results actually achieved do not coincide with these as a usual thing, the oscillations will not settle down to zero. For all changes made by individuals relate to the established value scale and this price-system will be subject to fluctuations due to unforeseen causes; consequently individual changes in arrangements will continue indefinitely to take place. The experiments by which alone the value of human judgment is determined involve a proportion of failures or errors, are never complete, and in view of human mortality have constantly to be recommenced at the beginning.

We turn now to consider in broad outline the two types of individual income implied in the enterprise system of organization, contractual income and profit.[215] We shall try as hitherto to explain events by placing ourselves in the actual positions of the men acting or making decisions and interpreting their acts in terms of ordinary human motives. The setting of the problem is a free competitive situation in which all men and material agents are competing for employment, including all men at the time engaged as entrepreneurs, while all entrepreneurs are competing for productive services and at the same time all men are competing for positions as entrepreneurs. The essential fact in understanding the reaction to this situation is that men are acting, competing, on the basis of what they think of the future. To simplify the picture and make it concrete we shall as before assume that there exists some sort of grouping of men and things under the control of other men as entrepreneurs (a random grouping will do as a start) and that entrepreneurs and others are in competition as above stated.

The production-distribution system is worked out through offers and counter-offers, made on the basis of anticipations, of two kinds. The laborer asks what he thinks the entrepreneur will be able to pay, and in any case will not accept less than he can get from some other entrepreneur, or by turning entrepreneur himself. In the same way the entrepreneur offers to any laborer what he thinks he must in order to secure his services, and in any case not more than he thinks the laborer will actually be worth to him, keeping in mind what he

[215] As already observed, the theoretical features of contractual income are those associated with rent in the conventional distributive analysis. From the point of view of our present assumptions, all productive goods being fixed in amount and in their distribution among the members of society, such incomes might naturally be called wages. As we have insisted that there is no significant causal or ethical difference in the sources of income it does not particularly matter what they are called.

can get by turning laborer himself. The whole calculation is in the future; past and even present conditions operate only as grounds of prediction as to what may be anticipated.[216]

Since in a free market there can be but one price on any commodity, a general wage rate must result from this competitive bidding. The rate established may be described as the socially or competitively anticipated value of the laborer's product, using the term "product" in the sense of specific contribution, as already explained. It is not the opinion of the future held by either party to an employment bargain which determines the rate; these opinions merely set maximum and minimum limits outside of which the agreement cannot take place. The mechanism of price adjustment is the same as in any other market. There is always an established uniform rate, which is kept constantly at the point which equates the supply and demand. If at any moment there are more bidders willing to employ at a higher rate than there are employees willing to accept the established rate, the rate will rise accordingly, and similarly if there is a balance of opinion in the opposite direction. The final decision by any individual as to what to do is based on a comparison of a momentarily existing price with a subjective judgment of significance of the commodity. The judgment in this case relates to the indirect significance derived from a twofold estimate of the future, involving both technological and price uncertainties. The employer in deciding whether to offer the current wage, and the employee in deciding whether to accept it, must estimate the technical or physically measured product (specific contribution) of the labor and the price to be expected for that product when it comes upon the market. The estimation may involve two sorts of calculation or estimate of probability. The venture itself may be of the nature of a gamble, involving a large proportion of inherently unpredictable factors. In such a case the decision depends upon an "estimate" of an "objective probabil-

---

[216]In actual society freedom of choice between employer and employee status depends normally on the possession of a minimum amount of capital. The degree of abstraction involved in assuming such freedom is not serious, however, since demonstrated ability can always get funds for business operations. A propertyless employer can make the contractual payments secure by insurance even when they may involve loss, and complete separation of the risk-taking and control function from that of furnishing productive services is possible if there is a high development of organization and a high code of business honor. But the conditions generally necessary in real life for the giving of effective guarantees must also be taken into account as we proceed.

ity" of success, or of a series of such probabilities corresponding to various degrees of success or failure. And normally, in the case of intelligent men, account will be taken of the probable "true value" of the estimates in the case of all estimated factors.

The meaning of the term "social" or "competitive" anticipation will now be clear. The question in the mind of either party to an employment agreement relates simply to the fact of a difference between the current standard of remuneration for the services being bargained for and his own estimate of their worth, discounted by probability allowances. The magnitude of the difference is altogether immaterial. The prospective employer may know absolutely that the service has a value to him ever so much greater than the price he is paying, but he will have to pay only the competitively established rate, and his purchase will affect this rate no more than if he were ever so hesitant about the bargain, just so he makes it. It is the general estimate of the magnitudes involved, in the sense of a "marginal" demand price, which fixes the actual current rate.

In many respects the nature of the organization we are now dealing with is the same as that described in chapter IV, with uncertainty and progress absent. The value of a laborer or piece of material equipment to a particular productive group is determined by the specific physical contribution to output under the principle of diminishing returns with increase in the proportion of that kind of agency in the combination, and on the price of this contribution under the principle of diminishing utility with increase in the proportion of productive energy devoted to making the particular product turned out by the establishment in question. But the facts upon which the working-out of the organization depends can no longer be objectively determined with accuracy by experiment; all the data in the case must be estimated, subject to a larger or smaller margin of error, and this fact causes differences more fundamental than the resemblances in the two situations. The function of making these estimates and of "guaranteeing" their value to the other participating members of the group falls to the responsible entrepreneur in each establishment, producing a new type of activity and a new type of income entirely unknown in a society where uncertainty is absent.

Even in the hypothetical situation dealt with in chapter IV there would be likely to be a concentration of certain control and coordinating functions in a separate person or group of persons in each productive group. But the duties of such persons would be of a routine character merely, in no significant respect different from those of any other operatives; they would be laborers among laborers and their incomes would be wages like other wages. When, however, the managerial function comes to require the exercise of judgment involving liability to error, and when in consequence the assumption of responsibility for the correctness of his opinions becomes a condition prerequisite to getting the other members of the group to submit to the manager's direction, the nature of the function is revolutionized; the manager becomes an entrepreneur. He may, and typically will, to be sure, continue to perform the old mechanical routine functions and to receive the old wages; but in addition he makes responsible decisions, and his income will normally contain in addition to wages a pure differential element designated as "profit" by the economic theorist. This profit is simply the difference between the market price of the productive agencies he employs, the amount which the competition of other entrepreneurs forces him to guarantee to them as a condition of securing their services, and the amount which he finally realizes from the disposition of the product which under his direction they turn out.

The character of the entrepreneur's income is evidently complex, and the relations of its component elements subtle. It contains an element which is ordinary contractual income, received on the ground of routine services performed by the entrepreneur personally for the business (wages) or earned by property which belongs to him (rent or capital return). And the differential element is again complex, for it is clear that there is an element of calculation and an element of luck in it. An adequate examination and analysis of this phenomenon requires time and careful thinking. The background of the problem should now be clear: the uncertainty of all life and conduct which call for the exercise of judgment in business, the economy of division of labor which compels men to work in groups and to delegate the function of control as other functions are specialized, the facts of human nature which make it necessary for one who directs the activities of others to assume responsibility for the results of the operations, and finally the competitive situation which pits the judgment of each entrepreneur against that of the extant business world in adjusting the contractual incomes which he must pay before he gets anything for himself.

The first step in attacking the problem is to inquire into the meaning of entrepreneur ability and its conditions of demand and supply. In regard to the first main division of the entrepreneur's income, the ordinary wage for the routine services of labor and property furnished to the business, no comment is necessary. This return is merely the competitive rate of pay for the grade of ability or kind of property in question. To be sure, it may not be possible in practice to say exactly what this rate is. Not merely is perfect standardization of things and services unattainable under the fluctuating conditions of real life, but in addition the conditions of the entrepreneur specialization may well bring it about that the same things are not done under closely comparable conditions by entrepreneurs and non-entrepreneurs. Hence the separation between the pure wage or rent element and the elements arising out of uncertainty cannot generally be made with complete accuracy. The serious difficulty comes with the attempt to deal with the relation between judgment and luck in determining that part of the entrepreneur's income which is associated with the performance of his peculiar twofold function of (a) exercising responsible control and (b) securing the owners of productive services against uncertainty and fluctuation in their incomes. Clearly this special income is also connected with a sort of effort and sacrifice and into the nature and conditions of supply and demand of the capacities and dispositions for these efforts and sacrifices it must be pertinent to inquire.

It is unquestionable that the entrepreneur's activities effect an enormous saving to society, vastly increasing the efficiency of economic production. Large-scale operations, highly organized industry, and minute division of labor would be impossible without specialization of the managerial function, and human nature being as it is, the guaranteeing function must apparently go along with that of control; indeed, in the ultimate sense of control the two are not even theoretically separable. Thus there would be a large saving even outside of any question of the superior abilities of certain individuals over other individuals for the performance of this function. And there is still another gain of large magnitude through the reduction of uncertainty by the principle of consolidation, which also is independent of the personal attributes of the entrepreneur. But these economies, due to the system as such, and not to activities of the individuals performing a special function, accrue to society; no cause can be discovered in this connection alone which would give rise to a special distributive share.

As to the actual comparative magnitude of the various elements of gain secured through the enterprise system it would be rash to guess, but certainly a very large real gain is secured through the selection of managers having superior fitness for the work. Now it is of supreme importance that such selection is possible only because and in so far as such fitness can be identified in advance of its demonstration in each particular case. The prospective entrepreneur himself has an opinion of his own suitability, in so far as he forms an estimate of the true value of his prognostications and policies. Other persons may or may not agree with his opinion of himself. A man may actually get into the position of entrepreneur in several ways. If he has property or known personal productive powers of a technological sort he may assume the functions of entrepreneur without convincing any one outside himself of any special fitness to exercise them. As long as his own resources safeguard the interests of the persons to whom he agrees to pay contractual incomes these persons need not worry about the correctness of the judgments on which the entrepreneur's policies are based. If he cannot make such guarantees he must, of course, convince either the persons with whom he makes wage or rent bargains or some outside party who will underwrite the guarantees for him. The effect of this transfer of the guarantee function on the nature of entrepreneurship is a subtle question and will be taken up presently. It might even conceivably happen, in the third place, that a person not judging himself especially fit to control industrial policies would get into the place of entrepreneur, if other persons have a sufficiently high opinion of his abilities and trustworthiness. This case is more complicated still and its treatment must also be deferred. Discussion of divided entrepreneurship will lead naturally to the problem of the hired manager, most difficult of all. Let us consider first the simple case of unique and undivided exercise of the function, the control and uncertainty-bearing being all concentrated in the same individual, under the assumption that outsiders whether employed by him or not have neither opinions upon nor interest in the question of his competence. It will further simplify the problem if we begin by assuming that this is the only type of entrepreneurship in our society.

First, a further word as to the character of the process by which the entrepreneur's income is fixed. It may be distinguished from the contractual returns received for services not involving the exercise of judgment, and which are paid by the entrepreneur, by pointing out that the latter are imputed, while his own income is residual. That is, in a sense, the entrepreneur's income is not "determined" at all; it is "what is left" after the others are "determined." The competition of entrepreneurs bidding in the market for the productive services in existence in the society "fix" prices upon these; the entrepreneur's income is not fixed, but consists of whatever remains over after the fixed incomes are paid. Hence we must examine the entrepreneur's income indirectly, by inquiring into the forces which determine the fixed incomes, in relation to the whole product of an enterprise or of society.

Assuming perfect competition in the market for productive services, the contractual incomes are fixed for every entrepreneur by the competitive or marginal anticipations of entrepreneurs as a group in relation to the supply of each kind of agency in existence. Whether any particular individual becomes an entrepreneur or not depends on his believing (strongly enough to act upon the conviction) that he can make productive services yield more than the price fixed upon them by what other persons think they can make them yield (with the same provision that the belief must lead to action). After any individual has become an entrepreneur, the amount of his income depends on his success in producing the anticipated excess, and in this sense is a matter of the correctness of his judgment. But it is clear that his success is equally a matter of (a) the failure of the judgment, or (b) an inferiority in capacity, on the part of his competitors. The two factors of (a) capacity and (b) judgment of one's capacity are inseparably connected, and business capacity is again compounded of judgment (of factors external to the person judging) and executive capacity.

Moreover, there is in the exercise of the best judgment and highest capacity an inevitable margin of error. A successful outcome in any particular case cannot be attributed entirely to judgment and capacity even taken together. The best men would fail in a certain proportion of cases and the worst perhaps succeed in a certain proportion. The results of one trial or of a small number of trials can at most establish a certain presumption in favor of the view that ability has or has not been shown.[217] A dependable estimate of ability can

[217]As has been well observed in connection with games of skill. It is not necessarily a proof of high skill to make a twenty-foot putt in golf or pierce a two-inch bull's-eye at a hundred yards with a rifle; nor a lack of skill to miss a three-foot putt or strike outside the eight-inch circle. Either would happen sometimes with good shots or poor; only the proportion of successes and failures in a fair number of trials gives any indication of real ability to do the trick.

only come from a considerable number of trials. Even then there are differences in kind of ability, as well as degree. And in business management no two instances, perhaps, are ever very closely alike, in any objective, describable sense. It is one of the mysteries of the workings of mind that we are able to form estimates of "general ability " which have any value, but the fact that we do is of course indisputable.

Still further, the venture itself may be a gamble, as we have repeatedly pointed out. Most decisions calling for the exercise of judgment in business or responsible life in any field involve factors not subject to estimate and which no one makes any pretense of estimating. The judgment itself is a judgment of the probability of a certain outcome, of the proportion of successes which would be achieved if the venture could be repeated a large number of times. The allowance for luck is therefore twofold. It requires a large number of trials to show the real probabilities in regard to which judgment is exercised in any given kind of case as well as to distinguish between intrinsic quality in the judgment and mere accident. And bearing in mind again the extreme crudeness of the classification of instances at best, the marvel grows that we are able to live as intelligently as we do. Let us now attempt to state the principles determining entrepreneur income more accurately and in the form of laws of demand and supply.

The demand for a productive service depends upon the steepness of the curve of diminishing returns from increasing amounts of other kinds of services applied to the first. In the familiar case of land, the more rapidly the returns from increased applications of labor and capital applied to a given plot of land fall off, the higher will be the rent on land. Now there is evidently a law of diminishing returns governing the combination of productive services with entrepreneurs. It is based on the fact already stated of limitation in the space range of foresight and executive capacity. The greater the magnitude of operations which any single individual attempts to direct the less effective in general he will be — "beyond a certain point," as in other cases of the law. The demand for entrepreneurs, again, like that for any productive agency, depends directly upon the supply of other agencies.

The supply of entrepreneurs involves the factors of (a) ability, with the various elements therein included, (b) willingness, (c) power to give satisfactory guarantees, and (d) the coincidence of these factors. If society as a whole secures a high quality of management for its enterprises it will be through a coincidence of ability with willingness, or of all three factors, as well as through an abundant supply of the elements separately. Willingness plus power to give guarantees, not backed up by ability, will evidently lead to a dissipation of resources, while ability without the other two factors will be merely wasted. To find men capable of managing business efficiently and secure to them the positions of responsible control is perhaps the most important single problem of economic organization on the efficiency side.

The supply of entrepreneur qualities in society is one of the chief factors in determining the number and size of its productive units. It is a common and perhaps justifiable opinion that most of the other factors tend toward greater economy with increasing size in the establishment, and that the chief limitation on size is the capacity of the leadership. If this is true the ability to handle large enterprises successfully, when it is met with, must tend to secure very large rewards. The income of any particular entrepreneur will in general tend to be larger: (1) as he himself has ability, and good luck; but (2), perhaps more important, as there is in the society a scarcity of self-confidence combined with the power to make effective guarantees to employees. The abundance or scarcity of mere ability to manage business successfully exerts relatively little influence on profit; the main thing is the rashness or timidity of entrepreneurs (actual and potential) as a class in bidding up the prices of productive services. Entrepreneur income, being residual, is determined by the demand for these other services, which demand is a matter of the self-confidence of entrepreneurs as a class, rather than upon a demand for entrepreneur services in a direct sense. We must see at once that it is perfectly possible for entrepreneurs as a class to sustain a net loss, which would merely have to be made up out of their earnings in some other capacity. This would be the natural result in a population combining low ability with high "courage." On the other hand, if men generally judge their own abilities well, the general rate of profit will probably be low, whether ability itself is low or high, but much more variable and fluctuating for a low level of real capacity. The condition for large profits is a narrowly limited supply of high-grade ability with a low general level of initiative as well as ability.

The analysis of profit is much simplified for students of political economy by the fact that the conventional distribution has placed such (misguided) emphasis on the concept of residual income, notably, of course, in the treatment of rent. Yet it will not do to press the parallel too far, for there is this important difference: Rent — and as every one now understands, any other share as well — is residual after the products of the other shares are deducted (product being the marginal contribution of a single unit multiplied by the number of units). But profit (under the simplified conditions we are now dealing with) is the residue after deduction of the payment for the other agencies, determined by the marginal bid of entrepreneurs as a class for all agencies as aggregates. The residue in the latter case is not a product residue, but a margin of error in calculation on the part of the non-entrepreneurs and entrepreneurs who do not force the successful entrepreneurs to pay as much for productive services as they could be forced to pay.

As the argument is quite complicated, it will be well to recapitulate. We have assumed in this first approximation that each man in society knows his own powers as entrepreneur, but that men know nothing about each other in this capacity. The division of social income between profits and contractual income then depends on the supply of entrepreneur ability in the society and the rapidity of diminishing returns from (other factors applied to) it, the size of the profit share increasing as the supply of ability is small and as the returns diminish more rapidly. If men are poor judges of their own powers as well as ignorant of those of other men, the size of the profit share depends on whether they tend on the whole to overestimate or underestimate the prospects of business operations, being larger if they underestimate. These statements abstract from the question of possession of means to guarantee the fixed incomes which they contract to pay; limitations in this respect act as limitations on the supply of entrepreneur ability. If entrepreneur ability is of such high quality that it practically is not subject to diminishing returns, the competition among even a very few such men will raise the rate of contractual returns and lower the residual share, if they know their own powers. If they do not, the size of their profits will again depend on their "optimism," varying inversely with the latter.

A man's knowledge of his own powers involves knowledge of the amount of uncertainty he deals with in trusting his own judgment, which, if the scale of operations is large enough, means the absence of uncertainty in the effective sense, if the knowledge is complete.

Even if judgment itself subject to error is exercised in regard to the real probabilities in an intrinsic gambling situation, we have for the uncertainty in the situation as a whole an objective probability with predictable results for a large number of cases. The presence of true profit, therefore, depends on an absolute uncertainty in the estimation of the value of judgment, or on the absence of the requisite organization for combining a sufficient number of instances to secure certainty through consolidation. With men in complete ignorance of the powers of judgment of other men it is hard to see how such organization could be effected. Yet so elusive is the mechanism by which we know our world, so great the capacity of mind for seizing upon indirect methods of increasing certainty, that a further sweeping reservation must be made. If men, ignorant of other men's powers, know that these other men themselves know their own powers, the results of general knowledge of all men's powers may be secured; and this is true even if such knowledge is (as it is in fact) very imperfectly or not at all communicable. If those who furnish productive services for a contractual remuneration know that those who bid for the services know what they are worth to themselves, the bidders, or if each bidder knows this to be true of the others, the latter will be forced to pay all that they are willing to pay, which is to say all that they can pay. To be sure, competition under such conditions would be likely to take on the character of a poker game, a bluffing contest. But it must be admitted that actual wage bargains are in no slight degree of this character.

The case of European exploiters among primitive peoples illustrates the possibility of large profits to be made by a small number of men who know what they are doing among a large number who do not. But if they compete among themselves there must come a time, if their number increases, when they will force prices to their competitive level without any action on the part of the exploited masses more shrewd than that of accepting a larger offer in preference to a smaller one. The number of competitors required to bring about this result depends upon the steepness of the curve of diminishing returns from entrepreneurship, upon the limitation of the scope of enterprise one man can deal with effectively. And the idea of scope must be extended to include the variety of situations to be dealt with. The question of diminishing returns from entrepreneurship is really a matter of the amount of uncertainty present.[218] To imag-

[218]The diminishing returns of management is a subject often referred to in

ine that one man could adequately manage a business enterprise of indefinite size and complexity is to imagine a situation in which effective uncertainty is entirely absent.

The entire foregoing argument has dealt with a simplified situation inasmuch as the members of our society have been assumed to know something about the true value, each of his own judgment and ability to control events in accordance with it, but to know these things about each other only as the other man's own opinion of himself is manifested in his dispositions to act. In fact men form judgments of other men on the basis of watching their performances over a period of time, and in addition form impressions having some claim to validity from mere personal appearance, conversation, etc. Such knowledge of others is one of the most important factors in our efforts to live together intelligently in organized society. It is the most difficult to discuss scientifically of all the data connected with the practical bearings of knowledge and uncertainty.

Estimates of the worth of other men's opinions and capabilities probably form by far the largest part of the data on which any individual makes decisions in his own life, at least in the sphere of economic activity where such activity is highly organized. Such estimates function as an indirect indication of what we may expect to happen in any set of conditions; we know and give ourselves credit for knowing nothing of value about the problem itself, but we know what is the belief of other men whose judgment we respect and which we accept in place of an opinion of our own. The degree of confidence which we feel in our own situation is simply the degree

economic literature, but in regard to which there is a dearth of scientific discussion. For an interesting, but in the present writer's view fundamentally unsound, treatment, see H. C. Taylor, Agricultural Economics, chap.VI. Our own discussion of the theory of enterprise is admitted to be vague and unsatisfactory. A complete and logically rigorous discussion would be a large undertaking. In view of the extreme complexity of the elements involved in uncertainty, most of which may be independent variables, the number of possible suppositions which might be followed out is prohibitive. At least it would require so much space and be so difficult to follow, and of so little practical significance, that the probability of its being read does not justify the attempt. It is hoped that the above discussion covers the principal points of interest. The essential factors are men's ability in the entrepreneur field, which includes foresight and executive capacity, and their knowledge of their own powers and disposition to trust them in action. The factors likely to be neglected are the last two, self-knowledge and self-confidence or initiative, which are closely related, but not identical. In addition, knowledge of, and willingness to trust, other mens powers and judgment is a still more important consideration, not yet discussed.

of confidence we feel in the value of the judgment of the "authority" whose pronouncement we accept as the best information available on the merits of the case. To be sure, the mode of formation of these opinions of others' opinions is complex and obscure, and is rarely free from all passing of judgment on the case itself independently. There is a mutual reinforcement; we have some ideas of our own in the premises, and these agree with the views of some authority. We often if not in general believe what we do because the authority believes it, but to some extent we believe in the authority because he holds the view to which we were already inclined. In large measure we even believe in ourselves because and in the measure that we think others believe in us, though, on the other hand, again, . . . But it is enough to indicate the complexity of the relations between our own and others' opinions without attempting to set all these relations out in logical statements. The importance of indirect knowledge of fact through knowledge of others' knowledge is the point we wish to emphasize.

Correspondingly, the uncertainty of the knowledge on the basis of which we act is in large measure the margin of error in our estimates of the authorities whom we elect to follow. The uncertainties of business are predominantly of this character, and the genus calls for particularly careful study. Our discussion hitherto has assumed pure and undivided entrepreneurship, which would follow from the impossibility of knowledge by one person of another person's capabilities. In the absence of such knowledge it is clear that no one would put his resources under the direction of another without a valid guarantee of the payment agreed upon, and no one could become an entrepreneur who was not in a position to make such guarantees without assistance,[219] it being equally clear that no one would make such a guarantee for another. That is, entrepreneurship would be completely specialized in a pure form, responsibility and control completely associated. When men have knowledge, or opinions on which they are willing to act, of other men's capacities for the entrepreneur function, all this is changed; entrepreneurship is no longer a simple and sharply isolated function. This is, of course, the state

[219]It does not follow that he would have to own property, though in the real world this is the practical consequence. It is easily conceivable, however, that one might secure the payment of his obligations by pledging his own earning power. Such an arrangement need not call for more difficult feats of organization or involve greater strain on human nature than is true of indemnity insurance at present.

of affairs in real life, and it is this partially specialized and more or less distributed entrepreneurship which merits most careful consideration. Several forms of organization and modes of distribution of the function call for notice.

The simplest division of entrepreneurship which we can think of is the separation of the two elements of control and guarantee and their performance by different individuals. This is a natural arrangement, for it must often happen that entrepreneur ability will not be associated with a situation on the part of its possessor enabling him to make satisfactory guarantees of the contractual incomes promised. Under such circumstances it may be mutually profitable for him to enter into agreement with some one in a position to underwrite his employment contracts, but not himself possessed of the ability or disposition to undertake the direction of enterprises. The form of this partnership and conditions of division of the profit may be highly various. As a matter of fact we know that it commonly takes the shape of a new wage bargain, the guarantor hiring the director in much the same way as the latter hires the productive services which he organized and controls. This transfer of function involves a transformation in character also which must be considered at length, and will be taken up in the next chapter. Let us note here that it is usually impracticable to separate all the guaranteeing responsibility from the control of the enterprise. It is rare that a hired entrepreneur receives a contractual income as his only interest in the business. He is usually a part owner, or at least his salary is so adjusted as to make it clear that his continuance in the position is contingent upon its prosperity under his direction.

An effect of the evaluation of ability nearly as important as the transformation in entrepreneurship with its partial transfer to another individual is that the specialization of the function within the enterprise may be quite incomplete. That is, it is no longer true that men are necessarily unwilling to entrust productive services, of person or property, to an outsider without an effective material guarantee of the fixed payment agreed upon. If they have confidence in the manager's ability and integrity they may gladly work with only a partial or imperfect security for their remunerations. To the extent that this is the case such owners of productive services manifestly share in bearing the uncertainty or "taking the risk" involved in the undertaking. That they also share in the effective control will appear in the course of a more careful examination of the entrepreneur function under the complicated, vague, and shifting conditions of real life (except that progress is still abstracted), which is the next stage in our inquiry.

Chapter 10. Enterprise and Profit (*continued*) - The Salaried Manager

THE typical form of business unit in the modern world is the corporation. Its most important characteristic is the combination of diffused ownership with concentrated control.[220] In theory the organization is a representative democracy, of an indirect type. The owners elect directors whose main function is to choose the officials who are said actually to carry on the business of the company. The directors themselves, however, exercise real direction over the general policies of the corporation. Moreover, if it is a large enterprise, the executive officials chosen by the directors have only a general oversight over business policy, and their chief function in turn is to select subordinates who make most of the actual decisions involved in the control of the concern. And of course the process does not stop there; there may be many stages in the hierarchy of functionaries whose chief duties consist of choosing still other subordinates.

The first necessary step in understanding the distribution of control and responsibility in modern business is to grasp this fact: What we call "control" consists mainly of selecting some one else to do the "controlling." Business judgment is chiefly judgment of men. We

[220]That is, the most important characteristic from the standpoint of organization. Of perhaps equal importance is the legal nature of the corporation as an entity separate from its member owners. The term "limited liability" is not descriptive. The members of a corporation have, strictly speaking, no responsibility at all; only the property of the corporation, which property does not directly belong to the owners, is liable for the corporation's obligations.

know things by knowledge of men who know them and control things in the same indirect way. Nor can this conclusion be escaped, as there is some tendency to pretend, by distinguishing between judgment of ends and judgment of means. The only problems with which we have any concern are all problems of means. There is only one end, finally, to business activity, and this is already decided upon before the business is founded; that is, to make money. The decisions made by members of the business organization all relate to means, at whatever state of "generality" they may be taken; the difference between decisions as to general policy and operative detail is one of degree only, in which all degrees exist; it is an arbitrary distinction. Decisions as to ends in any proper sense are made only by consumers — persons outside the productive organization altogether.

These statements hold good in fact for all other departments of organized social activity as well as for business. They are even more true of political organization. It is hardly an exaggeration to say that the political officeholder's business is to get the job and then find some one else to perform its duties. In the field of organization, the knowledge on which what we call responsible control depends is not knowledge of situations and problems and of means for effecting changes, but is knowledge of other men's knowledge of these things. So fundamental to our problem is this fact that human judgment of things has in an effective sense a "true value" which can be estimated more or less correctly by the man possessing it and by others — so fundamental is it for understanding the control of organized activity, that the problem of judging men's powers of judgment overshadows the problem of judging the facts of the situation to be dealt with. And if this is true of knowledge it is manifestly true of uncertainty. Under organized dealings with our environment, attention and interest shift from the errors in men's opinions of things to the errors in their opinions of men. Organized control of nature in a real sense depends less on the possibility of knowing nature than it does on the possibility of knowing the accuracy of other men's knowledge of nature, and their powers of using this knowledge.

The fundamental principle underlying organized activity is therefore the reduction of the uncertainty in individual judgments and decisions by grouping the decisions of a particular individual and estimating the proportion of successes and failures, or the average quality of his judgments as a group. It is an application of the broader principle of consolidation of risks, but the circumstances are peculiar. The result can never be calculated, either from a priori data or from tabulations of instances observed. It is an estimate in the purest sense, an estimate into which previous observation may enter little. We form our opinions of the value of men's opinions and powers through an intuitive faculty of judging personality, with relatively little reference to observation of their actual performance in dealing with the kind of problems we are to set them at. Of course we use this sort of direct evidence as far as possible, but that is usually not very far. The final decision comes as near to intuition as we can well imagine; it constitutes an immediate perception of relations, as mysterious as reading another person's thoughts or emotions from subtle changes in the lines of his face.

The great complexity and difficulty in the analysis of business uncertainty and of profit as the remuneration connected with meeting it arises from this peculiar distribution of responsibility in the organization. There is an apparent separation of the functions of making decisions and taking the "risk" of error in decisions. The separation appears quite sharp in the case of the hired manager, as in a corporation, where the man who makes decisions receives a fixed salary, taking no "risk," and those who take the risk and receive profits — the stockholders — make no decisions, exercise no control. Yet a little examination in the light of the preceding discussion of indirect knowledge and indirect responsibility will show that the separation is illusory; when control is accurately defined and located, the functions of making decisions and assuming the responsibility for their correctness will be found to be one and indivisible.

The phenomena can be best elucidated by beginning at the very "bottom" of the scale, with the "routine" duties of the common, unskilled laborer. It will be evident on reflection that even the coarsest and most mechanical labor involves in some sense meeting uncertainty, dealing with contingencies which cannot be exactly foreseen. It seems to be the function of all conscious life to deal with "new situations." Consciousness would never have developed if the environment of living organisms were perfectly uniform and monotonous, conformable to mechanical laws. In such a world organisms would be automata. There is a manifest tendency to economize consciousness, to make all possible adaptations by unconscious reflex response. In human life we see complex adaptations such as performing on a musical instrument drop below the threshold when learned. If the requisite movements were constant from generation to generation there is little doubt that they would become fixed in the germ plasm by the slow process of natural selection if we eliminate the more direct method by inheritance of acquired characters.

Moreover, in industrial life, purely routine operations are inevitably taken over by machinery. The duties of the machine tender may seem mechanical and uniform, but they are really not so throughout the operation. His function is to complete the carrying-out of the process to the point where it becomes entirely uniform so that the machine can take hold of it, or else to begin with the uniform output of the machine and start it on the way of diversification. Some part of the task will practically always be found to require conscious judgment, which is to say the meeting of uncertainty, the exercise of responsibility, in the ordinary sense of these terms.

But from the standpoint of organization the work of the common laborer does not involve uncertainty or responsibility in the effective sense, on account of the principle of indirect knowledge and transfer of responsibility discussed above. Even when it is impossible to reduce the work itself to routine sufficiently for a machine to handle it — due usually to lack of uniformity (i.e., uncertainty) in the material worked with — it is possible to judge with a high degree of accuracy the capacity of a human individual to deal with the sort of irregularities to be met with in the occupation. It is the function of the operative in industry to deal with uncertainty as a matter of routine! The exact movements he shall have to perform cannot be foretold, but his ability to perform them can be, and so the uncertainty is eliminated as an element in the calculations; ignorance of the environmental situation gives place to knowledge of human judgment.

The contrast again, even in case of the humblest operative, is not absolute. Most such persons occasionally meet with contingencies in regard to which they are expected to appeal to judgment and ability superior to their own. Nor can the operative's ability to handle his job be known with complete accuracy to his superior. The operative must exercise judgment over his own capacities in knowing when to go ahead independently and when to appeal for guidance. And the official who assigns the operative to his job and fixes his remuneration for performing it must exercise a rather higher quality of judgment in estimating the powers of the operative. The net effect is that uncertainty and responsibility are not quite eliminated, but are partially transferred to the superior in the scale of organization. The true uncertainty in the case relates to this official's judgment of his man in relation, of course, to the position he is to fill. As far as the lowest man in the scale is concerned, he is freed from all responsibility beyond the ("routine") duty of using his best judgment as occasion requires. His superior is responsible for him, and he accordingly receives a fixed wage.[221]

It will already be clear that this process of transferring responsibility does not end with the first step at the bottom of the scale, and the goal to which the argument will lead is in fairly plain view. The foreman (let us say) who passes judgment on the abilities of operatives and takes the responsibility for their performing in accordance with his expectations finds himself in turn in a similar relation to his own ranking superior in the organization. His capacity to judge operatives is passed upon and reduced to a routine function in the same way that he passes upon their capacities to do their work, and likewise his capacity to deal with those more exceptional contingencies in which operatives are likely to appeal to him; and his responsibility is in turn transferred to the higher official (superintendent or what-not) who selects him, assigns him to his work, and hears appeals in those still rarer questions which he refers higher up for decision. The knowledge on which the higher control is based is again, and still more, knowledge of a man's capacity to deal with a problem, not concrete knowledge of the problem itself. The higher official may in fact be very competent to deal with the problem directly, but he does not do so. And it is noteworthy that he may not be competent in this sense. Some superintendents would doubtless make better foremen than their foremen, and only serve in the higher capacity because of the still greater rarity and value of the ability to judge and handle foremen. But it is unquestionable that a great many men make very good superintendents who would not make good foremen at all, and perhaps this is the more common case.

---

[221]It need hardly be pointed out that the principle of consolidation of risks is operative here to a certain extent. The employer of men passes judgment on their "average" competency to do the things that they are expected to do, an average in the case of each individual and an average involving a further canceling-out of errors if he selects a number of employees. A still higher order of responsible judgment is involved in laying-out and subdividing the work of the establishment so that the task of each single employee is adapted to a certain fairly uniform grade of ability.

On up the scale the same relations hold good until we come to the supreme head of the business. For simplicity we may suppose that this individual combines all the managerial functions in his single person, that he is president, general manager, and so forth, that his directors exercise no control over him whatever beyond giving him his place and salary and a perfectly free hand. Even such an individual is in a position similar in essential respects, as far as the problem of organization is concerned, to that of the lowly machine tender. His capacities to deal with the kind of situations he has to deal with are subject to evaluation, are evaluated. His work is also a "routine" task of exercising his best judgment — and leaving the consequences to others. The real responsibility is again shifted back, as the effective uncertainty is in the judgment which placed him in his position. The responsible decision is not the concrete ordering of policy, but ordering an orderer as a "laborer" to order it. And this final responsibility necessarily takes the consequences of its decisions. The apparent separation between control and risk taken turns out, as predicted, to be illusory. The paradox of the hired manager, which has caused endless confusion in the analysis of profit, arises from the failure to recognize the fundamental fact that in organized activity the crucial decision is the selection of men to make decisions, that any other sort of decision-making or exercise of judgment is automatically reduced to a routine function. All of which follows from the very nature of large-scale control, based on the replacement of knowledge of things by knowledge of men, as our analysis has shown.

We must refuse to be misled by the superficial similarity between the daily work of the hired manager and that of the man in business on his own account. The difference is far more fundamental. The former has had his task cut out for him by others and been set to perform it; the latter has cut out his own task to fit his own measure of himself, and set himself at it. Here is the really responsible decision, made for the hired manager, by the independent enterpriser. Whenever we find an apparent separation between control and uncertainty-bearing, examination will show that we are confusing essentially routine activities with real control.[222]

Like a large proportion of the practical problems of business life,

---

[222]Cf. Hawley's contention (Quarterly Journal of Economics, vol. XI, p. 88) that the hired manager makes decisions, but the enterpriser takes the consequences of decisions, and that the former is therefore not an enterpriser.

as of all life, this one of selecting human capacities for dealing with unforeseeable situations involves paradox and apparent theoretical impossibility of solution. But like a host of impossible things in life, it is constantly being done. Though we cannot anticipate a concrete situation accurately enough to meet it without the intervention of conscious judgment at that moment, it can be foreseen that under certain circumstances the kind of things that will turn up will be of a character to be dealt with by a kind of capacity which can be selected and evaluated. That large-scale organizations are formed and operate successfully demonstrates that this principle is sound, that for these impossible problems solutions more right than wrong are actually found. Partly through operation of the principle of reduction of uncertainty by consolidation, partly for reasons embodied in our faculties of interpreting personality and which seem to be inscrutable, knowledge of men's capacities to know turns out to be more accurate than direct knowledge of things.

Another phase of entrepreneurship based on the same fundamental facts of transfer of responsibility, and which still further complicates its analysis, is the incompleteness of specialization. We may introduce the problem as a continuation of the above argument by inquiring into the question, To whom is the responsibility ultimately transferred when the entire conduct and policy of a business are in the hands of a hired manager? The answer is obvious: to the owners of the productive services used in the business; i.e., to the very shoulders from which the same responsibility is taken in the case of the specialization of function involved in contracting with an independent entrepreneur. In the latter case the entrepreneur, who selects himself, takes over all the uncertainty of the business along with control over it. But in view of the difficulty of any single individual giving adequate security for the performance of his contracts in the case of a large undertaking, such a form of organization has a very limited opportunity for growth. For it is clear that only the possessor of transferable wealth already produced (consumers' or producers' goods) or of future productive capacity in some form can make guarantees or really bear uncertainty or take risks for other persons. And it is nearly inevitable that the man who "undertakes" any line of business as entrepreneur will commit a part of his own wealth or productive powers to that business. What naturally happens, then, in any case is that the control of enterprise falls into the hands of the owner (or owners) of a part of the productive services used in the enterprise, which resources are placed in an exposed position with regard to losses in the business and so guarantee the owners of the remaining "land, labor, and capital" against failure to receive their full contractual remuneration.

It is impossible for entrepreneurship to be completely specialized or exist in a pure form, except in the rare and improbable case of a man who owns nothing in a particular business and contributes nothing to it but responsibility. Even a man who conducted a business entirely with borrowed funds and hired labor, but managing it himself, would not exemplify pure entrepreneurship, for a large part of the work of management is as we have seen reducible to routine and can be paid for with a fixed wage. The nearest approach to an entrepreneur only would be a man who borrowed all the resources for operating a business and then hired a manager and gave him an absolutely free hand. And such a man would have to be more than an entrepreneur in relation to some other business, or he would not be a true entrepreneur, making responsible decisions, in the business in question.

The natural result is a complicated division or diffusion of entrepreneurship, distributed in the typical modern business organization by a hierarchy of security issues carrying every conceivable gradation and combination of rights to control and to freedom from uncertainty as to income and vested capital. The feature of the system apt to be overlooked is a large element of real control disguised under a nominal contract for a fixed return. It is seldom true that the guarantees given can be regarded as absolute. If they are not, the owner of resources is taking a certain share of responsibility or risk, obviously. That he is also exercising control becomes apparent if we consider that his decision to allow the use of his labor or property under the conditions affects the scale of operations of the business. Control is completely absent from the function of furnishing productive services to a business only in case an accurately determined competitive value of the services is effectively guaranteed, so that everything but the money remuneration is made completely indifferent to their owner.

As a matter of fact we know that it is common for those who furnish resources to an enterprise to retain a large amount of direct consultative authority in regard to the conduct of the business. The voting trust is a device for securing this end and owes its importance to the necessity of providing for security owners an assurance of competent control when adequate protection of their interests cannot otherwise be achieved, especially when the value of the property depends largely on its intelligent employment in the particular use to which it has been committed. With the increasing specialization of industry such conditions become more and more common, effective guarantees become harder and harder to make, and investors find it necessary to insist more and more on sharing in the control of business. The distinction between stocks and bonds tends to fade out.[223]It is hard to find an illustration of an unconditional transfer of productive resources to a business for its use for a pecuniary consideration alone without an outright transfer of ownership. The owners of limited issues of first-mortgage bonds have an ultimate recourse to the courts to compel honest management of the concern if their interests are jeopardized. Only in such a case as the lease of pure site value which is indestructible and not changed in any way by use can we find an example of an income entirely freed from the element of responsible control.

The case of labor is somewhat peculiar, owing to the disposition of laboring people to gamble recklessly with life and limb as well as income. Under free competition there is little doubt that a considerable proportion of the losses of enterprise would fall upon labor, since laborers show themselves ready to engage in hazardous enterprises at their own risk for an increase in wages which is a fraction of an adequate compensation for the chances they take. But the social interest in the man who cannot afford the loss comes to the rescue with prior claim laws, mechanics' liens, and the like, so that the wages of labor are in fact generally a fair approximation to a guaranteed contractual return. The element of control which would be involved in a dependence of business upon laborers' choice of the ventures they would engage in, is correspondingly absent, as the effective contracting-out of the risk places different lines of employment on a plane of indifference at the wages fixed.[224]

---

[223]Of course, the machinery by which control is exercised becomes more indirect and the control itself more remote. Stocks approximate to the real position of bonds as well as bonds to that of stocks. One form of the change is a tendency to cover a larger proportion of investment by stock issues (as compared with bonds) than formerly. The increased recourse to borrowing from banks shows the same tendency, for banks in particular keep in touch with the management of businesses in which they invest.

[224]The case of the ultimate entrepreneur, dealing with and knowing men rather than things, suggests again the analogous political problem. The progress of

The relations between profit and the contractual shares call for a few further remarks. As observed in our historical introduction (chapter II) the older English economists used the term "profit" to designate the income of the owner of a business, who was regarded as essentially an investor. Hence, as the classical economics was essentially a long-time theoretical treatment, little distinction was drawn between profit and interest. A wage element was recognized in the income, and also a risk factor. Little was made of the latter as constituting a distinction between profit and interest, as ordinary contract interest so obviously contains an element of payment for risk also. And in view of our argument above that the assumption of risk in this connection involves the exercise of effective control to the same extent, the relegation of this factor into the background is still further justified.

American economic discussion developed under the influence of the marginal utility theory, which is essentially a short time view of the valuation problem. There is some connection between this fact and the greater emphasis given in this country to "wages of management" and the separation of this element from the entrepreneur's income, leaving "profit" or "pure profit" in a narrower sense than that given the term by the older writers. For management is more conspicuous in American industry, due to the more "dynamic" conditions of this country. In a longtime view or "static state" it would be relatively much less important. The greater emphasis given the risk factor in American (as in German) discussions is explained in the same way, a more dynamic background and greater interest in short-period changes.

With the recent development of accounting theory, the question

---

democracy toward intelligent efficiency seems to depend on a tendency for the ultimate sovereign, the electorate, to center its attention on the selection of competent agents, leaving to them the actual formulation of policies and conduct of affairs. Commission government, and still more the manager plan of municipal government, is a case in point. In the political sphere there is a real problem of ultimate ends, which must, of course, be dealt with by the electorate if the system remains democratic. And perhaps more than in the case of business the voter's judgment of the candidate must be connected with passing an opinion upon the issues, partly because major issues to some extent involve a question of ultimate social ideals. Professor Cooley (Social Organization, p. 129 and chap, XIII) bases an optimistic view of democracy on a belief in the capacity of the populace, admittedly ignorant in regard to political issues and the technique of government, to select men wisely on the basis of a sort of intuitive recognition of personal superiority.

whether interest on investment should be counted in profit has become acute from another point of view and has tended to constitute an issue between accountants and economic theorists. This is of course entirely uncalled-for, as the difference in position is a matter of obvious difference in standpoint. Economic theory is interested in the forces which determine the prices of goods, and in costs of production as a condition of supply. It goes without saying that, in the long run again, a return on capital equal to the competitive rate of interest is a condition of production, and so from this point of view a cost. (That things may be different from a short-time viewpoint serves to increase the confusion.) The accountant is interested in proprietorship, the relations between a business and its owners, and in cost as a deduction from the owner's income. Moreover, scientific accounting is an outgrowth of corporation problems, and in the corporation the responsible owner is thought of as an investor, his interest as a capital interest, whether he has put any money in the business or not and whether or not it has any value above its debts. And profit, being a return on investment, is naturally thought of as a rate of return.

In most cases it would not be fruitful to attempt an accurate separation of profit from interest.[225] For on the other side of the relation, pure interest is almost as rare a phenomenon and as elusive a concept as pure profit. The specialization of the entrepreneur function is a fundamental fact in business organization, but for reasons which should already be clear, it cannot be carried to theoretical completeness. The entrepreneur must almost of necessity own some property and the owner of property used in a business can hardly be freed from all risk and responsibility. It is useful, however, to distinguish between the return actually realized by an entrepreneur and the "competitive" rate of interest on high-class "gilt-edge" securities where the risk and responsibility factor is negligible. The difference would be profit, or "pure profit" in the sense in which economic theory uses the term.

Even at last some reservation must be made in calling interest on the entrepreneur's investment a cost of producing the commodity.

[225] By "interest" is here meant property income merely. The relation between interest and rent is essentially a "dynamic" problem, and will be taken up for discussion in the following chapter. It is questionable whether interest would be met with at all in an unprogressive society, and certain that the distinction between interest and rent would be of small importance. Cf. also above, chapter V.

It is generally admitted that if this rate of return is not realized on the average and in the long run the investment will not be held in the business in question. But the truth accurately stated evidently is that the owner must expect in the future to receive a return equal to that which he can be sure of elsewhere, on the investment which he is free to transfer to other uses. And of course allowance must be made for the connection between different elements of investment as well as technological fluidity. If half the investment in an enterprise represents machinery, working-capital, land, or what-not which can be transferred to other lines, and the other half represents permanent commitment, worthless outside the particular business, the cost of producing the output of that business (after the commitment has been made) is only the (anticipation of the) competitive return on the removable half of the capital alone. Of course this half could not be removed without rendering the remainder worthless.

The association of profit with income on property is valid, within the limits discussed, for the greater part of business enterprises, but there are important exceptions. The independent entrepreneur is not yet by any means an extinct species. Such a person typically furnishes both property and labor services to a business, meaning by labor services personal activities which might be hired and paid for with a fixed wage. The entrepreneur income in a case of this sort contains an element of wages as well as an element of interest. The contention of some accountants that a salary should be allowed for the owner's work and the residue considered as a return on his investment does not seem to be well founded. It is based on a bias derived from the habitual (and proper) procedure in corporations, where the responsible owner furnishes property services only. It would be just as logical to deduct from the owner's income a competitive rate of interest and call the residue wages or wages of management. The only significant distinction is that between the total income and a "pure profit" secured by deducting both competitive wages for the work and competitive interest on the investment furnished by the owner. The determination of the proper wage rate will be fraught with the same sort of difficulties that have been referred to in the case of pure interest, but in a much more aggravated form; it is far more difficult to appraise labor and find similar services in the competitive field as a basis of comparison than in the case of property.[226]

---

[226]We must again refer to the use of the term "interest" as meaning property income merely, though superficially this is not quite consistent with treatment

In some instances, though perhaps a relatively small proportion of real enterprises and those probably of small average size, the independent entrepreneur may have no property investment in his business, furnishing labor services only. It is in reference to such a situation that the conventional (American) treatment of profit and wages of management has most significance. It must be very unusual, for reasons already pointed out, for a man to hire the use of the labor and property of others without putting up some property as well as labor of his own. It would be possible, within limits, for such a man to give adequate security for payment of the fixed remuneration of outside agencies, if his own earning capacity were high.[227]

But in reality this probably does not happen on any considerable scale, or with enterprises of large magnitude. However, allowance must be made for the ownership of property used in other enterprises, and also for the "moral backing" of wealthy relatives or friends. And such "moral backing" may or may not constitute a division of the entrepreneur's responsibility. The only ultimate security may still be the potential earning power of the entrepreneur himself, which, however, might not be marketable on account of a moral hazard without being underwritten by property-owning connections.

On the whole we must say that the discussion of profit in relation to wages of management has been greatly overworked. The connection with property income is enormously more common, direct, and close. The residual share of income falls of necessity to the person in responsible control of a business; hence, in most cases to a person who also receives a property income. He may or may not also receive a labor income as well. The important distinction for the purposes of theoretical analysis is that between pure residual income or pure profit and property income. The relation to labor income is incidental in importance comparatively, and being of the same character, at any rate, does not call for much space in a discussion of profit. If a distinction is made between land and capital, it must be recognized that the profit receiver may be also a recipient of rent, in addition to interest or wages or both. And in exceptional cases he may receive rent only, as, for instance, a farmer who owns his land, but borrows

---

of it as a "rate." Pure interest is much more easily defined than a pure competitive return on actual property, but even the latter offers less difficulty than an appraisal of the competitive value of the services of an independent entrepreneur.

[227]To the extent that he does not give adequate security the owners of the productive services exposed to loss are the true entrepreneurs.

all his working capital and hires all his work done. In such a case the practical problem would be to distinguish pure profit from rent. But such a situation is somewhat artificial, and the distinction between land and other property is from this point of view even more so.

The importance of property-ownership in connection with profit will be even greater and more apparent if "good-will," business connection, and established reputation, etc., be regarded as property. If these categories are capitalized and included in investment the cases are rare indeed where an employer of others' labor and capital has no investment of his own in the undertaking. As to the proper procedure in dealing with these items, whether they should or should not be regarded as property, the answer depends on whether they are salable. If good-will is separable from the other elements in a business, the test of which is that it can be sold away from them without affecting their value, then it is property on its own account, and the competitive rate of return on its sale value must be deducted from the owner's income before a pure profit is arrived at. If good-will is inseparable from some other property element, such as a site, it is a factor in the value of that piece of property, and income on the total value must similarly be considered a property income, not a pure profit. If the good-will inheres in the person of the owner, however, it is not property, but an element in the personal service of the owner, and its proper income is a wage; again not a profit. In so far as its value (in the capital or revenue sense) can be appraised, it must be considered as entitled to a contractual return and does not give rise to profit in the narrow sense.

Our discussion of the meaning of profit may now be summed up in a few brief statements. Organization involves the concentration of responsibility, placing resources belonging to a large number of individuals under centralized control. Examination shows that the human functions in production involve making decisions, exercising control, but that this control is not final unless combined with assumption of the results of the decisions. The responsible decision relates to men rather than things; the ultimate manager is he who plans the organization, lays out functions, selects men for functions and appraises their value to the organization as a whole, in competition with all other bidders in the market. For this ultimate management there is but one possible remuneration, the residuum of product remaining after payment is made at rates established in competition with all comers for all services of men or things for which competition exists.[228] This residuum is profit; it is the remainder out of the value realized from the sale of product after deduction of the values of all factors in production which can be valued, or after all the product has been imputed to productive elements which can be imputed by the competitive mechanism. Profit is unimputable income, as distinguished from the total income of the owner of the business. Normally there are other elements in this total income, which, since they are not paid out by the business, may be said not to be imputed, or they may be described as "residually imputed."

Pure profit is theoretically unimputable, in the sense in which the competitive system of industrial organization imputes product value to agencies concerned in production. In this competitive process, all the product value which can be associated with any agency will accrue to that agency. The essence of the process is the bidding of entrepreneurs or would-be entrepreneurs for the use of productive services in the future, the rates of remuneration being determined by a present general competitive estimate of the values of the services in the market, while the return finally received from their use may diverge from this estimate in view of the fact of uncertainty or liability to error in all human prognostications. As far and as fast as any portion of income can be known in advance to be connected with the exercise of superior judgment, it will be imputed to the person possessing the unusual powers, and will become a wage (of management), no longer a profit. Wages of management are not different in principle from wages for routine work; management is routine work when the term is properly understood in the present connection. The true uncertainty in organized life is the uncertainty in an estimate of human capacity, which is always a capacity to meet uncertainty.

In general practice the ownership of property is necessary to the assumption of genuine responsibility, and in the typical modern business organization the responsible owner furnishes no labor services to the business, but property services only. In such a case profit in our sense of the term appears as a difference between the rate of return on the owner's investment and a competitive rate of return on investment generally. The scientific use of the term "profit" must therefore be distinguished from the various loose uses of the term in business, and particularly from the net revenue of the owner; it

[228] Including, of course, monopoly elements in the situation. Cf. above, chapter VI.

is well to use a special expression, such as "pure profit," to distinguish the share which is accurately residual, theoretically different from the returns from routine functions, imputed by competition to the agents which earn them. We must bear in mind, however, that the imputed or competitive element in the owner's income does not bear quite the same relation to the price of the product as outlays actually incurred. The expectation of such a return at the general competitive rate is a condition of the production of that business's contribution to the total supply of a commodity, but its realization cannot be said to be necessary.

If it is necessary to distinguish between profit and wages, it is just as vital to contrast profit with payment for risk-taking in any ordinary use of the terms. An insurer, in so far as his business is reduced to a science, takes no risk; the risk in the individual case of the insured is obliterated on being thrown in with the multitude of cases of the insurer. And it is immaterial whether the "cases" are a homogeneous group of similars or whether each is objectively in a class by itself, if the true probability can be ascertained. The "risk" which gives rise to profit is an uncertainty which cannot be evaluated, connected with a situation such that there is no possibility of grouping on any objective basis whatever. For while it is true that decisions made by an individual tend to approximate an objective value when considered as a group, decisions of this character reduce to routine and do not involve ultimate responsibility; in so far as the powers of the entrepreneur become evaluated, a definite return is imputed to his activity, and this return is no longer a profit, but a wage.[229]

The only "risk" which leads to a profit is a unique uncertainty resulting from an exercise of ultimate responsibility which in its very nature cannot be insured nor capitalized nor salaried. Profit arises out of the inherent, absolute unpredictability of things, out of the

[229]The hiring of men to meet uncertainty can be illustrated by many examples from different fields. Corporations employ at set, fixed wages inventors, experimenters, prospectors for minerals, weather and crop forecasters, market predictors, speculators, etc. Gambling-houses pay men weekly salaries to play poker with their clients. It is clear that such employees, like the hired manager, make decisions as a matter of routine, without taking responsibility. The responsible decision is made by the employer, who selects them for their tasks, and the operation of the principle of consolidation of uncertainties is also apparent. The latter point is not so clear in other cases; the doctor makes decisions, but his patients take the responsibility for their correctness!

sheer brute fact that the results of human activity cannot be anticipated and then only in so far as even a probability calculation in regard to them is impossible and meaningless. The receipt of profit in a particular case may be argued to be the result of superior judgment. But it is judgment of judgment, especially one's own judgment, and in an individual case there is no way of telling good judgment from good luck, and a succession of cases sufficient to evaluate the judgment or determine its probable value transforms the profit into a wage.

The fundamental fact of organized activity is the tendency to transform the uncertainties of human opinion and action into measurable probabilities by forming an approximate evaluation of the judgment and capacity of the man. The ability to judge men in relation to the problems they are to deal with, and the power to "inspire" them to efficiency in judging other men and things, are the essential characteristics of the executive.

If these capacities are known, the compensation for exercising them can be competitively imputed and is a wage; only, in so far as they are unknown or known only to the possessor himself, do they give rise to a profit. The powers and attributes of leadership form the most mysterious as well as the most vital endowment which fits the human species for civilized or organized life, transcending even that power of perceiving and associating qualities and relations which is the true nature of what we call reasoning. It is the margin of error in this most ultimate faculty of judging faculties whose exercise is the essence of responsible control, which constitutes the only true uncertainty in the workings of the competitive organization (as of any other organization). And it is uncertainty in this sense which explains profit in the proper use of the term, the sense toward which economic usage has been groping, that of a pure residual income, unimputable by the mechanism of competition to any agent concerned in its creation.

It remains to follow out this line of reasoning in detail, to show how a large part of the phenomena of current economic life, on the organization side, are the natural results of the fact of uncertainty and this fundamental method of meeting it. But it seems best to postpone this further discussion until we have examined the bearings of progressive change on the amount and kind of uncertainty involved in economic life. These two chapters have dealt only with the more fundamental features of free enterprise which would be met with even in a society as nearly static as material possibility admits, and in which a minimum degree of uncertainty would be present. We have abstracted from many important features of entrepreneurship which are connected with the fact of progress or the presence of the conditions of progress, for progress involves uncertainty in a high degree and in very special forms. We turn now to consider the bearings upon economic organization of the various dynamic factors or elements of progress[230] and the uncertainty connected with them.

[230]See chapter V.

Chapter 11. Uncertainty and Social Progress

THE general character of the connection between progress and uncertainty has been dealt with at various points in the course of our inquiry. Change of some kind is prerequisite to the existence of uncertainty; in an absolutely unchanging world the future would be accurately foreknown, since it would be exactly like the past. Change in some sense is a condition of the existence of any problem whatever in connection with life or conduct, and is the actual condition of most of the problems of pure thought, since these are after all more or less related to practical requirements. We live in a world full of contradiction and paradox, a fact of which perhaps the most fundamental illustration is this: that the existence of a problem of knowledge depends on the future being different from the past, while the possibility of the solution of the problem depends on the future being like the past. The key to the paradox, as we have argued above (chapter VII), is to be found in two facts. In the first place, we analyze our world into objects which behave more or less consistently. That is, we recognize in things the unchanging property of changing in certain ways. If this process could be carried out to completeness, we should have a completely knowable world. It would also, however, be in the practical sense an unchanging world. It is a fact familiar to students of our thought processes that we thus explain change by explaining it away. The historic problem of thought is this of real change. The point for us here is that change according to known law (whether or not we call it change) does not give rise to uncertainty. What we practically mean by a static world is one in which all change is of this character.

But the process of formulating change in terms of unchanging "laws" (properties or modes of behavior of "things") cannot be carried to completeness, and here our minds invent a second refuge to which to flee from an unknowable world, in the form of the law of permutations and combinations. A law of change means given behavior under given conditions. But the "given conditions" of the behavior of any object are the momentary states and changes of other objects. Hence the dogma of science, that the world is "really" made up of units which not only do not change (atoms, corpuscles, ether, or what-not), but whose laws of behavior are simple and comprehensible. But it is contended that there are so many of these units that the simple changes which they undergo (ideally movements in space alone) give rise to a variety of combinations which our minds are unable to grasp in detail. We have examined this dogma and been forced to the conclusion that whatever we find it pleasant to assume for philosophic purposes, the logic of our conduct assumes real indeterminateness, real change, discontinuity.

Even the assumption of real indeterminateness, however, gives mind a new means of prediction, through grouping phenomena into classes and applying probability reasoning. This device enables us to predict what will happen in groups of instances where we find it impossible to derive laws fitting individual cases. The second fundamental fact of uncertainty is that this method also has its limits. Both methods in fact, prediction by law in individual cases and by probability reasoning in groups of cases, have rather narrow limitations in everyday life in consequence of the organic costs of applying them and the time required to get the necessary data; both outlay and time are commonly much greater than circumstances will allow us to consume in deciding upon a course of action. The actual procedure of making decisions in practical life is a rather inscrutable or "intuitive" formation of "estimates," subject to a wide margin of error or uncertainty.

The significance of change is that it gives rise to the problem of the control of action, and in this respect the difference between predictable and unpredictable change is conspicuous. The succession of day and night or the alternation of the seasons, the vital processes and changes of our own lives, waking and sleeping, work-time and meal-time and play-time, infancy, maturity, and age — such events call for action, but give rise to no problem of action; they are predictable. Problems of action arise out of departures from routine in changes of all sorts. It is a common observation that irregularities would be of much less magnitude and consequence in the absence of social progress, and a common practice to distinguish between "static" and "dynamic" risks. The fundamental difference, as we have seen, is one of degree only, and consists in the greater unpredictability of some actual progressive changes. In the first place, it is impossible to draw a sharp and significant distinction between progressive change and fluctuations. Everything depends on the periodicity of the change. If it is self-compensating in an interval short as compared with the length of human life, it does not involve uncertainty, and the increasing perfection of organization devices designed to secure consolidation constantly extends the period over which effective self-compensation may come about. On the other hand, all our progressive changes may be ultimately periodic for all we know.

Again, progressive change does not necessarily carry unpredictability with it; indeed, a merely progressive change does not. If the change takes place uniformly, or in accordance with any known mathematical function of time, the future may be foreknown as accurately as if there were no change. It is fluctuation after all which is the true cause of the uncertainty, fluctuation in progress. In fact some changes are fairly "constant" in their operation and do not give rise to uncertainties of the sort which disturb the operation of competition. Of this sort are the increase of population and the accumulation of capital. Others are highly capricious in their action and continually upset the calculations upon the basis of which entrepreneurs' bids for productive service are made.

Scrutiny of the character of the progressive changes which we have recognized (chapter V) as significant in the study of economics reveals some interesting similarities and differences among them. If we begin by distinguishing between natural changes and changes due to human action, we note that we do not have to consider any progressive changes under the former head. Natural changes are either of the nature of fluctuations from a constant condition or else, like the supposed cooling-off of the solar system, so slow as to make no difference for human calculations. The changes due to acts of man are, however, of two different kinds. Some are produced by deliberate intent and others come about more or less incidentally as a result of actions directed toward other ends. A study of the "real" motives of action would lead far afield, and probably yield no very clear and satisfactory results at last, but we can make a rough distinction. The improvement of technology and in large part the discovery of natural resources are directly willed, though the latter is to a more considerable extent accidental. The accumulation of capital may be treated as deliberately effected, though with some reservations, and the various redistributions of things among persons may be similarly treated, but with more reservations. The improvement of wants is partly a deliberate matter, partly incidental to other endeavors, and partly it "just happens." The increase in population is hardly willed at all; the matter of its innate quality is even less affected by volitional interference (and in fact unquestionably shows rapid retrogression under modern industrial conditions); while the education and training of the individual are controlled by a baffling mixture of planned action and accident.

Another dichotomy of fundamental importance for the study of uncertainty relates to the production as contrasted with the consumption of wealth. This distinction is also well recognized in discussions of uncertainty, the technological "risks" being separated from those connected with market changes. It is interesting to observe in the evolution of the modern industrial organization how the marketing function has consistently dominated that of production proper. We have already pointed out that the most fundamental determining fact in connection with organization is the meeting of uncertainty. The responsible decisions in organized economic life are price decisions; others can be reduced to routine and men can be hired to make them. The uncertainties of the market resist elimination or reduction by grouping more doggedly than do those connected with technological processes. Even in the transition period between the mediaeval and modern eras it was the marketing guilds which gravitated into positions of control, became the "Liveried Companies" and employed the producers and set them at their tasks, owning the materials they worked upon and the product when completed.

It will be observed that the main uncertainty which affects the entrepreneur is that connected with the sale price of his product. His position in the price system is typically[231] that of a purchaser of productive services at present prices to convert into finished goods for sale at the prices prevailing when the operation is finished. There

[231]In many instances, of course, this situation is inverted; the selling price is known in advance by contracting and it is the cost outlays which are uncertain.

is no uncertainty as to the prices of the things he buys. He bears the technological uncertainty as to the amount of physical product he will secure, but the probable error in calculations of this sort is generally not large; the gamble is in the price factor in relation to the product. But changes in the prices of producers' goods affect him indirectly, because they are likely to be connected with changes in product prices; they form one of the factors to be taken into account in forecasting the sales market. This is probably a secondary consideration, however, except in so far as capital values are involved, a fundamental exception, to be sure, which will have to be discussed at length presently. The main immediate sources of uncertainty are the amount of supply to be expected from other producers and the consumers' wants and purchasing power.

The most fundamentally and irretrievably uncertain phases or factors of progress are those which amount essentially to the increase of knowledge as such. This description evidently holds for the improvement of technological processes and the forms of business organization and for the discovery of new natural resources. Here it is a contradiction in terms to speak of anticipation, in an accurate and detailed sense, for to anticipate the advance would be to make it at once. Yet even here, as we have seen, change and the uncertainty of change are in some degree separable factors. Though we cannot describe a new invention in advance without making it, nor say what quantity and quality of new natural productive capacity will be developed and where, yet it is possible in a large degree to offset ignorance with knowledge and behave intelligently with regard to the future. These changes are in large part the result of deliberate application of resources to bring them about, and in the large if not in a particular instance, the results of such activity can be so far foreseen that it is even possible to hire men and borrow capital at fixed remunerations for the purpose of carrying it on.

Two further general observations are called for before we can take up in detail the effects of the uncertainties involved in progress upon the form and workings of the competitive economic organization. It is common to think of the economic process as the production of goods for the satisfaction of wants. This view is deficient in two vital respects. In the first place, the economic process produces wants as well as goods to satisfy existing wants, and the amount of social energy devoted to the former and neglected phase of activity is very large and constantly growing. The second point is that the production of the indirect means of want-satisfaction is by no means altogether directed to the ultimate satisfaction of wants in any direct sense of the terms. The increase in wealth is to a large extent an end in itself as well as a means to the increase of income, and this also again to a rapidly increasing degree as the standards of life are advanced. Men work "to get rich" in a large proportion of cases, not merely in addition to, but in place of, consuming larger amounts of goods. It is a grave error to assume that in a modern industrial nation production takes place only in order to consumption. It is true to a great and ever-increasing degree that consumption is sacrificed to increased production. Whatever our philosophy of human motives, we must face the fact that men do "raise more corn to feed more hogs, to buy more land to raise more corn to feed more hogs to buy more land," and, in business generally, produce wealth to be used in producing more wealth with no view to any use beyond the increase of wealth itself.

From the standpoint of effects upon organization we must distinguish between the various phases of progress already enumerated (in chapter V), the increase of population, education and training, accumulation of capital, improvement in technology and business organization, discovery of new natural resources, and changes in the character of human wants. The most important of these from our point of view and at the same time the one easiest to discuss intelligently is the accumulation of capital.

Let us begin with the relation of capital in the sense of material goods to the fundamental structure of society. The facts of progress will be seen to have an intimate connection with the very institution of private property. In an unprogressive society private property in the modern sense of the term need not exist. The social justification of private ownership is that the coupling of control of resources with enjoyment of the fruits of their use is supposed to give an incentive to use the goods effectively in production. The abolition of slavery or property in human beings rests on the fact that slaves do not work as effectively as free men, and it turns out to be cheaper to pay men for their services and leave their private lives under their own control than it is to maintain them and force them to labor.

The same reasoning applies to property in material things, but in an unprogressive state the force of the argument is relatively weak. When production methods are a matter of routine, as in the Middle Ages, and there is no thought of progress, common ownership of land and tools is the rule. The problem of control becomes acute when methods are changing, and the incentive to change methods is mainly the desire to increase property values, to "get rich." We can hardly over-emphasize the fact that the dynamic urge back of modern economic life is the desire to increase wealth, rather than a desire to consume goods, though there is a psychological connection of an irrational sort between the two considerations. Even when improvement in standards of living does result from the increase of wealth, it cannot be assumed that this was the motive; for as we have previously emphasized, a permanent net increase of wealth must come from a surplus production on the part of individuals which they never plan to consume, but expect to die and leave behind them.[232]

The most direct connection of the uncertainties of progress with economic theory in the conventional use of the term is in relation to the explanation of interest. Interest is a phenomenon connected with the increase of the material equipment of society and dependent on the uncertainty involved in the process. It might or might not exist in a "static" society, depending largely on how rigidly the term "static" is interpreted. If productive goods were not changeable in either form or amount or distribution there would be no occasion for the lending of free capital, and interest would not exist; if all equipment were fixed in form and amount, but transferable from one individual to another, it might exist; with productive goods fixed in amount (no net saving or consumption of "capital" taking place), but changeable in form, interest would doubtless be found, but would make no appreciable difference in the distribution of income, as it would differ in very little but name from rent.[233]

[232] A small amount of capital wealth would, of course, result from the temporary investment of savings later withdrawn and consumed. An adequate discussion of the motives involved in the production of such surplus wealth would be beyond the scope of this work. The writer would say, however, that the theory of an "instinct" of acquisition or accumulation seems to him to be even below the plane of scientific thinking of the famous "dormitive virtue" of opiates. The latter at least is a real property or mode of behavior of something, while the human activity of accumulation is not a distinctive reaction, but a manifestation of the same tendencies found in human conduct generally. The "creative" or "constructive" impulse is open to the same objection; the "pleasure of being a cause" used by Gross, Preyer, Cooley, and others seems to be the best description of action not directed to gratifying an immediate and conscious need of the organism as a vital machine. It is merely a confusing misuse of terms to call an undifferentiated and undirected tendency to action-in-general an "instinct."

[233] See above, chapter V, where it is shown that the "capitalization rate" which

To understand interest it is necessary to have clearly in view the mechanism of the creation of capital equipment through the process of saving and investment. The classical conception of capital as "advances to laborers"[234] is essentially sound at least as a starting-point, though it must be amended or qualified in two particulars. The description applies, first, only to new or "free" capital, capital in the process of formation; it is true in the sense that capital goods come into existence through an "advancement" of consumption goods. In the second place, the advances are not made to laborers only, but to owners of already existing capital goods (and natural resources if these are separated from capital goods) as well. The difficulties and confusions with which interest theory is beset arise largely from the use of terms, notably the ambiguity of the term "capital." In the discussion which follows we shall employ the expression "capital goods" to refer to "the produce of past industry used for further production," the concrete instruments and tools, and restrict the term "capital" to a much narrower meaning, relating to this antecedent stage in the creation of capital goods or to their value as distinct from the goods themselves.

The nature of capital creation has been made clear by many writers. The primitive man constructs his own equipment to increase the efficiency of his own labor, and what he dies possessed of is likely to be buried with him. In organized civilized life the process is different in two respects. In consequence of specialization certain persons devote their energies altogether to the production of equipment goods, others not at all; and in the second place, a great permanent fund of goods is built up and maintained and increased from generation to generation. Yet what happens on the whole is fundamentally the same, though the division of labor makes it somewhat more difficult to see. Those who are engaged in the making of equipment goods are naturally not at the same time making their own living; they must five out of a surplus of consumption goods either stored up in advance or diverted from the use of those who produce it contemporaneously. In either case the first requisite to capital creation is the

would determine or rather arise out of the sale-value of property on the second of the above assumptions is not interest in the proper sense of the term, and that its rate is determined by "psychological" considerations of "time-preference," very different from the forces which determine the rate of interest in the present world. These forces we now proceed to analyze more in detail.

[234]Substantially followed by Taussig, and rightly so. See Wages and Capital; also Principles of Economics, chaps. 38-40.

creation of a surplus, the production of more goods than are consumed, by somebody at some time prior to the coming into existence of the capital goods. This is the essential meaning of "saving."

In civilized society the makers of capital goods include landlords and owners of capital goods as well as laborers. All who furnish productive services of any kind to the capital goods producing operations are manifestly paid out of prior production or excess contemporary creation of consumption goods by other persons and equipment. The essence of the process is that a surplus of consumption goods, set aside by being "saved," makes possible the diversion of productive resources from the creation of consumption goods to the creation of producers' goods. This is what is meant by "advances."

The series of events is further complicated by the intervention of money, for a relatively small proportion of students of economics ever learn to think back of the exchange function of money to the transfers of real things mediated by it. Saving is erroneously thought of as the saving of money, and the income of the producers of capital goods as a money income. Of course the money is a mere medium of exchange. It represents to the saver the ownership of a certain amount of the wealth of society, which can be "drawn" or "cashed" in any form he pleases at existing prices. If the saving is "invested," used for capital creation, this wealth is transferred to those engaged in these operations and "cashed" by them in the form of the things they want, mainly consumption goods. The title to these things is what the saving is and what is transferred. The transferred goods maintain or support the producers of capital goods, including laborers, landowners, and owners of capital goods who would otherwise be engaged in making consumption goods for themselves or for exchange. Interest arises when saved wealth is not invested by the saver, but transferred by loan to another person, either direct from saver to investor or mediated by a bank or financial institution as middleman.

The loan at interest is thus a means of securing specialization of function, enabling one set of persons to save surplus wealth and another set to convert savings into capital goods by advancing them to the owners of productive services who then use these services to create the capital goods instead of the consumption goods which they would have been used to produce had no saving taken place. The operations could be carried on without specialization; division of labor here as elsewhere involves economy merely, but is not the only way of getting things done. The savers could advance their own surpluses to owners of productive services and create capital goods on their own account, either themselves exploiting these new productive goods or transferring them by lease to other entrepreneurs. The gains from having them transfer this function to others who make investment their business are of the same character as the gains from specialization in any other connection.

Notably the gains are the same as those which arise from the specialization of the entrepreneur or control-plus-responsibility function, for this is what is really involved in the loan. Let us suppose that the saver does his own advancing and comes out the owner of the capital equipment which results from his saving; what will he do with it then? He might also employ this new equipment himself in the production of the sort of goods to which it is adapted, continuing meanwhile the original business or profession out of which he made the first saved surplus. But we know that it is in general much better and much more likely to happen that he shall lease the equipment at a fixed rate to an entrepreneur for actual operation. Let us make it as clear as possible that exactly the same sort of gains are realized by his transferring the surplus of goods itself to an entrepreneur at a fixed remuneration and leaving to the latter the construction as well as operation of the new equipment (or leaving the construction and operation to two different outside entrepreneurs).

The saving of surpluses is clearly one function or operation and their use to make possible the creation of new equipment another and quite different one, just as the furnishing of productive services is one function and their use in the production of goods is another. In fact a little reflection will show that the operation of converting surplus goods into capital goods partakes in an especial degree of the characteristics which lead to the specialization of the entrepreneur function in the field of ordinary productive operations: namely, it involves special knowledge and foresight of future conditions. A surplus of consumption goods is fluid capital; it may be used to create any hind of concrete productive instruments whatever, within the limits of physical possibility and arbitrary social control. In a society which permitted such use it could be made to produce or increase a supply of slave labor. It can as a matter of fact be used to increase the supply of natural agents or to invent and discover new ways of doing things, even to create new wants for goods, and many things not conventionally considered capital creation.

The burning question in practice is, what form of new capital goods shall be created, where, by what methods, etc. The answer is an exercise of judgment of far the highest type called for in the business world. It is obviously inevitable that the function of answering this type of question will be specialized along the same lines and for the same reasons as the control of enterprise under static conditions. The individuals who control the conversion of saved surpluses into capital goods must take the responsibility for their decisions, though as in the former case the "control" may take the form of selecting some one else to exercise the immediate control as a routine task performed without responsibility for the results. The call for the exercise of judgment is greater as the uncertainties of progress are greater than those of routine operations, and the necessity that the responsibility be taken by the person who exercises the judgment — of the situation or of the human capacity to judge it — is correspondingly great.

Under freedom of contract the machinery which naturally grows up for effecting this specialization is the machinery of the market, working in the same way as in the case of entrepreneurs' bargains with the owners of productive services. Surplus consumption goods, or titles to these in the form of money or bank deposits, form a perfectly standardized commodity of an ideal sort for trading. It is also extremely mobile, still further adapting it to the operations of a market of the widest scope. Banks and financial institutions have this market highly organized. The actual workings of the market are the same as those of any other market. At any time there is a price established, which in this case is unusually definite and uniform. It is not, indeed, a single homogeneous commodity that is dealt in, for funds for different sorts of investment admit of the specialization of the entrepreneur function in widely different degrees. But after all the loan market represents a narrower range of prices according to grade and kind of the goods than is true of nearly any other market to be named. Men who are willing to purchase at the established price meet men who are willing to sell at that price; others do not enter the market. If more of the commodity is offered than will be taken at the existing price the price falls, and vice versa, keeping the price constantly adjusted to the point which equates the supply and demand.

The buyers' decisions to enter the market represent a judgment of an investment opportunity that will yield a profit (together with ability to give the security demanded in consideration of the rate on the particular kind of loan). The entrepreneur in this case must make an estimate of the future, involving a very complicated series of factors. The borrower of funds (like the hirer of other agencies) for routine productive operations estimates the physical product to be turned out by their use and the sale price of this product. The borrower for the purpose of creating new capital equipment[235] must estimate in physical terms the results of his constructive operations, the physical output of his equipment after it is in use, and both the cost and the salability of that product, all of which are in the future by the interval required to construct the equipment in addition to the period of production in the industry. Besides all which it must be kept in mind that the construction of a new productive plant includes getting it into operation, building up business connections in the markets for all the things the business must purchase as well as the things which it sells; and this normally requires a much longer time than the mere mechanical construction of the plant.

The specialization of entrepreneur activities may go farther than above indicated in various ways. In particular, the use of surplus goods, represented by money funds, in constructing new production goods may be separated from the operation of the new equipment when constructed. But for obvious reasons this is also likely not to be the case. Construction includes, as we have seen, an initial period of operation longer than the construction period itself in the narrow sense, and the overlapping in time makes them difficult to separate. It commonly happens, indeed, that ' the mechanical part of building a plant is turned over for a fixed consideration to another entrepreneur, a contractor. Of course the starting of new enterprises with a view to their sale or even lease to others for operation after they are established as going concerns is not at all unusual, but can hardly be said to be the typical procedure in most lines of business.

The importance of the distinction between capital and capital goods should now be clear. The business world thinks of capital as money funds. Money, however, is only a medium of exchange, and in the investment function represents a title to a surplus of wealth, practically speaking a surplus of consumption goods. This is the real meaning of free capital, which is a stage in the development

[235]Borrowing for the purchase of productive equipment already in existence (land or other goods) manifestly makes no difference in either the demand or supply of capital and hence has no effect on the interest rate.

of capital goods. The crux of current confusion in interest theory lies in the failure to see the significance of the fact that we live in a progressive society, that new net surplus production is constantly flowing through the loan market into the investment field and being converted into material equipment.[236] That is, it is surplus production on the part of the individuals and classes who save it; from the standpoint of society as a whole there is no surplus production of consumption goods; the surplus appears in the form of additions to capital equipment. In an unprogressive society where new saving was not being used to create new resources, there could not be interest in the sense in which the term has significance to economic theorists, — i.e., as a distributive share, — though interest could be paid for consumption loans. At present consumption loans are negligible in comparison with loans for conversion into new productive goods; when they are made they, of course, take the same rate of interest, allowance being made for degree of security against loss of interest and principal.[237]

Interest is the payment for the use of free capital; for the use of capital goods when employed by another than their owner, the payment is a rent. Interest is manifestly paid out of the produce of the property created with the resources obtained by the loan; it is part of the produce of the capital goods which were in the mind of the borrower when the loan was made, which the capital represented to him. This yield of property must again be distinguished from rent; the former is the actual return realized from the exploitation of the material things, while rent is the competitive market value of their use. Rent is paid out of the property yield if the property is actually leased; if it is managed by the owner, income should still be imputed to it on the basis of its fair rental value. The yield should include rent plus a profit, if the entrepreneur is to get any remuneration for the performance of his special function.[238]

[236]From the standpoint of an ultimate long-time treatment of interest theory it is important that this conversion is not usually utterly irrevocable. The process can generally be reversed, the capital withdrawn, and the wealth recovered in the form of consumption goods — more or less quickly and effectively — by under-maintenance of the capital goods.

[237]See chapter IV for a discussion of the possibility that interest might appear in connection with the use of property in a static state, and chapter V for a similar discussion with regard to a progressive society with uncertainty absent.

[238]Whether entrepreneurs as a class or on the average do secure remuneration for their services as entrepreneurs in the strict sense — i.e., exclusive of payment for their work and for the use of their property — is a point about which question

These three species of income thus form a sort of concatenated series, tied together by two forms of profit. The actual yield of the property includes the competitive rent, and the profit which pays the responsible entrepreneur who exploits it. The rent in turn includes competitive interest on the investment (the original value sacrificed to create it) plus a profit which is the remuneration for the entrepreneur function of converting the investment into the concrete goods.

One striking difference between rent and interest has been especially fruitful as a source of confusion in the theory. Both are expressed as rates, per dollar per year, but the explanation is very different in the two cases. Interest is naturally a rate, a ratio between two values. The object transferred from saver to entrepreneur is expressed in value terms, a certain amount of money, representing surplus consumers' goods to a certain value, and the return to the capitalist is also stated in value terms. If rent is stated as a rate of return on the investment, however, the relation is inverse; the investment in this case means not an original value magnitude, but the sale value of the property, which is the result of capitalization at the current rate of interest. For obviously in a progressive society where men are constantly lending funds of value at interest, freedom of exchange between value funds and productive goods will fix a value on the latter equal to the investment necessary to produce an equivalent return. It is this phenomenon of capitalization which to certain writers of the "psychological school"[239] has obscured the fact that what is transferred in a loan at interest is a fund of value which is not the result of a capitalization process, but is valued as an immediate utility.

Capitalization and property values are fundamental to an understanding of the phenomena which arise out of the uncertainties present in a progressive society, and call for some further discussion on their own account. When a new productive enterprise is once established and shows promise of yielding a profit above the

will be raised in the next chapter.

[239] Time preference or discount of the future, as more fully explained elsewhere, has nothing to do with the interest rate except in determining the supply of new capital (rate of saving). This indirect effect becomes appreciable only over long periods of time, since the saving made in any short period is negligible at best in comparison with the total investment previously made, or more strictly that part of this total which retains some degree of fluidity, and is also negligible in relation to the total demand for capital in the market.

competitive rates of return on the resources put into it and those necessary for its operation, this entire future yield, discounted to its present worth at the current rate of interest, can be drawn or cashed in at once by the sale of the property.[240] Taken in conjunction with the fact observed above, that the desire to own productive wealth is by no means merely an indirect desire to consume its revenue, this fact of the anticipation of future income by capitalization increases many fold the incentive to embark on new ventures. Even when the owner of the enterprise has no intention of selling the property, but considers only operating it to secure an income, the paper profit on the capital value must be considered a part of his remuneration more or less separable in his mind from the profit in the shape of an income above the competitive return on the investment.

It would be hard to overestimate the error involved in the psychological interpretation of economic motive as desire to consume goods alone. Even the desire for an income is not simply a desire to consume. For societies, or social classes in any society, near the subsistence margin, this is more nearly true. Even the so-called "subsistence margin," however, in any advanced society like the United States includes probably several times as much as is really necessary to gratify the animal wants and maintain health and physical efficiency. This does not mean that an individual can really live on a fraction of what those with the lowest incomes actually consume, for in a civilized society, the conventional necessaries may be as indispensable in fact as the animal necessaries. The motives for the consumption of even the conventional necessaries are none the less different from the animal needs. The desire (or necessity) for conforming to conventions is not the same thing as the need for food and protection; the easy fallacy is confusion of the requirement for food, clothing, and shelter of the conventional kinds with the requirement for food, clothing, and shelter as physiological necessities. A large part of the consumption of persons, in the lower income strata even, does not yield satisfaction as consumption; the motives and cravings are social in their origin and nature. It is a commonplace that many of the necessities of to-day did not exist or were not available for our ancestors a few generations ago, irrespective of their wealth.

In separating the desire to increase one's possessions from the desire to consume goods, we of course make no pretense of carrying

[240]Allowance must be made for the uncertainty of the permanence of the income.

our analysis back to "ultimate" motives, but an observation in this connection may not be out of place. Adverse reference has been made to the use of instinct psychology in economics. In the writer's view the lists of instincts given by Parker and others are superficial in the highest degree; yet it must be admitted that this literature represents progress, in comparison with the naive psychologizing of conventional economics. The instincts are a step in the right direction, carrying back the immediate lines of endeavor to more generalized motives and impulses. The defect in the procedure is that it stops halfway on the road to a rather obvious goal. Man has no instincts in the sense of tendencies to act in a definite way under definite circumstances, at least above a plane so low that they are as properly interpreted as reflexes. He has a few needs, of course, but the knowledge of their mode of satisfaction is not innate. We should never know, if untaught, what to eat, if indeed we should connect the pangs of hunger with the act of eating at all in the absence of knowledge gained by teaching through stimulating certain reflexes. And similar statements probably hold for sex behavior. It seems clear that in our whole higher life above the plane of food and sex and primitive pleasure-pain reactions, our activities result from a single unspecified, undirected tendency to act purposefully, the specific direction of the desire and activity being determined by suggestion from the environment and critical reflection upon such outside suggestion. All the instincts not directly connected with self-preservation (and the specific content of even these as we have seen is largely taught) are easily analyzed into each other; any one of them — or better, any pair, for they run largely in pairs of opposites — if interpreted broadly will account for most of our conduct. The only differentiation that would have any meaning would be the separation of an instinct of repose from the instinct of action; and repose is a mere negative.

Possibly thought is sometimes enough different from motor activity to justify a separation, but this would certainly be the case with exceptional individuals only, and the instinct theorists insist on universality as a criterion for a true instinct.[241]

[241]The correct line for a scientific interpretation of human behavior is in the writer's view well indicated in the "Methodological Introduction" (by Professor Thomas) to The Polish Peasant in Europe and America, by Thomas and Czaniecki. Professor Thomas's analysis runs in terms of "values" (social customs, conventions, or mores) and "attitudes," the result of individual criticism of the established values and tending constantly to modify and reconstruct the

The conclusion we are here interested in, however interpreted into human nature, is that social progress on the material side is largely motivated by a desire to possess wealth, and that the role of uncertainty in connection with capitalization is to make it possible for an individual through superior judgment or good luck to obtain a large increase in his wealth in a short time. In addition capitalization brings about a reduction of uncertainty through consolidation, in a way pointed out in an earlier chapter. Persons who are fitted for and enjoy making new ventures can specialize in this type of economic activity, selling the new enterprises when established. Thus by bringing many ventures within the scope of action of a single individual (or business unit) the errors tend more or less to cancel out; and an estimate can be formed of the objective value of the entrepreneur ability exemplified, still further reducing the margin of uncertainty in any particular venture.

It goes without saying that the phenomena of capitalization hold good for established enterprises as well as new ones. Any change in the current yield of any property whatever at once accrues, in so far as it is viewed as permanent, in the form of a change in the capital value of that property. These changes in capital value often overshadow in importance the changes in income. Such changes in capital values, depending on the anticipated future income of the property, do not necessarily wait forwent possible outcomes in a group of instances is known, it is possible to get rid of any real uncertainty by the expedient of grouping or "consolidating" instances. But that it is possible does not necessarily mean that it will be done, and we must observe at the outset that when an individual instance only is at issue, there is no difference for conduct between a measurable risk and an unmeasurable uncertainty. The individual, as already observed, throws his estimate of the value of an opinion into the probability form of "a successes in b trials" (a/b being a proper fraction) and "feels" toward it as toward any other probability situation.

As so commonly in this subject fraught with logical difficulty and paradox, reservations must be made to the above statement. In the first place, it does not matter how unique the instance, if a real probability can be calculated, if we can know with certainty

---

latter. This view is also harmonious with that of Professor Tufts, formulated in more general terms in the essay on "The Moral Life" in the volume entitled Creative Intelligence.

how many successes there would be in (say) one hundred trials if the one hundred trials could be made. If we know the odds against us it does not matter in the least whether we place all our wagers in one kind of game or in as many different games as there are wagers; the laws of probability hold in the second case just as well as in the first. But in business situations it so rarely happens that a probability can be computed for a single unique instance that this qualification has less weight than might be supposed. However, in so far as objective probability enters into a calculation, it is hard to imagine an intelligent individual considering any single case as absolutely isolated. The only exception would be a decision in which one's whole fortune (or his life) were at stake. The importance of the contingency and probable frequency of recurrence in the individual lifetime of situations similar in the magnitude of the issues involved should make a difference in the attitude assumed toward any one case as well as the mathematical probability of success or failure.

A second reservation of more importance is connected with the possibility referred to in the preceding chapter, of forming classes of cases by grouping the decisions of a given person. That is, even though we do not get a quantitative probability by the process of grouping, still there is some tendency for fluctuations to cancel out and for the result to approach constancy in some degree. There appear to be in the making of judgments the same two kinds of elements that we find in probability situations proper; i.e., (a) determinate factors (the quality of the judging faculty, which is more or less stable) and (b) truly accidental factors varying from one decision to another according to a principle of indifference. The difference between the uncertainty of an opinion and a true probability is that we have no means of separating the two and evaluating them, either by calculation a priori or by empirical sorting. But in the second case the difference is not absolute; the sorting method does apply to some extent, though within narrow limits. Life is mostly made up of uncertainties, and the conditions under which an error or loss in one case may be compensated by other cases are bafflingly complex. We can only say that "in so far as" one confronts a situation involving uncertainty and deals with it on its merits as an isolated case, it is a matter of practical indifference whether the uncertainty is measurable or not.

The problem of the human attitude toward uncertainty (not for the present purpose distinguishing kinds) is as beset with difficulties as that of uncertainty itself. Not merely is the human reaction to situations of this character apt to be erratic and extremely various from one individual to another, but the "normal" reaction is subject to well-recognized deviations from the conduct which sound logic would dictate. Thus it is a familiar fact, well discussed by Adam Smith, that men will readily risk a small amount in the hope of winning a large when the adverse probability (known or estimated) against winning is much in excess of waves. It is like the oft-cited advance of the tide up a beach, advance and recession alternating and obscuring even the fact that a small gain of an occasional wave constitutes a net advance. Economic progress under real conditions shows similar advance and recession, proceeding in cycles of a character now fairly well understood, but of such uncertain length that the consequences at the turningpoints are often catastrophic. A large part of the phenomenon is due to the fact that the creation of new capital is so closely bound up in the issue of circulating medium by commercial banks. Price levels and profit margins being even more dependent on this precarious exchange medium, the operations of business proper find themselves tied up to the tendencies of a credit currency under private control to expand to a point of instability and under the least shock to collapse. These phenomena enormously increase the uncertainty of business operations and create opportunities for making large gains through the exercise of superior foresight or by good luck.[242]

The above description of the uncertainty relations of one of the elements of social progress, brief and inadequate as it is, must suffice for the present sketch. Moreover, the other progress factors, though more complicated and difficult of treatment, will have to be disposed of very briefly by a mere indication of some of the similarities to and contrasts with the growth of capital. The increase of population may be briefly handled. In the aggregate, it is not subject to enough uncertainty to produce any noticeable effect on the organization of society. Over long periods the general increase, if it proceeds faster than new lands are opened, as it has since the industrial revolution, causes a rise in the value of "land." This change,

[242]Davenport (Economics of Enterprise) has emphasized the fact that the short-period changes in the interest rate are due to changes in the supply of bank funds. He is to be criticized for failing to make it clear that the long-time questions must be handled along wholly different lines. Cf. also Moulton, "Commercial Banking and Capital Formation," Journal of Political Economy, 1918, pp. 484 ff., 638 ff., 705 ff., 849 ff.

however, as an aggregate is so far overshadowed by the differences in the changes at different locations that it may be passed over. There is little question that in fact speculators in land make on the whole less than the competitive return on their investment, though this is difficult to prove conclusively. The outstanding phenomenon is the large gains and losses, especially the large gains from a few fortunate investments in real estate held over a period of generations by the same families. We shall recur to this theme in the next chapter. It is clear that the main cause of the differential rates of value increase is another one of our progress factors, the redistribution of the population over the soil. The mixture of foresight and pure luck in the production of gains from such uncertainties is an interesting question, but one about which there seems to be little comment worth making. Another phenomenon in connection with the increase of population over long periods is the redistribution of wealth and probably of ability among individuals. We know that the wealthier families increase much more slowly than the less wealthy, and there is every reason to believe that the same applies to the more as compared with the less capable. As wealth and ability are both inherited in varying degrees the consequences are obtrusive, in their general character at least. These facts do not affect the form or theory of competitive organization, but as they modify the material upon which the mechanism works the results are none the less subject to change.

Another progress factor, the increase in the available supply of natural resources, has been referred to incidentally above, and as the relations of "land" to "capital" were discussed in an earlier chapter, this topic need not detain us long. Discovery of new natural wealth may result from pure accident, in which case its value is all pure profit, which in consequence of the principle of capitalization may be cashed in at once by the finder. But this is not what usually happens. In the case of agricultural land the conditions and rewards of pioneering are fairly ascertainable. If any profit results from these operations it is an exceptional case or else it is remuneration for some special sacrifice undergone; i.e., is not a profit at all. With mineral resources things are different. Here there is an enormous amount of complete unpredictability. Under old-fashioned methods there is no question that prospecting for the precious metals involved in the aggregate enormous losses. In regard to other minerals, coal, oil, iron, copper, etc., the present writer has no ground for forming an opinion, but would "guess" that the search for these things being less feverish, the accidental gains are much less in arrear of the losses. Recently the search for precious metals has been placed on a much more scientific basis and there is doubtless in the aggregate less discrepancy than formerly between the returns realized and a normal competitive return on the resources invested.

The point which calls for emphasis is that where the possibility of securing wealth by the discovery of natural resources is known, along with something of the operations and outlays required, resources will be attracted into the field of searching for them in accordance with men's estimates of the chances of success in relation to the outlays to be incurred. The quest of wealth by this process thus becomes to those engaged in it an ordinary business operation, differing from the routine production of goods for immediate consumption in no matter of principle, though perhaps affected by a larger degree of uncertainty. And the same organization devices will be called into existence to deal with the uncertainty present — large-scale operations, the use of insurance where possible still further to broaden the base of the calculations, scientific research into the conditions of prediction and control of results, etc. Entrepreneurs engaged in exploration and development work bid in the same market against entrepreneurs in the fields of static industry for the same fundamental productive resources, and competition must fix a uniform price for both uses and bring about the same tendency to equality of cost incurred with output secured over the whole field of investment.

Another factor of progress having exceedingly complex uncertainty relations is the changes in human wants. These changes, again, may just happen, accidentally, or they may take place more or less in accordance with law and hence predictably, or they may be deliberately brought about by the expenditure of resources for the express purpose of effecting such a change. If they happen unexpectedly the disturbances in incomes and capital values which result must be classed as pure profit or loss. In so far as they can be foreseen, no profit will be realized. In so far as they result from a deliberate expenditure of resources, they become as all other economic operations. The amount of profit realized will then depend on the effectiveness of competition based on foreknowledge of the results of the activity. In this respect the "production" of wants is like the production of goods. In fact, as we have previously observed, the advertising, puffing, or salesmanship necessary to create a demand for a commodity is causally indistinguishable from a utility inherent in the commodity itself.

The last progress factor calling for notice is that of knowledge, or what may be designated by the term "invention" taken in a broad sense. It is a commonplace fact that one of the chief sources of uncertainty in business life is the improvement of technological processes, methods of organization, and the like. It is difficult to draw a rigid distinction in principle between the discovery of new facts and the production of change in the facts themselves as objects of knowledge. It is plain that the finding of new natural resources is equivalent to their creation and the difference in the case of human wants is also rather hazy and metaphysical. The important "practical difference between discovery and creation relates to the matter, referred to in a previous chapter, of the cost of reproduction of ideas as compared with things. The knowledge of a fact may be extensible almost without cost throughout the membership of competitive society. Of course — and this is an observation which students of the phenomena have neglected to make — it also may not be of this character; it may cost as much to get an idea into a head as it does to get matter from one form into another, and it always does cost some expenditure of energy somewhere. In general, however, a competitor can get the idea of a new method or process at less cost than he can get new material equipment, provided energy is not expended in preventing him from doing it. Moreover, the mere gratification of curiosity may be ample compensation for the effort required to get an idea, so that this cost can be entirely neglected or may even become negative.

The essential facts about new knowledge for our purposes center around the qualities of the productive equipment, including laborers, requisite for carrying it into effect. A new process usually calls for changes in the forms and attributes of productive agencies and necessarily involves new combinations among these. In very simple cases, however, little may be involved beyond new manipulations of old things. Like all the other phases of progress this one may result from accident or from the planned expenditure of existing resources. Even in the case of accident we cannot say that anticipation of and allowance for the change is entirely eliminated. For it is not meaningless to assert that even of things beyond our knowledge or control some are more likely to happen than others. We do make such judgments and in the large they are probably more right than wrong, however mysterious may be the basis upon which their value rests. In so far as the probability of a discovery can be estimated it is evident, as in the case of progressive changes previously discussed, that entrepreneurs will make allowance for its effects and in so far it will in the aggregate cause no competitive maladjustment and produce no discrepancy between the prices paid by entrepreneurs for productive services and the prices received for their products. The value of such estimates is naturally very small, and we may assume that most of the offsetting of gains and losses from disturbances due to accidental discoveries is itself accidental and not the result of calculation.

In the case of new knowledge which is the result of deliberate thought, investigation, and experiment, the element of predictability is of course greater. As inscrutable as with accidental discoveries, almost, are the operations by which we form an estimate of the chances of success in such operations, but the fact is inescapable that we do form such estimates and that they have considerable value. Much scientific and business research is now carried on under some approximation to competitive conditions by the employment of large-scale methods. That is, it is possible to foresee the average long-run results of the operations with sufficient accuracy to cause the employment of resources in the field up to a point where the return is approximately equated with the return from the same resources in the general competitive market. In any case it is clear that in so far as the results can be predicted the investment of resources in the acquisition of new knowledge will be so adjusted as to equate the return with the general competitive level, which is to say equate realized values to costs and eliminate profits.

The matter is indeed frequently, if not usually, complicated by the very low cost of indefinitely multiplying an idea when it is once secured. As a consequence of this fact the inventor or discoverer usually has to make some special provision to limit the use of his results to his own business operations. In certain fields this can be done through legal protection granted by the State in recognition of the value to society of the service. In others artificial measures for secrecy must be taken. In many cases no direct safeguards are available and the economic profitableness of the idea is limited to the period of time required for competitors to copy the new method. Regular commercial research in these fields is doubtless rare. Even legal protection is valid only for a limited period of time and secrecy cannot often be permanently maintained. When the idea becomes common property it is like any other superabundant element in production, a free good and no longer a productive factor in the effective economic sense.

It may often happen, however, that one of the results of a new departure is greatly to increase the value of some limited kind of material or human productive service. If this service be that of a non-reproducible natural agent the inventor may permanently secure that part of the value of his idea by purchasing such property. If the gain attaches to reproducible property he may prolong his differential gain by the period required to increase the supply, and even in case of a specialized human service a long-time contract may sometimes be utilized to retard diffusion of the results of superior methods. As observed in our discussion of monopoly it is immaterial whether we regard these cases as monopolization of the idea or method as such or as monopolization of the limited resources necessary for its exploitation. The losses which are equally likely to result from inventions fall upon the owners of the specialized human qualities or equipment goods.

Discussion of the conditions of permanence of the gains from improved methods of production leads naturally to the consideration of the general subject of economic friction and its opposite, mobility. We have already observed that the advocates of the "dynamic" theory of profit, the theory that profit is the result of progressive change, give an exceedingly important place to the phenomenon of friction in their analysis.[243] In this view, indeed, friction is a necessary condition to the occurrence of profit, as it is expressly stated that in the absence of friction profit would disappear as fast as it appeared and that it does constantly slip through the fingers of the entrepreneur and spread over society at large as fast as the friction can be overcome.

It will be apparent as soon as pointed out that this argument uses "friction" in an inadmissibly inclusive sense. To explain profit thus in terms of friction, the term must be made to cover every form of resistance to change and readjustment in productive operations. That is, to get rid of profit by eliminating friction, it would be necessary not merely to have a perfect market, perfect competition, and costless mobility, but in addition it would have to be possible without the consumption of time or effort to change the form of capital

[243]Cf . above, p. 34 f.

equipment and goods in process, not to speak of natural agencies and the existing labor force. In a world where this could be done, it is manifest that there would be no need for productive effort of any kind. Perhaps we may distinguish between the readjustments involving only the moving about and recombination of productive agencies of all kinds and those calling in addition for substantial alteration in the form of things. The latter it is clearly inadmissible to class under the head of overcoming "friction." But the same may be said even of mere movement of things. This also is a productive transformation, and undoubtedly the greater part of ordinary productive activity comes under the head of transportation, taken in a broad sense.

It is necessary to take up the problem under the heads of the different types of production costs and investigate the forces which retard the readjustment of each type to correspondence with the value of the productive contribution of the agency to which the payment is made. The first and simplest readjustment is that of values of services which undergo no change in either form or position as a result of the introduction of new methods. A new discovery will, as already noted, increase the value contributions obtainable by the use of some agencies and decrease those of others. It will ordinarily be true that changes in the market prices of these services will lag appreciably behind the changes in their theoretical values to the entrepreneur. Many of them are hired under contracts covering a longer or shorter period of time which prevent sudden changes in their rate of remuneration. During any such interval the employing entrepreneur must, of course, make a gain or loss by their use.

And even where the factor of a time contract does not enter, there will probably be a lag in the prices of productive services, i.e., in the costs of production, as compared with commodity prices. The former are, of course, in the aggregate caused by and reflected from the latter and the forces of competition which impute commodity values to the productive services upon which production depends do not operate instantaneously. The chief cause of this lag is again the difficulty and uncertainty of knowledge; it takes the owners of productive services and entrepreneurs some time to learn the facts. Most of this learning has to be done by crude and rather slow trial-and-error methods; there is generally no possibility of computing results in advance. In the interval necessary for every one to find out the exact relations of dependence between product values and the employment of each resource and of working out an ideal adjustment, it is clear that there will be many discrepancies between entrepreneurs' outlays and their returns, i.e., many occurrences of profit, positive or negative.

A somewhat special case is presented by goods in process when new methods are introduced. The general tendency must be to decrease the values of most of these, though not necessarily of all. The loss will fall on the owner in whose hands they are when the price change takes place, which may not be the owner at the time the new process is invented, for these price changes will also lag more or less. The loss in value will depend on several factors, the amount of superiority of the new process over the old, the amount of difference between the old intermediate goods and the corresponding new ones, and the possibility, and the cost, of changing the old intermediate goods in a way to have the manufacture carried to completion by the new process.

Material productive goods will fall more or less under the same head as goods in process according as they are or are not reproducible, short-lived, and amenable to change in form. We have seen that the difference between capital and land is one of degree, depending on these qualities in the agent. At one extreme, capital is typified by goods in process. At the other, "land" consists of these agencies whose supply is most rigidly fixed, the nearest approach to the theoretical limit being the element of site value. Taking this extreme first, a piece of pure land will gain or lose the capitalized value of the change in its income as soon as this is accurately adjusted. With ordinary capital equipment, allowance must be made for the life of the agency and also for the possibility and cost, including the time required, to adapt it to the new conditions. The adaptation may include both movement from one situation to another and change in form. Even a revolutionary invention, making buildings and machinery worthless for use in their present form, does not usually destroy all their value. At worst a scrap value of the material is recoverable of the original free capital invested in them.

Laborers present a still different case. The only thing to be considered from the standpoint of economic organization is here the lag in the readjustment of wages to the new real value of labor. Changes in the value of specialized skill accrue to the laborer as an individual only and cannot be capitalized. The same facts as to possibility of readaptation hold good as in case of material equipment goods, but again this is a matter of the individual's own personal economy and does not affect entrepreneurs. The peculiarities of labor in relation to readjustments form one of the main sources of injustice and hardship in an individualist economy. The risk of loss in the value of acquired knowledge and training means a constantly impending threat of indigence. Laborers are attached to their homes and even to their work by sentimental ties to which market facts are ruthless. But these matters hardly call for detailed discussion in a study of the present sort.

Chapter 12. Social Aspects of Uncertainty and Profit

Uncertainty is one of the fundamental facts of life. It is as ineradicable from business decisions as from those in any other field. The amount of uncertainty may, however, be reduced in several ways, as we have seen. In the first place, we can increase our knowledge of the future through scientific research and the accumulation and study of the necessary data. To do this involves cost, the expenditure of resources which must be drawn from other uses. Another way is by the clubbing of uncertainties through large-scale organization of various forms. This operation also involves costs, and not merely in the sense of expenditure of resources. There is also to be considered the loss of individual freedom involved in any possible plan of organization, a loss for the great mass of persons affected, though possibly a gain for a few who may secure wider powers and a larger range of action from the concentration of authority.

In the third place it is possible, also at a cost, to increase control over the future. And here again both sorts of costs must be faced, substantive outlays and human losses through organization. Finally, uncertainty might be further reduced almost indefinitely by slowing up the march of progress, which, of course, involves a direct sacrifice in addition to both the forms of cost already noticed.

All these proposals raise the fundamental issue as to the essential evil of uncertainty, how great it is and hence how much we can afford to sacrifice in other ways in order to reduce it. In this sort of calculation as in all economic problems we are dealing with a question of proportioning alternatives subject to a principle of diminishing relative importance. It would doubtless be possible to use all the resources of society with more or less effect in reducing uncertainty, leaving none for any other use. It is a question of how far to go. The question is complicated by the fact that the use of resources in reducing uncertainty is an operation attended with the greatest uncertainty of all. If we are uncertain as to the results of ordinary business operations we are doubly so as to the results of expenditures along any of the lines enumerated looking toward the increase of knowledge and control.

Quite as important as the question of reducing uncertainty is that of its distribution. This question raises again the same fundamental issue, this time from the individual point of view instead of the social, as to the intrinsic desirability of reducing uncertainty. How far the burden should be equalized, how far concentrated or specialized, depends on the individual attitude toward uncertainty, and especially on the tendency of the irksomeness to increase as the amount of uncertainty faced by an individual increases, and vice-versa. The steeper the curve of increasing disutility the more we must favor a relative dispersion of the burden. It is perhaps obvious that high degrees of "risk" are more irksome; most of us are reluctant to jeopardize our lives or the elemental requirements of life. But it is also evident that individuals differ widely in the extent to which they find this true. We have already noted the more or less paradoxical fact that the very idea of intelligent conduct implies an effort to reduce uncertainty, while none the less we recognize, on any calm, cool contemplation of the matter, that a life with uncertainty eliminated or perhaps even very greatly reduced would not appeal to us.

There is a close connection between the two notions, reducing the absolute amount of uncertainty on the whole and distributing it, for most methods of reducing it effect either a concentration or a distribution. On this head there seems to be no generalization which can be made with confidence and which is worth making.

It is not too much to say that the very essence of free enterprise is the concentration of responsibility in its two aspects of making decisions and taking the consequences of decisions when put into effect. It is therefore of the utmost importance to inquire critically and carefully into the facts as to the results of such a concentration in comparison with any possible alternatives. At the outset we shall raise no question as to large-scale industry; and it is evident that if we are to have large-scale organization with its advantages in efficiency we must assume a corresponding degree of concentration of control in the immediate sense of executive direction. This, however, as we have been especially concerned to emphasize, does not necessarily mean concentration of responsibility. We have seen that practically all human activity, even that of the purest routine character, is in some manner and degree forward-looking and involves meeting unexpected situations and making decisions. But these decisions do not necessarily involve responsibility. The outstanding feature of free enterprise organization is the transfer of the lower grades of responsibility to men whose decisions relate to the selection of men for the places under their control and to answering occasional questions in regard to exceptional contingencies. The two functions are, indeed, never quite separate. The ultimate responsibility consists chiefly in the selection of a man or a very few men to "organize" the establishment. But the ultimate authority usually if not always exercises some direct control over business policy. In most cases also the higher officials of an enterprise have a direct stake in the business beyond their fixed salaries. And down through the organization the subordinate functionaries may be said to have responsibility in the sense that the results which they secure must come up to the expectations of their superiors or they will lose their positions.

In the existing system of things the ultimate responsibility centers almost altogether in the ownership of the property "at risk" in the business. There are infinite variations and complications in the distribution of "risk" and control, but the general tendency is clear. The lower grades of labor take practically no risk and exercise correspondingly little control, and the same is only less true of the higher grades and of borrowed capital. We must remember that the two things, uncertainty-bearing and responsible control, are inseparable; in so far as the reward of any service is contingent upon the success of the undertaking, the owner of that service, in consenting to its employment for a contingent remuneration, exercises judgment and wields power over the enterprise. But the greater part of the uncertainty and power are centered in the ownership of certain property which is placed in the position of guaranteeing the contractual income of the other property and that of the labor used in the business.[244]

---

[244]Limited progress has been made in some countries in the development of organizations of laborers which engage in enterprise independently, borrowing any necessary capital and hiring supervision at fixed rates. Cooperative production in the ordinary sense may also be referred to, but neither of these cases affords a notable exception to the above generalization as the laborers borrow very little capital. It is one of the defects of our civilization that mechanism has not been involved to enable human ability to hypothecate its productive power in procur-

We shall not attempt to take up all the possible or actual arrangements in regard to responsibility and control, but shall limit the discussion to the general problem of concentration of uncertainty. It will be kept in mind that the basis of effective assumption of responsibility is necessarily either the ownership of property or the creation of a lien on future human productive power and is in fact almost altogether the former. Another preliminary reservation is that in a sense ultimate control rests with the consumer. But in so far as economic organization takes the form of free enterprise this control is exercised only after the fact, and the responsibility we are concerned with is that of meeting the consumer's demands at the end of the production process. We assume, then, that the entrepreneur system of organization, with production for the market impersonally, and concentration of direction, arises because it is superior to, or more satisfactory all around than any other free contract system. And the first step in our inquiry will be a brief examination into the meaning of free contract.

With the possible exception of the word "cause" and its equivalents, it is doubtful if there is a more abused word than "freedom"; and surely there is no more egregious confusion in the whole muddled science of politics than the confusion between "freedom" and "freedom of contract."[245] Freedom refers or should refer to the range of choices open to a person, and in its broad sense is nearly synonymous with "power." Freedom of contract, on the other hand, means simply absence of formal restraint in disposal of "one's own" It may mean in fact the perfect antithesis of freedom in the sense of power

---

ing resources to make it effective under its own direction and responsibility. A notable tendency in modern business development is to specialize and subdivide uncertainty and control in all possible degrees. Corporations multiply securities representing every conceivable gradation from the position of a pure creditor with absolute safety and complete indifference to the conduct of the business at one extreme to risk and control so highly concentrated that slight fluctuations in earnings make the difference between high dividends and assessments at the other. In mercantile business and even in industrial concerns credit instruments pass through the hands of a lengthening series of middlemen who add their guarantees of soundness and pass them on at a little higher price or lower return. Bond houses, bill brokers, and acceptance banks are an interesting development in this field. In the labor field the same tendency is manifest. Intermediate employers may hire labor for rehiring to actual exploiters, as in the familiar case of the padrone, and in some lines of professional work. Every development of profit-sharing is similarly a redistribution of risk and control.

[245]Sir H. S. Maine and Herbert Spencer are especially responsible for this vicious and question-begging perversion of thought.

to order one's life in accordance with one's desires and ideals. The actual content of freedom of contract depends entirely on what one owns.

Ownership, as we have seen, consists essentially of the combination of the rights of control and of usufruct. The point to be emphasized here is that in a social system based on pure freedom of contract, ownership and control are interchangeable terms;[246] there is no other form of control. To be sure, there would have to be a "state" of some sort, an authoritative organization, to maintain such a system, but its sole function would be the enforcement of contract and prevention of non-contractual relations. Its necessity arises from the fact that contracts are not often executed on both sides simultaneously and the further fact that men might prey upon each other. That is, the role of the State in such a system would be merely to restrict human relations to the mutually voluntary, or contractual. In such a system, to repeat, those who owned nothing could not exist unless by the sufferance and generosity of those who did own, and the amount of freedom possessed by any person would be equal to the amount of his ownership.

Now, what one owns is under ideally simple conditions a result of three factors. The first and by far the most important is the historical "brute fact" of what he has "to begin with," his inheritance from the past. This is purely a matter of status — hence the fundamental absurdity of Maine's contrast between status and contract as descriptions of the position and condition of the individual. All free contract can mean is that status can be changed by voluntary agreement with another party, and cannot be changed without one's consent. The second factor in ownership is thus the result of previous contracts. And the possibility of change in status by mutually voluntary agreement depends on one's status — i.e., what one owns — at the time of the agreement, and hence finally on what one owned to begin with. The third factor in ownership or present status is change resulting from the voluntary and independent employment or transformation by utilization of one's own in the past. This element is also clearly a matter of change only, going

[246]It is obvious that pure freedom of contract is impossible in a continuous society, as children and the aged and many others can control nothing. In order to deal with the concept in a pure form we are compelled (see chapter IV) to assume that all dependent persons were absolutely dependent, which is to say virtually "owned" by the freely contracting members of the society.

back to initial status or what one owned to begin with. In a pure free contract system there is no power (control) except ownership; only change in ownership (which is to say really in status) has any connection with the exercise of free choice, and the range of choice depends absolutely on previous status and hence ultimately on the initial status in which the individual finds himself on his first entry into the system of contracting persons.

All the above, however, assumes that contracts and the activity directed to increasing ownership by "productive" transformation of what one already owns are intelligently carried out. In the world as it is, where all human designs and acts are fraught with uncertainty, a fourth factor must be added, the result of luck. Furthermore, we are still assuming complete independence and non-interference among the contracts and activities of different individuals. In the world as it is the interests affected by contracts are never all represented in the agreements. This is really a limitation on the assumption of pure freedom of contract, a failure to restrict human relations to the mutually voluntary sphere, but it is a fact which has to be taken into account, like deliberate predation.

These facts are so obtrusive that no one has in practice ever advocated pure freedom of contract, the restriction of the action of society as a whole to the negative function of preventing non-contractual relations. No question is ever actually raised as to the State limiting freedom of contract in many directions and encouraging agreements of other sorts. It also necessarily appropriates through taxation a considerable part of the usufruct of things privately "owned," thus modifying ownership in both its phases. And this modifying influence on private property extends rapidly in scope as the laissez-faire theory of the State loses ground in the modern world.

It is a fundamental fact that the possible objects of ownership fall into two main classes, personal powers inherent in the individual, and material things. If an individual does not have some form and degree of ownership in the former he is a slave, the property of some outside party, and outside the system altogether. The modern world is, of course, pretty well committed to private property in the individual's own personal powers in all adults not dangerously abnormal or incompetent, subject only to general limitations. It is difficult to secure effective utilization of these under any other system, and the live questions relate only to the ownership of material things.[247]We

[247]We make no distinction between natural agents and produced equipment

have seen in different connections that the importance of the difference between these two classes is at least much exaggerated, that generic natural differences are hard if not impossible to find in relation either to their cause-and-effect bearings on price theory and economic organization or to their moral standing. The conditions of demand, conditions of supply, and relation to the possessing individual turn out on examination to be much alike, and differences which exist at all are mostly artificial and conventional. But from the standpoint of our human interests outside the production and consumption of goods we must recognize that the ownership of one's self is in a somewhat higher position than the ownership of external objects. Yet in a civilization where man is highly and increasingly dependent on access to and use of material things for his very life this distinction tends to fade out, and recognition of this fact accounts for much of the current ferment and change in the social attitude toward "property" (used narrowly as property in things).

Another line of argument on the question of the relations between ownership of one's own powers and ownership of material things follows somewhat parallel lines to a somewhat similar uncertain or negative conclusion, beginning from an opposed point of view. The starting-point of our inquiry is the fact, clearly brought out by our study of enterprise, that the drift under non-interference is toward placing the control of industry, the ultimate entrepreneurship, in the hands of property-owners and not the owners of the human services, the workers. The ostensible reason for this is that a business venture offers opportunity for actual absolute loss, as well as merely a greater or less gain, and that only property can in the nature of the case make the guarantees against this net loss. This fact seems at first sight to afford the basis for another distinction between labor and property services, namely, that laborers are only used in industry, while material goods are used up, that only the services are consumed in the one case, while the thing itself may be destroyed in

---

goods, as we have shown that under competition no final distinction can be drawn between preemption and production. (See the discussion of land and capital in chapters IV, V, and XI.) In this connection we may remark here that we are not necessarily in disagreement with a separation of land from capital from the point of view taken by Marshall (Principles of Economics, book IV, chap. I). From the standpoint of a single political unit occupying a limited area of the earth whose natural resources are thoroughly explored, they stand in a different relation as to new supply from that which they occupy in a world economy or a vast and relatively new country like the United States.

the other.

A little critical reflection will show that this also is not really the case. Perhaps it ought to be so, but it is not, and cannot be. In the first place, the risk of destruction and total loss is perhaps as great in fact in the case of the laborer as in the case of the property-owner, and where in the latter case the owner loses only productive power the former loses health or bodily members or his life, which mean vastly more. The real merits of this situation are also being recognized by society and we see the growth of legislation designed to transfer the hazard of loss of the economic value of the laborer as a productive agent (and this only, so far) to the business and through it to the consumer of the product. There is another side to the question in the hazard of loss of specialized skill and training. These are acquired in connection with and for use in the particular business. The cost of acquisition is borne chiefly by the worker and if the business proves unprofitable, the loss generally falls on him. Yet these "risks," seemingly so much greater than those incurred by the property-owner, do not carry with them the control of the business, nor do the bearers of the risks even secure under competitive free contract (as is perfectly well known) anything like fair compensation in the form of a higher contractual return. And it must be added that the actuarial value of the worker's risks depends quite as much on the quality of the management as is the case with those of the owner of material property.

The only visible explanation of this state of things is an appeal to a "fact of human psychology" that the owners of "things" are less willing to trust those "things" to the control of others without an adequate guarantee in kind than are men who own only themselves to hazard such outside control without even the poor safeguard of a guarantee against economic loss.[248]

It is manifestly impossible to carry on production without incurring both sorts of uncertainties, uncertainty as to the results and as to the preservation intact of the means of production employed, both human and material. Since production must precede consumption and requires time, all those concerned in it must be maintained during the production period out of the fruits of previous production. And these products must be advanced by those who own them. It

[248]It is interesting to observe the concern of the management for the personal security of the workers brought about by compensation laws, and especially the remarkable results of the "safety first" movement in reducing accidents.

is not physically necessary that they be permanently hazarded by the owners, that the actual producers should get their entire wage in advance of the completion of the process, but this is the way it works out under free contract. Nor is it inevitable that these products be owned by any individuals at all, a point which we must next take up. At the same time the chance of loss of equipment must be borne, temporarily, by those who have equipment to lose, if equipment is privately owned. The permanence of the loss to an individual owner is not physically prescribed, in case of the owner of material things or of human powers in their purely economic aspect. But this again is the way it does work out under the "obvious and simple system of natural free contract." We must now glance briefly at the social bearings of free contract in a more fundamental sense.

There is naturally no intention of implying that freedom of contract is to any appreciable extent a result of the deliberate adoption by society of a reasoned policy of organization. However, the continuation of the system is a question which has been much discussed on its merits and which may ultimately be decided on the basis of discussion. To discuss the issue systematically we shall first eliminate and postpone for later notice the point as to personal self-ownership and limit ourselves provisionally to the ownership of material productive goods, the more or less live issue between individual and social property in these things. And we must further distinguish at the outset between two different and to a large extent opposed sets of interests involved in social organization. The conventional view in economics treats social organization as a mechanism for the satisfaction of "wants" which are assumed to be fixed conscious desires and tendencies to action, subject to the principle of diminishing relative utility. The limitations of this view have been emphasized throughout our study, but we have to consider this aspect of economic life in purity and isolation if we are to use the scientific method of analysis. Other interests are just as fundamental, notably the desire for freedom and power for their own sakes and the preference for certain qualities of human relations. It is largely this second set of interests which, directly and indirectly, have finally abolished slavery and established self-ownership.

Viewing society, then, as a want-satisfying machine and applying the single test of efficiency, free enterprise must be justified if at all on the ground that men make decisions, exercise control, more effectively if they are made responsible for the results of the correctness, or the opposite, of those decisions. If property were socialized we should still have to concentrate the function of the actual making of decisions, but it would be in a far greater degree than now a routine task, with the remuneration independent of the results. In the light of our previous discussion there is a difficulty here and we must be careful to make the meaning clear. Two things, specifically, would happen. Businesses in which men now work directly with their own resources would be transformed into public enterprises under the management of hired functionaries. In this case the nature of the change is clear enough. More obscure is the case of the corporation, now controlled by a hired manager. Here the change is the substitution of the public, organized in some political way, for the stockholders, and the position of the immediate decision-maker is superficially not much changed.

But only superficially. It is true that the growing similarity of large-scale business to the political democracy is one of the socialist's strongest arguments against a probable loss of efficiency in the exchange of private for public ownership. But we must emphasize the fact that the similarity is much exaggerated — in fact by both parties to the controversy, from different motives, of course. The insistence on the large number of stockholders in some of our great corporations is definitely misleading. Most of these do not regard themselves and are not regarded as owners of the business. In form they are such, but in substance they are merely creditors, and both they and the insiders count upon the fact. The great companies are really owned and managed by small groups of men who generally know each other's personalities, motives, and policies tolerably well. Hence in the first place the salaried manager under a socialist government, whether appointed by a political superior or chosen in some way by a democratic constituency, would really be in a very different position from the president or manager of a present-day corporation. He could not conceivably be so directly accountable to the ultimate entrepreneur, society, as he now is to the ultimate entrepreneur, the small group of "insiders" who are the real owners of the business.

But the greater change would consist in the substitution of the public at large for the small group of owners. The main difference is an inevitable concomitant of the mere size of a group. The insuperable difficulty of cooperative production has been to make the individual feel that the results depend upon his own activity. The individual feels lost in the mass, helpless and insignificant. Political democracy, of course, encounters the same difficulty. Perhaps we may believe that some progress is being made in solving the problem in the political sphere where decisions are really much less important in that the alternatives among which choice is made relate to less vital matters. If so, it may be possible that some generations of political democracy might train the individual in a sense of personal responsibility which would make industrial democracy more feasible.

But this is at best an exceedingly superficial view of the problem. At bottom it is a matter of feeling for the large property-owner as well as for the masses served by industry. He is really a social functionary now. Private property is a social institution; society has the unquestionable right to change or abolish it at will, and will maintain the institution only so long as property-owners serve the social interest better than some other form of social agency promises to do. Of course there is a lot of moral flub-dub about natural rights, sacred institutions of the past, etc., and it has some power to hold back social change. But in the end, and a not very distant end either, the question will be decided on the basis of what the majority of the people think, in a more or less cold-blooded way, about the issues. If we get more effective management through the system of concentrated private ownership than we would through some democratic machinery, it is because men plan better when they do not feel like government officials doing things for other people, when they feel their work as their own and identify their personalities with it.

And this even though the same men know "in their hearts," subconsciously if not consciously, that they are the agents of the democracy and ultimately responsible to it for their trust. For it is clear that the "personal" interests which our rich and powerful business men work so hard to promote are not personal interests at all in the conventional economic sense of a desire to consume commodities. They consume in order to produce rather than produce in order to consume, in so far as they do either. The real motive is the desire to excel, to win at a game, the biggest and most fascinating game yet invented, not excepting even statecraft and war.

The suggestion which inevitably comes to mind is that a democratic economic order might conceivably appeal as effectively to the same fundamental motives. What is necessary is a development of political machinery and of political intelligence in the democracy itself to a point where men in responsible positions would actually feel their tenure secure and dependent only on their success in filling the position well. It is not mainly a matter of salary, though undoubtedly such men would have to live conspicuously well in an economic sense also — just as the officials of our political democracy expect to do, even when patriotic and public-spirited. The essential problem is wisely to select such responsible officials and promote them strictly on a basis of what they accomplish, to give them a "free hand" to make or mar their own careers. This is the lesson that must be learned before the democratization of industry will become a practical possibility. If we substitute for business competition, bad as it is, the game of political demagoguery as conventionally played, with rotation in office and "to the victors belong the spoils" as its main principles, the consequences can only be disastrous.

Another interesting misconception in regard to the public official should be pointed out before we leave this topic. It is common and natural to assume that a hired manager, dealing with resources which belong to others will be less careful in their use than an owner. The view shows little insight into human nature and does not square with observed facts. The real trouble with bureaucracies is not that they are rash, but the opposite. When not actually rotten with dishonesty and corruption they universally show a tendency to "play safe" and become hopelessly conservative. The great danger to be feared from a political control of economic life under ordinary conditions is not a reckless dissipation of the social resources so much as the arrest of progress and the vegetation of life.

This point leads naturally to the question which has been much discussed in treatments of risk and profit: does the private business man really abhor risk and uncertainty, and tend also to "play safe"? Other phases of the same question, the close relations of which are not always recognized, but which turn out to involve the same issue, relate to the social cost of risk-taking and the tendency of profits to a minimum.

The conventional view is, of course, to regard risk-taking as repugnant and irksome and to treat profit as the "reward" of assuming the "burden." This is, of course, the business man's own idea of the matter,[249] and students of the problem have often held the same

[249] See Merril, J. C. R, article on "Speculation," Price Current Grain Reporter, September 29, 1915, pp. 26-27: "It is a universal axiom of business that the greater the risk involved in any line of business the greater must be the profits

opinion. Thus Willett[250] argues that society pays for the sacrifice of assuming risk through higher prices for commodities in whose production it is a factor, for the reason that men are deterred from entering these occupations by their unwillingness to assume risk and that the supply of such commodities is consequently reduced. Ross also assumes[251] that risk is repugnant and draws the same conclusion, and Haynes[252] lays still greater emphasis on the influence of risk as a deterrent to production, quoting Andrews[253] to the same effect. Other writers have been more hesitant in generalizing or have made distinctions, or positively disagreed with this view. Thus v. Mangoldt[254] remarks that it is notorious that more money is lost than made in most forms of speculative activity and asserts the belief that this is true of business enterprise in communities which are in comfortable circumstances and have a reasonable surplus for embarking in venturesome undertakings. Professor F. M. Taylor also analyzes the problem with some care,[255] insisting that the profits of entrepreneurs may be either larger or smaller than the amount necessary to make up an insurance fund to cover actual losses. He holds it probable that they are for small risks larger and for large risks much smaller than the necessary insurance fund, but concludes that society has to pay a higher price for a particular commodity or service than it would have to pay if risk were eliminated.

There are several confusions of thought to be avoided in arguing this question. In the first place it is inaccurate to speak of profit as the reward of risk-taking or as the inducement to take risk. It is of the essence of the situation that the profit is in the future and uncertain when the decision is made and hence it is the *prospect* or *estimated probability*[256] of profit which "moves men's wills" (Taylor). Hence we cannot assert a connection between actual profit and the irksomeness of risk in the individual instance. And from the stand-

---

to those engaged in it, or . . . profits are in proportion to risks!"

[250]Economic Theory of Risk and Insurance, pp. 55-56. 8 Op. cit. (Annals, Am. Acad., 1896), p. 119.

[251]Op. cit. (Annals, Am. Acad., 1896), p. 119.

[252]Quarterly Journal of Economics, vol. ix, no. 4, p. 414.

[253]Institutes of Economics, p. 54.

[254]Unternehmergeivinn, p. 85. 7 Principles of Economics (1913), pp. 366-67, 383-84.

[255]Principles of Economics (1913), pp. 366-67, 383-84.

[256]J. S. Mill stated that chances of profit tend to equality, but in the fifth edition changed the word "chances" to "expectations." See Principles, Ashly edition, p. 412.

point of aggregate profit in the society as a whole the question is whether there is any such share or not, whether entrepreneurs as a class make a profit or suffer a loss (speaking, of course, of net or "pure" profit, after remunerations for *all* productive services are counted out).

Let us recall for clearness the precise situation of the profit-seeking business man. He contracts for productive services in advance, on a basis of what he expects to be able to make by their use. Like the purchaser of any commodity, he as an individual finds a price fixed and buys more or less at the established price, while in the aggregate the competition of all purchasers adjusts the price to the point where an entire existing supply can just be taken out of the market. It will be seen that the prices of productive services at any time, the entrepreneurs' costs of production, represent under perfect competition what entrepreneurs expect their products to be worth when sold, while the entrepreneurs' incomes represent the facts at a later time as contrasted with the anticipations at an earlier. The condition, then, under which entrepreneurs as a group will realize a positive profit is that they *underestimate* the prospects of their business relatively to their dispositions to venture. If, on the contrary, they overestimate their prospects (considering the degree of conviction necessary to move their wills), they will in the aggregate suffer loss, and if they estimate correctly on the whole, neither will occur. If the estimates are a matter of pure chance it would seem that the variations in the two directions would be equal, the average correct, and the general level of pure profit zero. Many writers, notably Hawley,[257] have assumed that such a distribution of errors necessarily obtains, though in the absence of a correct theory of profit the appropriate conclusion is not drawn.[258]

It may be objected that it is impossible that enterprise on the whole should suffer a net loss, but a little consideration will show that this is not true. The entrepreneur, as society is organized, is almost always a property-owner and must necessarily be the owner of productive power in some form. It may then well be that entrepreneurs lose more than they make, the difference coming out of the returns due them in some capacity other than that of en-

[257] See above, chapter II, p. 42.

[258] Hawley sometimes holds that profit is negative (Quarterly Journal of Economics, vol. XV, p. 609) and at other times that it is positive. (Ibid., P. 79.)

trepreneur. The question of fact is thus whether entrepreneurs as a class receive on the average more or less than the normal competitive rate of return on the productive services of person or property which they furnish to business.

The question does not admit of any definitive answer on inductive grounds. Such evidence as is available in the form of statistics points to the conclusion that the net result is a loss, but it is inconclusive.[259] Perhaps the best that can be done is to argue the case on a *priori* grounds and attempt nothing beyond an opinion as to the probable facts. The writer is strongly of the opinion that business as a whole suffers a loss. The main facts in the psychology of the case are familiar, and some of them have been stated above. The behavior of men in lotteries and gambling games is the most striking fact. Adam Smith pointed out the tendency of human nature to exaggerate the value of a small chance of large winnings. Senior[260] thought that the imagination exaggerates the large odds in favor of either gains or losses. Cannan[261] holds that both unusually risky and unusually safe investments are especially attractive to large classes of men and yield too small a return while ordinary hazards are neglected and hence yield more. Professor Carver contributes the suggestion[262] that business risks are predominantly of the character in which the odds are not great and the possible losses larger than the probable gains, that these have a negative appeal to the gambling instinct and that profit is a positive quantity. But in view of the possibility of

[259]M. Porte, Entrepreneurs et profits industriels (Paris, 1905), argues to this conclusion from certain figures on business failures in Massachusetts. The results of studies of farm accounts by the New York State College of Agriculture indicate that farmers commonly make less than fair wages and a fair return on the investment, and investigations of public utility ventures have yielded similar results. The best study of the distribution of income in the United States, by Dr. W. I. King, reaches the conclusion that the average profit per entrepreneur in this country is about one and four tenths times the average wage per laborer. (See Wealth and Income of the People of the United States, p. 165.) It seems safe to assume that entrepreneurs have greater ability than laborers in a larger ratio than this, especially since a large proportion of the wage-earners reported by the Census are women and young persons and children. But Dr. King's division of income into shares and his estimates of the numbers of recipients of each type are both replete with long-range deductions and assumptions leaving so much room for error that little if any confidence can be placed in the result.

[260]Cited by Cannan, History of Theories of Production and Distribution, p. 369.

[261]Article on "Profit" in Palgrave's Dictionary of Political Economy.

[262]Distribution of Wealth, p. 283.

capitalizing the entire future return of a venture into present wealth this view of the nature of business risks seems very questionable. The point we wish to emphasize is that these "risks" do not relate to objective external probabilities, but to the value of the judgment and executive powers of the person taking the chance. It is certainly true that as Smith and v. Mangoldt both observed, most men have an irrationally high confidence in their own good fortune, and that this is doubly true when their personal prowess comes into the reckoning, when they are betting on themselves. Moreover, there is little doubt that business men represent mainly the class of men of whom these things are most strikingly true; they are not the critical and hesitant individuals, but rather those with restless energy, buoyant optimism, and large faith in things generally and themselves in particular.

To these considerations must be added the stimulus of the competitive situation, constantly exerting pressure to outbid one's rivals, as in an auction sale, where things often bring more than any one thinks they are worth. Another large factor is the human trait of tenacity, also conspicuous in bourgeois psychology. Men may possibly be timid and critical on first embarking in new ventures, but once committed, it seems unquestionable that the general rule is to hold on to the last ditch, and the greater part of the bidders for productive services are owners of businesses already established. The prestige of entrepreneurship and the satisfaction of being one's own boss must also be considered. It therefore seems most reasonable to suppose that the prices of these are fixed at a level above rather than below that which the facts actually warrant, and as we have noticed, the statistics, such as they are, point to the same conclusion.

So much for the pure profit of entrepreneurs. We have already emphasized the fact that profit and imputed income are never accurately separated on either side of the dividing line. As there is no income which is pure profit so there is none which does not contain an element of profit. This is perhaps most conspicuous, or at least most familiar, in connection with interest. It is recognized that "pure interest" is impossible of identification, that ordinary interest includes an element of "risk premium." It is no less true that wages contain a variable element which is to be explained by the uncertainty of the return. The earnings of professional men form the notorious case. Men are attracted into these callings more by the lure of the small chance of conspicuous success than by the position achieved by the rank and file. Adam Smith was sure, and the opinion is still corroborated by common observation, that an occupation offering a small chance of attaining a high position and a large income will yield a lower average return to the same ability than one in which earnings are more uniform. That is, there is a negative premium on risk-taking in these cases also.

With most kinds of labor the chance element amounts to relatively little in all probability, and in any case it is perhaps best regarded as a return on the investment in special knowledge and skill rather than on effort directly. In any case, if Smith's reasoning is sound it appears that risk-taking is the opposite of irksome, that men work (or labor to acquire the capacity for work) more cheaply on the average for an uncertain than for a fixed compensation. To the landowner there is virtually no risk of actual loss involved in leasing it, and usually little or none of failure to receive the contract rental. In lending capital we find risk of loss of principal as well as interest and a great deal of attention is paid to the risk element in fixing the rate of return. A rate of pure interest is a concept to which it is so difficult to attach any definite meaning that it seems futile to speculate as to the adequacy of the excess of contract interest above this level to constitute an insurance fund to cover losses. The question, as before, is whether the actual receipts from contract interest and repayments of principal form on the average an amount equal to or less or more than the pure interest and the original principal. The writer sees no way of forming an opinion on this subject.

From the standpoint of social policy, two questions are to be raised. From one point of view, "society" is a husbandman or " wirtschaf tender Mensch" interested in getting its work done as well and as cheaply as possible. The foregoing considerations seem to indicate that from this pure productive efficiency point of view and with all the factors measured in competitive pecuniary terms it is better to let the individual "take the risk. It seems probable that with society and human nature as they are, the individual not only charges nothing for this service, but pays something for the privilege of rendering it — on the average. But we must remember that in the case of property he really does not take the risk, and it is a question of making him feel that he does, for property is and always has been "really" social and ownership a social function. It is not clear that the illusion of ownership, with the possibility and actuality of enormous waste and dissipation involved, is in fact a cheap way for society to remunerate the management of its material wealth. As with all questions involving human motives, however, only negative statements can be made on this subject until we begin to know something of what men as individuals and as society really want. The quality of management secured has, of course, to be taken into account along with the cost of securing it, but we have already said all that it seems worth while to say in the present connection on this head.

The second question raised is whether it is really good for the individual, and hence for society which is the individual in the aggregate, to have the risks of industry assumed by the former even if he is willing to do it at a loss, on the average, to himself. Some light on the proper answer is to be gained by considering the attitude which we actually take toward lotteries and gambling generally. Clearly there are limits to the terms on which the members of society are to be allowed to take chances, and notably when the independent members have dependent upon them other members in whom society is peculiarly interested. Rapid progress is at present being made toward prohibiting the laborer from unwisely contracting to assume hazards, and no theoretical objection can be made to extending the principle to property risks where the fundamentals of a decent and self-respecting existence are at stake.

The protection of a minimum standard of life is only one of many questions of the human interests involved in the distribution of risk and control, but we cannot here go into or even attempt to classify or enumerate a list. In concluding the discussion of the topic we shall only insist again on the limitations of the economic view of social organization as a mechanism for satisfying human wants in any static and hence scientifically describable sense of the term. Man's chief interest in life is after all to find life interesting, which is a very different thing from merely consuming a maximum amount of wealth. Change, novelty, and surprise must be given large consideration as values *per se*, and since at best most of us must doubtless spend more time in producing wealth than in consuming it, the dynamic and personal factors must be taken into account on the production side of economic conduct, and weighed against the element of efficiency. One of the things we surely want is the society of other people on a basis of mutual agreeability, respect, and affection, irrespective of the question, itself inescapable in any serious reflection on the issues of life, as to whether personality has some sort of cosmic value. Hence each individual must be given responsibility, freedom of choice, a wider sphere of self-expression than he can have in a system of organization where control is specialized and concentrated to the last degree. Whether this is practicable and how it is to be done is the great problem which confronts the advocates of industrial democracy.

To conclude our study notice must be taken of certain long-time aspects of the problem of uncertainty and control. The distinction between "static" and "dynamic" "risks" is a much-labored but a fundamental point in connection with our subject. We have emphasized in this study also that uncertainty is dependent upon change, and in fact largely upon progressive change. The problem of management or control, being a correlate or implication of uncertainty, is in correspondingly large measure the problem of progress. In an unprogressive society knowledge of the future could be perfected to a high degree through actual forecast and control or the effect of certainty secured through the grouping of cases and application of probability reasoning. Under such conditions the problem of management would be indefinitely simplified as activity would follow in the main an established routine and real decisions would rarely be required. The actual form of economic control, free contract, and especially private property in material goods, is closely connected with the acute form of the problem of management which arises from the highly "dynamic" character of the society we live in and the extreme degree of uncertainty connected with change. Before the modern industrial era began, as we know, the economic life of Europe was unprogressive, and its organization of control was collectivistic. The establishment of individualism was the result of the desire for improvement, even though it would be misleading to say that it came about directly through a social conviction of its superiority over collectivism in this respect.

The social theory of private property rests, then, not so much on the premise that productive resources will be more effectively used in the creation of goods for consumption, as on the belief that there will be a greater stimulus to progress through inducing men to take the risks of action increasing the supplies of productive resources themselves, including both material things and technical knowledge and skill. We have shown in our discussion of interest the fallacy in the view that accumulation and forward-looking sacrifice can be explained on the basis of time preference in consumption. A sacrifice of present to future consumption does not generally increase the total consumption by the individual making it, and in addition the mere postponement of consumption would give rise to no considerable net increase in social equipment. The "abstinence" must be permanent, and not a mere matter of waiting. It follows that the premise of the justification of private property must be that the mere desire of ownership is a more potent motive to bring about sacrifice and effective control in this field than the desire to consume a larger amount of goods. The social policy of private property is sound, if at all, because the craving to own wealth will lead men to sacrifice consumption and take risks of complete loss in order to increase their property.[263] The truth or falsity of this premise is not our present concern, but it seems worth while to point out some facts in connection with its application.

Practically all forms of social economic progress represent, as has been pointed out, different modes of increasing the productive power of society through the sacrifice or "investment" of present consumption. These different ways are open, competing alternatives, quite comparable generally speaking in quantitative terms. One may invest his present goods in creating new equipment goods (the conventional way, and type of all), or in finding and developing new natural resources, or in developing his own personal powers (or even to some extent those of other men), or in inventing, or in improving business organization, or in creating new social tastes and wants. The first two modes of investment give rise to new property and this society, generally speaking, grants to the successful investor in fee simple and to his heirs and assigns forever.

Investment in one's own person likewise gives rise to undisputed possession of the new capacities, but these are not permanent, passing out of existence with the end of the individual's own active life. It would be interesting, if it were possible, to compare the attractiveness of these two forms of investment, for the effectiveness of control beyond one's own lifetime as an incentive to investment is one of the principal issues in the theory of enterprise. We shall recur to this topic presently.

The case of investment in invention is different again. Here, owing to the low cost of indefinitely multiplying an idea, it is usually difficult to capitalize an increase in productive power. Society gen-

[263] An accurate and exhaustive discussion of this point would have to distinguish between the motives of the entrepreneur and those of the owner who transfers the use of his property to an entrepreneur for a fixed return.

erally permits an inventor or his assigns to keep his idea secret as long as possible or to safeguard it in any manner. But this is so commonly impracticable and the social value of new inventions so manifest that the patent system has come into general use establishing and protecting by law a *temporary*, and rather short-lived, property right in the improvement. It is manifest that this is an exceedingly crude way of rewarding invention. Not merely do the consumers of the product pay, which is doubtless fair, but large numbers of other persons suffer who are prevented from using the commodity by the artificially high price. And as the thing works out, it is undoubtedly a very rare and exceptional case where the really deserving inventor gets anything like a fair reward. If any one gains, it is some purchaser of the invention or at best an inventor who adds a detail or finishing touch that makes an idea practicable where the real work of pioneering and exploration has been done by others. It would seem to be a matter of political intelligence and administrative capacity to replace artificial monopoly with some direct method of stimulating and rewarding research.

The improvement of business organization and methods offers still less chance of securing any permanent gain, since the result is usually neither patentable nor capable of being kept secret. Yet this form of progress also represents an investment of present wealth which could have been placed in fields yielding perpetual property rights. Surely there is no evidence of any unwillingness to make expenditures in this form of improvement, and the fact raises interesting questions as to the motives which actually operate in inducing men to make the present sacrifices which promote economic progress. Expenditure in creating new wants can be made to yield a more permanent advantage through the use of distinctive brands and legal protection of trade marks and trade names. Some of these, of course, become pieces of property of great value and ready salability.

Remains, then, the final question of the relative importance as stimuli to save and invest, of property rights and the right to transfer such rights to other individuals or project control beyond one's own lifetime. We cannot enter here at length into the question of inheritance. Still more than ownership in the strict sense, of which it is no essential part, inheritance rests on no conscious theory, but has simply happened. The attribute of inheritance more or less naturally inheres in personal effects where the family system exists, and it becomes transferred to productive goods as these increase in importance, while property in productive goods also enormously strengthens and isolates the private family sentiment. Voluntary bequest outside the family represents a later development and in a sense the reverse tendency.

The "theory" of the rights of transmission and bequest is, of course, that they form an important element in the inducement to conserve and accumulate wealth. The writer is extremely skeptical as to the soundness of this view, but there are considerations which must give pause to any rash advocacy of fundamental change. The difficulty , again, is to suggest an alternative plan which seems workable. The public confiscation of wealth at the death of the owner raises the question of what would be done with it. For those who are dubious of the direct management of productive enterprise by public agency, a leasing system or sale at auction in exchange for income rights in the form of debentures or the like perhaps offer a possible way out. This is much like some of the suggestions of the Saint-Simonian school of socialists.[264] Even then the practical problem of distributing the income among the people or of its public utilization gives rise to misgivings.

Somewhat similar problems again arise in connection with the personal powers of individuals, which, as we have seen, obstinately resist generic separation from material goods in their economic bearings. Innate ability, in the sense in which there is such a thing, is inevitably hereditary, and nothing can be done about it except to modify the conception of the individual's property rights in his own powers. But culture in all its subtle significance, as well as education and training in their cruder forms, are also more or less transmissible and more or less subject to voluntary bestowal, and the factor of personal influence or "pull" can by no means be left out of account. The significance of control over these things is very great and would probably be multiplied rather than diminished in a society which abolished property in material things. It seems that real equality of opportunity, a true merit system, is hardly conceivable, and that no very close approach to such a consummation can be expected in connection with the private family. Plato, of course, recognized this fact, which most of his modern successors have a tendency to blink.

The ultimate difficulties of any arbitrary, artificial, moral, or rational reconstruction of society center around the problem of social

[264]See also Alvin S. Johnson, "The Public Capitalization of the Inheritance Tax," Journal of Political Economy, February, 1914.

continuity in a world where individuals are born naked, destitute, helpless, ignorant, and untrained, and must spend a third of their lives in acquiring the prerequisites of a free contractual existence. The distribution of control, of personal power, position, and opportunity, of the burden of labor and of uncertainty, and of the material produce of social industry cannot easily be radically altered, whatever we may think ideally ought to be done. The fundamental fact about society as a going concern is that it is made up of individuals who are born and die and give place to others; and the fundamental fact about modern civilization is that it is dependent upon the utilization of three great accumulating funds of inheritance from the past, material goods and appliances, knowledge and skill, and morale. Besides the torch of life itself, the material wealth of the world, a technological system of vast and increasing intricacy and the habituations which fit men for social life must in some manner be carried forward to new individuals born devoid of all these things as older individuals pass out. The existing order, with the institutions of the private family and private property (in self as well as goods), inheritance and bequest and parental responsibility, affords one way for securing more or less tolerable results in grappling with this problem. They are not ideal, nor even good; but candid consideration of the difficulties of radical transformation, especially in view of our ignorance and disagreement as to what we want, suggests caution and humility in dealing with reconstruction proposals.

Index

www.ingramcontent.com/pod-product-compliance
Lightning Source LLC
LaVergne TN
LVHW010722210926
848485LV00007B/1419/J
9781622730049